THE STUDY OF RELIGION IN THE PUBLIC SCHOOLS: AN APPRAISAL

COMMITTEE ON RELIGION AND EDUCATION*

Appointed by the American Council on Education

F. *Ernest Johnson,* Study Consultant, National Council of the Churches of Christ in the U.S.A.; *Chairman*

Paul J. Braisted, President, Edward W. Hazen Foundation

Eugene E. Dawson, Dean of Administration and Students, Kansas State Teachers College; subsequently President, Colorado Woman's College

Louis Finkelstein, Chancellor, Jewish Theological Seminary of America

Jacob Greenberg, Deputy Superintendent of Schools, New York City

John O. Gross, Executive Secretary, Division of Educational Institutions, Board of Education of the Methodist Church

James L. Hanley, Superintendent of Schools, Providence, Rhode Island

Rt. Rev. Msgr. Frederick G. Hochwalt, Executive Secretary, National Catholic Educational Association

Galen Jones, Director, Council for Advancement of Secondary Education

Kenneth E. Oberholtzer, Superintendent of Schools, Denver, Colorado; *Vice-Chairman*

Herbert L. Seamans, Director, Commission on Educational Organizations, National Conference of Christians and Jews, Inc., New York City; subsequently Consultant on Human Relations, University of Miami

Paul H. Vieth, Horace Bushnell Professor of Christian Nurture, Divinity School, Yale University

Roscoe L. West, President, New Jersey State Teachers College, Trenton; subsequently retired

Arthur S. Adams, President, American Council on Education, *ex officio*

* Membership at the time of the conference.

THE STUDY OF RELIGION
IN THE PUBLIC SCHOOLS
An Appraisal

Report of a Conference on
Religion and Public Education
Sponsored by the
American Council on Education at
Arden House, Harriman, New York
March 10-12, 1957

Edited by NICHOLAS C. BROWN

Papers contributed by F. ERNEST JOHNSON
ARTHUR E. SUTHERLAND · BERT JAMES LOEWENBERG
JACK ALLEN · JOHN THOMAS FARRELL
SISTER MARY NONA, O.P. · EUGENE E. DAWSON

American Council on Education   Washington, D. C.

Conference Participants

Aaron I. Abell, Professor of American History, University of Notre Dame

Jack Allen, Professor of History, George Peabody College for Teachers

Florence O. Benjamin, Coordinator of Social Studies, Abington Township School District, Pennsylvania

Max Birnbaum, Educational Consultant, The American Jewish Committee, New York City

Samuel M. Blumenfield, Director, Department of Education and Culture, The Jewish Agency, Inc., New York City

Henry Bragdon, History Department, Phillips Exeter Academy

Paul J. Braisted, President, The Edward W. Hazen Foundation, Inc., New Haven 11, Connecticut

Brother E. Thomas, F.S.C., Central District Catholic High School, Pittsburgh, Pennsylvania

†*Walter R. Cleminson,* Principal, Grosse Pointe High School, Michigan

Jules Cohen, Secretary, Joint Advisory Committee of the Synagogue Council of America and the National Community Relations Advisory Council, New York City

Rev. Joseph F. Costanzo, S.J., Fordham University

Eugene E. Dawson, Dean of Administration and Students, Kansas State Teachers College; subsequently President, Colorado Woman's College

W. Marshon DePoister, Administrative Dean, Chapman College, California

Rev. Charles F. Donovan, S.J., School of Education, Boston College

Benjamin R. Epstein, National Director, Anti-Defamation League of B'nai B'rith, 515 Madison Avenue, New York City

John Thomas Farrell, Professor of History, The Catholic University of America

Isaac Franck, Executive Director, Jewish Community Council of Greater Washington, 1420 New York Avenue, N.W., Washington 5, D.C.; Lecturer in Philosophy at American University

Foye G. Gibson, President, Scarritt College for Christian Workers

James L. Hanley, Superintendent of Schools, Providence, Rhode Island

† Deceased.

Rev. John Hardon, S.J., Professor of Theology, West Baden University, Indiana

Ellis Ford Hartford, Chairman, Division of Foundations of Education, University of Kentucky

Rt. Rev. Msgr. Sylvester J. Holbel, Superintendent of Schools, Diocese of Buffalo, New York

R. Lanier Hunt, Executive Director, Department of Religion and Public Education, National Council of the Churches of Christ in the United States of America, New York City

F. Ernest Johnson, Study Consultant, National Council of the Churches of Christ in the United States of America, New York City

Galen Jones, Director, Council for Advancement of Secondary Education, Washington, D.C.

Dumont F. Kenny, National Program Director, National Conference of Christians and Jews, Inc., New York City

Milton R. Konvitz, Professor, School of Industrial and Labor Relations and Law School, Cornell University

Edward A. Krug, Professor of Education, University of Wisconsin

Jordan L. Larson, Superintendent of Schools, Mount Vernon, New York

Bert J. Loewenberg, Department of History, Sarah Lawrence College

Rev. Neil G. McCluskey, S.J., Education Editor, *America,* New York City

Very Rev. Msgr. William E. McManus, Assistant Director, Department of Education, National Catholic Welfare Conference; subsequently Archdiocesan Superintendent of Schools, Chicago, Illinois

Annabelle M. Melville, State Teachers College, Bridgewater, Massachusetts

Sam H. Moorer, Director of Instructional Field Services, Department of Education, State of Florida, Tallahassee, Florida

Thomas P. Neill, Professor of History, Saint Louis University, St. Louis, Missouri

Rt. Rev. Msgr. Timothy O'Leary, Superintendent of Schools, Archdiocese of Boston, Massachusetts

Prentiss L. Pemberton, Associate Director, The Danforth Foundation, St. Louis, Missouri

Leo Pfeffer, Director of the Commission on Law and Social Action, American Jewish Congress, New York City

Marvin G. Pursinger, Chairman, Department of Social Studies, Willamette High School, Eugene, Oregon

Gerald Read, Associate Professor of Education, Kent State University

George H. Reavis, Editorial Consultant, Field Enterprises, Inc., Chicago, Illinois

Harrison Sasscer, Assistant Director, Division of Legislation and Federal Relations, National Education Association, Washington, D.C.

Samuel Schafler, Department of Education, The United Synagogue Commission on Jewish Education, New York City

Herbert L. Seamans, Director, Commission on Educational Organizations, National Conference of Christians and Jews, Inc., New York City; subsequently Consultant on Human Relations, University of Miami

A. L. Sebaly, National Coordinator, Teacher Education and Religion Project of the American Association of Colleges for Teacher Education, Oneonta, New York

Herman Shibler, General Superintendent of Schools, Indianapolis, Indiana

Albert J. Silverman, 5002 Norwood Avenue, Baltimore 7, Maryland

Sister Mary Janet, S.C., Consultant, Commission on American Citizenship, The Catholic University of America

Sister Mary Justine, O.P., Resurrection School, Minneapolis, Minnesota

Sister Mary Nona, O.P., President, Edgewood College of the Sacred Heart, Madison, Wisconsin

Isidore Starr, 44-59 Kissena Boulevard, Flushing, New York

Arthur Eugene Sutherland, Professor of Law, Harvard University

Eleanor W. Thompson, Vice-Principal, Philadelphia High School for Girls, Pennsylvania

Ronald B. Thompson, Registrar and University Examiner, Ohio State University

Clyde F. Varner, Supervisor of Social Studies, Department of Instruction, Board of Education, Cleveland, Ohio

Paul H. Vieth, Horace Bushnell Professor of Christian Nurture, The Divinity School, Yale University

Rt. Rev. Msgr. John J. Voight, Secretary of Education, Archdiocese of New York, 451 Madison Avenue, New York City

Roscoe L. West, President, New Jersey State Teachers College, Trenton

Fremont Philip Wirth, George Peabody College for Teachers

Herman E. Wornom, General Secretary, Religious Education Association, New York City

Elsie O. Zeccola, 309 Mosholu Parkway, N., New York City

Arthur S. Adams, President, American Council on Education

Francis J. Brown, Staff Associate, American Council on Education

Nicholas C. Brown, Staff Associate, American Council on Education

Foreword

THIS REPORT is the outcome of the Conference on Religion and Public Education, which was sponsored by the Committee on Religion and Education of the American Council on Education and held on March 10–12, 1957, at Arden House in Harriman, New York. It is the fourth in a series of reports, published by the American Council on Education, on the appropriate relationship of religion to public education in the United States.

The Council has been concerned with this complex and vexing problem since 1944 when the Committee on Religion and Education was established, following the publication of *Religion and Public Education*. Activities of the committee resulted in two additional publications—*The Relation of Religion to Public Education* (1947) and *The Function of the Public Schools in Dealing with Religion* (1953).

Because of the mounting interest in this basic problem of American education, the committee voted in the fall of 1955 to hold a conference for the purpose of seeking, first, an appraisal of its published position and, second, a considered recommendation for its future work. Accordingly, after the Council's Executive Committee gave its approval early in 1956, the proposal for a conference was submitted to the Edward W. Hazen Foundation and the Danforth Foundation. Both foundations responded with generous grants that made it possible not only to conduct the conference but also to publish this report.

When the conference plans were finally drafted by a special subcommittee in the fall of 1956, invitations were sent to a group of persons who were known to have a vital interest, a definite concern, and perhaps a special competence in the field of religion and public education. The response was remarkably enthusiastic—especially in

ix

view of the fact that it was to be a "working" conference extending over a period of three days and involving a large measure of individual participation.

Sixty-three persons, representing the three major faiths in the United States and coming from approximately twenty-five states, participated in the conference. They included officials of national organizations, representatives of higher education, local school administrators, curriculum and textbook experts, and classroom teachers. These participants gave special attention to the committee's main recommendation in its 1953 report. In this report, the committee approached the problem of the relation of religion to public education from the point of view of *the requirements of a fundamental general education* rather than from the point of view of what religious groups themselves desire; however, in so doing, it took full account of the problems and issues involved as viewed by responsible educational and religious leaders. Thus, a great deal of spirited but constructive discussion at the conference focused on the committee's conclusion in its last report that the factual study of religion points the way to a democratic solution of this persistent problem.

Careful preparations for the conference were made to ensure useful results. In order to furnish a background of common information and to provide a definite focus for profitable discussions, seven papers were written and distributed to all delegates well in advance of the meeting. These papers were then summarized briefly by their authors at the conference before they were discussed in the general sessions. Following the general sessions, five table groups, each an occupational and religious cross section of the entire group, debated the issues in detail and later reported to the whole conference.

Arranged in a logical sequence, the seven papers attempted on successive days to provide "The Approach," to define "A Specific Problem," and to pose "The General Problem." Thus, papers I and II set the broad limits for the discussion; papers III, IV, V, and VI focused attention on the specific problem of how and when religion should be dealt with in teaching American history at various levels; and paper VII posed the general problem of the relationship of religion to public education.

The Council makes grateful acknowledgment to the Edward W. Hazen Foundation and the Danforth Foundation, which made this undertaking possible. The foundations are not, however, the authors or publishers of this publication and are not to be understood as approving, by virtue of their grants, any of the statements made or views expressed herein.

The Council is also indebted to all the delegates whose cooperation and participation made this publication possible. The Council hopes that this volume will prove helpful to others who are likewise concerned with these important issues.

ARTHUR S. ADAMS, *President*
American Council on Education

August 1, 1957

Contents

CONFERENCE PARTICIPANTS   v

FOREWORD   *Arthur S. Adams*   ix

The Approach:
Setting the Limits for the Discussion

OPENING REMARKS   *Arthur S. Adams*   3

SUMMARY OF POLICIES AND RECOMMENDATIONS OF THE
AMERICAN COUNCIL ON EDUCATION COMMITTEE ON RELI-
GION AND EDUCATION   *F. Ernest Johnson*   5

DISCUSSION BASED ON DR. JOHNSON'S PAPER   18

PUBLIC AUTHORITY AND RELIGIOUS EDUCATION: A BRIEF
SURVEY OF CONSTITUTIONAL AND LEGAL LIMITS
                                          Arthur E. Sutherland   33

DISCUSSION BASED ON PROFESSOR SUTHERLAND'S PAPER   47

A Specific Problem: How and When Should References
to Religion Be Made in the Teaching of
American History at Various Levels?

RELIGION IN THE HISTORY OF AMERICAN IDEAS
                                        Bert James Loewenberg   77

DISCUSSION BASED ON DR. LOEWENBERG'S PAPER   86

RELIGIOUS MATTER IN THE TEACHING OF AMERICAN HISTORY   *John Thomas Farrell*   97

DISCUSSION BASED ON PROFESSOR FARRELL'S PAPER   113

THE STUDY OF RELIGION IN HIGH SCHOOL AMERICAN HISTORY   *Jack Allen*   122

DISCUSSION BASED ON PROFESSOR ALLEN'S PAPER   132

SOME RELIGIOUS ASPECTS OF ELEMENTARY AMERICAN HISTORY   *Sister Mary Nona, O.P.*   139

DISCUSSION BASED ON SISTER MARY NONA'S PAPER   154

TABLE REPORTS AND DISCUSSION   163

DISCUSSION BASED ON TABLE REPORTS   175

The General Problem: What is the Proper Relationship of Religion to Public Education?

THE NEXT DECADE OF RESEARCH AND EXPERIMENTATION RELATING TO RELIGION AND PUBLIC EDUCATION
                                    Eugene E. Dawson   187

DISCUSSION BASED ON DR. DAWSON'S PAPER   200

TABLE REPORTS AND DISCUSSION   206

DISCUSSION BASED ON TABLE REPORTS   213

NOTES   223

The Approach:

Setting the Limits for the Discussion

Opening Remarks

ARTHUR S. ADAMS
President, American Council on Education

ON BEHALF of the American Council on Education, I take special pleasure in welcoming you to this Conference on Religion and Public Education. From your letters, I know that many of you made considerable sacrifices to come here, and I know *all* of you set aside important tasks to come to this mountaintop with its magnificent view to share with us your thought and experience on this central issue in American education. We are indebted to you, and we are grateful for your presence.

The fact that classroom teachers, curriculum experts, textbook writers, local officials, college people, and individuals from national organizations have assembled here from approximately twenty-five states is clear indication that we are dealing with a matter of basic and national concern. It also illustrates in a very concrete way one of the aims and functions of the American Council on Education.

The Council regards itself as just what the name implies, a *council* of organizations and institutions. It seeks to offer a forum for the exchange of educational opinion. It does not primarily seek to be an operating agency, although this role sometimes devolves upon it when issues arise involving actions which no other educational organization is in a position to undertake.

Because the Council has some operating activities, some persons may be inclined to think that it is primarily an operating organization. This is not so. The Council's central function is to undertake an enterprise of just this sort, to bring together interested and knowledgeable people, concerned with a particular educational problem, to explore the total problem from many points of view, and to try to reach whatever consensus is possible.

In this connection, I want to say that I have great confidence in the democratic process of discussing difficult issues and reaching general consensus. We are not so foolish as to expect that everyone will leave here of one mind on any particular issue, but we are hopeful that, through a realistic and friendly exchange of views, we can find and enlarge the area of common agreement. To do this, we need to keep uppermost in our minds the best interests of the pupil and his education.

I think we all recognize that dealing with this subject is like trying to pick up mercury from a slippery table top with a table knife. It is not easy to do. We are dealing with a subject in which the words themselves become elastic and somewhat elusive. It is hard to define their meaning in precise terms.

As we go forward in the next two days of discussion, people will say with great earnestness, "You see, you can't do it this way," and then someone else will say, "How about this way?" This is the kind of discussion we want. Only by conscious thought, careful expression, considerate listening, and conscientious revision of our thought can we come to firm agreements on this exceedingly important subject.

Because of the careful provisions for informal discussion and because of the unique qualifications of each delegate, each person here should feel not only a complete freedom to express his or her point of view, but also a special responsibility to do so.

Now it is my pleasure to introduce someone who doesn't really need an introduction. I present him because he is the dean of all those who have been involved in this venture. He has been involved in these affairs from the very beginning, and he has contributed mightily to the progress that has been made: Professor F. Ernest Johnson.

Summary of Policies and Recommendations of the American Council on Education Committee on Religion and Education

F. ERNEST JOHNSON

Dr. Johnson, chairman of the Committee on Religion and Education, is chief study consultant for the Department of the Church and Economic Life, Division of Christian Life and Work, National Council of the Churches of Christ in the U.S.A., and professor emeritus of education, Teachers College, Columbia University. He was director of research and editor of Information Service *in the Federal Council of the Churches of Christ in America, and subsequently in the National Council of Churches. He is author of* The Church and Society *and editor of* American Education and Religion *and a number of other books.*

THE PURPOSE of this paper is fourfold:

1. To state and interpret the position that has been presented and defended by the American Council's Committee on Religion and Education with respect to the place of religion in public education;

2. To summarize briefly the committee's findings with reference to existing practices and prevailing attitudes with respect to this problem;

3. To call attention to developments since our committee's first report was issued in 1947 which have given us encouragement and moral support;

4. To consider the implications of the present situation for future strategy.

I wish to make it clear at the outset that opinions expressed in this paper, except where offered as representing the committee's position, are my own, and not necessarily the opinions of the committee. At the same time I believe that what I shall say is in line with the main currents of the committee's thought and with the results of its inquiries.

The Committee's Position

It will be recalled that the American Council pioneered in this field by convening, in cooperation with the National Conference of Christians and Jews, a conference of educators on religion and public education, which was held in Princeton, New Jersey, in May 1944.[1] At that time criticism was being aimed at public education because of the scant attention given to religion in its curriculum. On the other hand, many prominent educators were expressing concern lest the growing demand for "more religion in the schools" might lead to a breaking down of the "wall" between church and state. As a result of the Princeton conference the Council created the Committee on Religion and Education.

The committee issued its first report, *The Relation of Religion to Public Education,* in April 1947.[2] It took a firm position against religious instruction—in the sense of indoctrination—in tax-supported schools, but contended vigorously for including in the public school program, for objective study, religious subject matter wherever it is intrinsically related to a given school discipline. This would mean that the study of literature should take in our religious classics; the study of history should include the religious aspects of the period studied; the social studies program should provide for visitation and observation of religious institutions as well as those related to business, industry, and social welfare; and so on. We have held that religious literacy is an essential goal of a liberal education.

This approach to religion has been widely characterized as "study *about* religion." The term has been found useful by many educators, though it is sometimes contended that "study about" is not really education at all, since it does not require or produce that personal *involvement* which is essential to a genuine educative experience. I think it appropriate here to point out that the kind of study of religion for which our committee has contended is definitely characterized by personal involvement since it is in essence not mere curious inspection, but reverent inquiry. The word *reverent* here denotes an attitude implicit in democracy, since a reverence for individual persons surely implies reverence for what men have immemorially held to be holy.

It should also be said that controversy has arisen from time to time over the relation of such objective study as we have advocated to the act of personal commitment which is characteristic of religious experience at its best. Let us recall what the committee said on this point:

The intensive cultivation of religion is, and always has been, the function of religious institutions. To create an awareness of its importance is a responsibility of public education. In creating such an awareness the school is but rounding out its educational task, which culminates in the building of durable convictions about the meaning of life and personal commitments based upon them. The school cannot dictate these convictions and commitments, but it can, and should, foster a sense of the obligation to achieve them as a supreme moral imperative and to that end bring its students into contact with the spiritual resources of the community.[3]

This passage has been thought by some to be ambiguous. Perhaps it is, when read out of context. However, I think the report as a whole made it quite clear that we were unwilling to assign to the tax-supported school any role that involved indoctrination in religious beliefs, or pressure toward commitment to their espousal or advocacy. If I, as the person who drafted the passage just quoted, may be permitted to interpret it, it means that the enterprise of general education includes the confrontation of growing persons with spiritual values and influences in accord with their actual magnitude in the culture and the general estimate of their importance in the life of the community. All democratic education is weighted—biased, if you please—in subject matter and emphasis in accord with the value system of the community to which the school belongs.

But—to use again the language of the report—to "impel the young toward a vigorous, decisive, personal reaction to the challenge of religion" must detract in no degree from the respect and reverence due the individual conscience whose honest response to that challenge is negative rather than affirmative. Honest response, not acquiescence or conformity, is the primary goal. Religious liberty is an ultimate value. I must confess to a personal concern lest some of the efforts to correct a long-standing deficit in public education may result in pressures that do violence to personal freedom.

Clarification seems to be needed at two points. A common error is the characterization of the approach we and many others have advocated as "nonsectarian." We sought from the beginning to show that advocacy of *any* creedal proposition is regarded as sectarian from the point of view of some elements of the population. Our approach is not nonsectarian but, so to speak, multisectarian. That is to say, we have urged that religion in the various forms in which it appears today in our culture and in which it has influenced history be respectfully studied in the interest of achieving a culturally adequate education.

Our committee has maintained that nonsectarian religion—that is to say, an aggregate of common elements in the several faiths represented in the community—would be something *less* than would seem authentic and adequate to any one religious group, and something *more* than a substantial part of the average community would be willing to have authoritatively propagated. Presumably such considerations underlie the United States Supreme Court's persistent ban on religious instruction in the schools in spite of the very liberal doctrine laid down in the Zorach case in 1952.[4]

A second error is to assume that insistence on the study of religious classics, institutions, and movements in secular schools is in some sense a disparagement of the secular as such. This is the reverse of what we have stood for. Our primary concern is to oppose the artificial separation of the sacred and the secular—the setting-apart of religion from the common life. The cultural evil against which we have protested is the nonrelevance of spiritual ideals and sanctions to everyday life, whether in business, politics, or education.

Existing Practices and Prevailing Attitudes

Our second report, which was published in 1953 under the title, *The Function of the Public Schools in Dealing with Religion,*[5] was an attempt to survey existing practices in this area and the opinions of educational and religious leaders with respect to the position which the committee has advocated. I will summarize briefly the principal findings.

We found a conspicuous lack of anything approximating an

"American way" with respect to the relation of religion to public education. There were evidences of more or less deliberate avoidance of religious subject matter even when it was clearly intrinsic to the discipline concerned. On the other hand, we found planned religious activities widely prevalent—activities that, in many cases, could by no stretch of imagination be reconciled with the rigid prohibitions set up by the United States Supreme Court in the Everson and McCollum cases.[6] Finally, we found some attempts to steer a course between these extremes by means of objective study of religion in the culture.

A significant result of the study, in retrospect, was the apparent impossibility of designing any one policy, with or without judicial sanction, that would meet the widely diverse conditions existing in different parts of the country, especially in communities that are relatively homogeneous with respect to religion. It was a painful experience to discover in the schools religious practices well established by custom and supported by strong community sanctions which did patent violence to the religious liberties of minority groups as any discriminating court might define them. Yet nothing was more apparent than the prospect of disrupted community life, with perhaps devastating consequences to the minority groups themselves, that would result from arbitrary interference with deep-seated community customs.

At the same time, the study showed a high degree of receptivity on the part of educational leaders toward the general position which the committee had formulated and a corresponding readiness for experimentation designed to test its practicality. The committee has long been convinced that only through carefully planned, adequately financed experimentation involving cooperation between local school systems and teacher education institutions could the feasibility of its proposals with respect to the public school program be established with any assurance.

It should be noted that the chief focus of attention of the American Council's committee has been secondary education. The main thesis of its reports, to which I have called attention, is manifestly more relevant to the secondary level than to the elementary. This constitutes a limitation which I now regard as unfortunate and to which I shall return later. It was probably inevitable because of our preoccupation with a controversial issue that centered in doctrine and beliefs. That issue intrudes itself chiefly at the secondary level as far as the public schools are concerned.

As for higher education under public auspices, the committee's interest has been, in the main, restricted to teacher-education institutions and the teacher-education activities of liberal arts colleges. It soon became evident, however, that the factors limiting attention to religion at the higher level were of a different kind from those encountered in the public schools and that the problems we have been chiefly concerned with were basically public school problems.

Developments since 1947

I turn now to developments during the decade since our committee published its first report which tend to validate its approach and to give support to its main endeavor. To those of us who undertook ten years ago to arouse public interest in the role of religion in general education and who encountered sharp opposition in some quarters and apathy in others, the change of mood and the growth in interest have been amazing. The mood that prevailed earlier in influential circles was not consciously hostile to religion as such, but it indicated a two-sphere conception of religion and the state: not only were *church* and *state* to be separate, but government-sponsored activities, including public education, were to let religion alone. With the handing down by the U. S. Supreme Court of its decisions in the now famous Everson and McCollum cases, in 1947 and 1948, respectively, this position was made official.

We shall have before us an authoritative presentation of the legal and judicial aspects of our subject. I am impelled to refer to them, however, to the extent of their impact on the thinking of educational and religious leaders, and their bearing on our committee's position. Regardless of the merits of the particular matters decided in those two cases, the judicial doctrine to which they gave rise was so rigid and absolute as to be conspicuously out of line with policies and practices that had long been generally accepted. Indeed, a major result of the Court's ruling in the McCollum case—a rather startling one—was a sort of bewilderment which apparently prevented its being taken seriously. The public got one clear impression: religious classes should not be held in schoolrooms. The judicial position developed by the Court never took hold in the public mind.

What was novel in the Everson-McCollum doctrine—the crucial point appears in both of these cases—was the use of the three words "aid all religions" in the prohibition announced by the Court. No laws may be passed which "aid one religion, aid all religions, or prefer one religion over another." The ban against *preferring* one religion had been taken for granted since established churches were done away with. Patently, "aid" in varying degrees is given by government to religion in general in many forms which have been enumerated again and again. Some of the most conspicuous are the chaplaincy in the Armed Forces, in penal institutions, and in legislative bodies; the exemption of church property from taxation and the protection of title to such property in courts of law; the issuance of religious proclamations by Presidents and governors; provision of secular textbooks for children attending parochial as well as for those attending public schools; and similar provision of free transportation to and from school. The textbook matter had been previously settled by the Supreme Court and the constitutionality of unrestricted free transportation was affirmed in the Everson case itself, in which the doctrine of no aid to "all religions" was first formulated. It seems clear that so rigid a doctrine, regardless of what history may have to say of its judicial merit, was bound either to undergo revision or to bring about drastic changes in common practice which is quite unrealistic to contemplate.

What amounted, from a lay viewpoint, to a revision of the rigid doctrine the Court had promulgated in 1947 and 1948 came in the Zorach case, decided in the spring of 1952. In practical effect, the principle of cooperation between state and church, within certain limits, was substituted for that of absolute separation. The Court said: "When the State encourages religious instruction or cooperates with religious authorities by adjusting the schedule of public events to sectarian needs, it follows the best of our traditions. For it then respects the religious nature of our people and accommodates the public service to their spiritual needs."

A layman can hardly avoid the impression that the majority of the Court felt the necessity to recede from the absolutist position embodied in the earlier decisions and to render a judgment nearer to the realities of the American situation—not to say, within the bounds of enforcibility. Thus, the present judicial situation creates a pre-

sumption in favor of the position which this committee has taken
from the beginning. While I have never thought that our proposals
would be subject to a Supreme Court ban, even in the light of the
McCollum case, it must be said that the philosophy of our committee
is much more in line with that which is reflected in the ruling opinion
in the Zorach case.

It is doubtless gratuitous to speculate on the possible relationship
between judicial decisions and the course of events. Yet I am con-
strained to point out that the promulgation by the Supreme Court of
an absolutist doctrine seems to have been the signal for a re-examina-
tion by educational leaders of the whole question—a process characterized by a pragmatic approach in line with historical development
—and that the subsequent modification of the Court's position in turn
indicated a departure from absolutist doctrine concerning the separation of church and state.

The new constructive interest in the place of religion in public
education has been manifested during the last few years in an impressive number and variety of ways.

The Educational Policies Commission, which has rendered liberal
educational leadership of a high order, issued a highly significant
report in 1951 under the title, *Moral and Spiritual Values in the
Public Schools.*[7] Many members of this conference have, I am sure,
made good use of it. In the section dealing with religion the commission set forth with emphasis a recommendation substantially iden-
tical with that which our committee had made in 1947—objective
study of religion as empirical cultural fact. The commission designated
this approach as "teaching about religion." "The public schools,"
said the report, "can teach objectively about religion without advocating or teaching any religious creed. . . . Knowledge about religion
is essential for a full understanding of our culture, literature, art,
history, and current affairs."

A noteworthy conference on religion in teacher education was
held at Yale University in 1952, at which active interest in this field
was reported from a large number of teacher education institutions.

The American Association of Colleges for Teacher Education, with
the aid of a grant from the Danforth Foundation, initiated in 1953
a novel project of great promise with which members of this conference are familiar. In that project teachers colleges and schools of

education in various parts of the country are conducting coordinated efforts to "discover and develop ways and means to teach the reciprocal relation between religion and other elements in human culture in order that the prospective teacher, whether he teaches literature, history, the arts, science, or other subjects, shall be prepared to understand, to appreciate, and to convey to his students the significance of religion in human affairs."

The workshop on Moral and Spiritual Values in Education,[8] established some years ago at the University of Kentucky, is now well known. Among the proposals formulated there is the following: "The school should create respect for the various forms of religious beliefs and practices through an understanding of the historical and social conditions under which they have arisen. Through visitation and observation the school should give the pupil an understanding and appreciation of the expressions and operations of religion in the local community."

Kent State University is another center of significant exploratory activity. It has conducted in-service workshops in local school systems in Ohio, designed to discover and develop moral and spiritual values in the public schools. The role of religion is considered in this context.

Columbia University conducted a fruitful conference on religion and education in 1954 as a feature of its bicentennial program.[9]

Union Theological Seminary has for the past five years conducted a seminar with workshop features for selected public school teachers and administrators who wish to clarify their vocational responsibility with respect to religion. The project, which has been financed by the General Service Foundation, is carried out within the general framework of our committee's analysis.

Among official religious bodies there has been much activity in the field we have been exploring. The National Council of Churches of Christ in the U.S.A. has a well-established Department of Religion and Public Education which, in the development of its program, has made constructive use of materials developed by our committee or pursuant to its exploratory studies.

The Roman Catholic position with respect to the place of religion in general education is well known. Because it has been authoritatively formulated, and because it is a matter of faith, we cannot point to any specific impact of the work of the American Council's committee on Catholic policy. It should be noted, however, that in recent years authoritative Catholic pronouncements have stressed the essential role of the public school in meeting the needs of American youth, and the resulting necessity of a positive attitude toward religion in schools which, in the nature of the case, must be under secular control. Monsignor William McManus, assistant director of the Department of Education, National Catholic Welfare Conference, when asked in the course of a workshop program what Catholics expected of the public schools, replied:

Catholics expect them to teach the regular subjects in an objective, complete and integral manner so that the students on all levels will discover for themselves the significant role of religion in human affairs, past and present. They expect public schools to refrain from indoctrinating pupils in a doctrinaire, secularistic philosophy of life which avowedly discounts the importance of religion in all affairs.[10]

Jewish educational leaders have given protracted and critical study to the reports issued by our committee. As a minority group having a huge stake in free, democratically controlled public schools, Jews are naturally apprehensive of any hint of sectarian intrusion into the school program. I think this apprehension is not without warrant insofar as it is inspired by overzealous efforts on the part of non-Jewish religious groups to bring sectarian influence to bear on the schools. I am impressed, however, by the readiness of Jewish leaders to accept *in principle* our basic contention concerning the responsibility of the public schools in this area. For example, the American Jewish Committee has said:

The schools should also foster an appreciation of the impact of religion on our civilization. Indeed, this knowledge is intrinsic to a well-rounded education. Such events as the Crusades, the Reformation and the colonization of America would be hopelessly distorted if religious motivations were not given proper weight. It would be equally wrong to omit the Bible from courses in literature or to ignore religious influences in the study of art.[11]

An interreligious approach to the problem has been effectively fostered for several years by the Religious Education Association through conferences, seminars, local chapter meetings, and the magazine *Religious Education*. The association is currently stressing the problems of higher education in this area, which are relevant to our main concern because of their bearing on the preparation of teachers.

Surely, this series of developments—only a partial list—abundantly warrants the venture the American Council on Education has made in territory that had previously been insufficiently explored. Indeed, the new interest and activity in this field might almost be called a movement.

Implications of the Present Situation

I shall venture now to comment on certain aspects of the present situation which seem to me to call for serious thought as we consider future strategy.

First, we must face the fact that the position our committee has taken in opposing everything in the nature of a theological commitment on the part of the public school itself is challenged as too conservative by many educational and religious leaders. We were sharply criticized at the outset on the ground that we had loose ideas about the separation between church and state. Now, the climate of opinion has changed to the extent of putting us on the defensive for taking separation too seriously.

Mr. Justice Douglas, in the ruling opinion in the Zorach case, wrote a sentence that has probably been quoted more often than any other judicial utterance in recent years. "We are," he said, "a religious people whose institutions presuppose a Supreme Being." I believe that sentence is strictly true, but I am troubled by the possibility that it may be taken as signifying a belief to which all teachers are expected to subscribe. The matter is by no means academic. Indeed, the major present concern of many religious and educational leaders with respect to the issue here under discussion seems to be that public education shall be definitely committed to a theistic position.

Some large school systems are shaping their curricula in this direction. An official publication of the Department of Instruction of the St. Louis Public Schools (1954) contained these directions for the teacher: "He shall endeavor to develop in his pupils principles of morality, love of God, and love of man. No teacher shall exercise any sectarian influence in the schools. . . ."

A "Guide to Moral and Spiritual Education" prepared for the San Diego (California) public schools in 1953 and authorized for experimental use contains the following paragraph:

American traditions, ideals, and institutions are founded on a belief in God and in recognition of His existence. Through great documents, which record historic decisions, and the instruments of government that set the pattern for democracy, Americans have demonstrated unswerving belief in God's existence. As the Pilgrims drew up their Mayflower Compact "in the presence of God" and as the signers of the Declaration of Independence attributed their rights to their "Creator," so today, in our schools, we assume that our students believe in God as defined for each of them in their home and church.

The much-publicized school prayer proposed by the Board of Regents of the State of New York is noteworthy in this connection. The Regents said: "We believe that at the commencement of each school day the act of allegiance to the Flag might well be joined with this act of reverence to God: 'Almighty God, we acknowledge our dependence upon Thee, and we beg Thy blessings upon us, our parents, our teachers and our Country.' "

The trend, in mood or in practice, indicated by these citations must be taken into account by all students of the problem. Of somewhat similar import are certain pronouncements of Protestant and Catholic organizations.

The National Council of the Churches of Christ in the U.S.A. has declared: "In some constitutional way provision should be made for the inculcation of the principles of religion, whether within or outside the precincts of the school, but always within the regular schedule of a pupil's working day."

A president-general of the National Catholic Educational Association has said: "We must appeal to American honesty and ingenuity to find a solution to the problem of restoring religion to the curriculum of all schools, without injury to the rights of any parent, and with equal justice to the rights of every child."

Especially in the matter of religious observances in connection with the great Christian festivals, it seems quite impracticable to enforce any one pattern designed as normative for the nation as a whole. A community that is relatively homogeneous and strongly religious is likely to insist that some token of its common faith find a place in the school program. That the sensibilities of minority groups which are deeply committed to a faith of their own are often offended in this way is a grievous fact. There are situations in which it seems practically impossible for the majority to enjoy in reasonable degree the "free exercise of religion" without the hazard of embarrassment and chagrin to members of a small minority. Here a large measure of understanding, forbearance, and restraint is called for. Yet I am strongly inclined to the view that the democratic process, informed by spiritual discipline, is our first and chief resource—not legislatures or courts. Appeal to the courts is an indispensable recourse for redress of an actual infringement of liberty, but is it not now sufficiently clear that the conditions of genuine freedom have to be discovered and defined in a context of the social and cultural environment?

I have come to believe, as a result of experience during the period here under review, that the effort to construct a national procedural norm with respect to the vital and vexing issue we are here confronting has been a serious mistake. It is one thing to do this in the matter of race segregation, which, in spite of many negative instances, is opposed by the very genius of American institutions; it is something quite other to set arbitrary limits—important though limits are —to the expression of religious faith and devotion, which is a major characteristic of the American people and deeply embedded in our tradition.

These considerations do not, I am persuaded, invalidate the position we have consistently defended—that religion should be studied objectively in the schools rather than taught dogmatically on public school authority. At the same time it is evident that in this controversial area we "face a condition and not a theory"—that in the past there has been too great a tendency on both sides of the argument to be doctrinaire. In practice, the demands of the local community are bound to be a powerful determinant in the making of school policy. Moreover, we have a significant tradition of local control over education which is at this moment being strongly emphasized. The boundary between state or federal control and local autonomy is tenuous and shifting. Recent experience with reference to religion in the schools indicates that the line cannot be arbitrarily drawn without political and social hazard.

It is in this connection that I have felt regret over the all but exclusive preoccupation of our committee with the secondary level of public education, for the most insistent demands that come from the community for explicit recognition of religion in the school program have to do with religious ceremonial and symbolism to which young children are particularly responsive. Paradoxically, it is the most intense forms of religious expression—the ritualistic forms—that the secular school finds hardest to avoid. Here is where the popular urge is strongest. We shall not solve our problem in terms of "study about religion" to the exclusion of those phases of the problem that are quite as relevant to the elementary level. Here I am not sure that even the right questions have been formulated.

We must also give serious thought to the role of religion in counseling—in what is commonly called guidance. While subscribing to the principle laid down by the Educational Policies Commission that religious sanctions may not be authoritatively invoked—that is, declared to be binding on individual conscience—in the public school, I nevertheless believe that these sanctions have an indispensable place in any guidance program. By this I mean, not sanctions imposed by the teacher or by the school, but sanctions that a wise counselor finds to be authentic in the personal and family life of the individual under guidance. Competent counseling makes use of all the personal resources in hand. If it be said that this involves hazards, the obvious reply is that all counseling is hazardous, but no hazard is greater than failure to make use of an authentic spiritual resource when we are trying to lead growing persons to higher moral and spiritual levels of life.

In conclusion, I wish to say that I believe the task assigned our committee has been measurably accomplished but that the American Council should continue to be active in this field. What is most urgently needed now is laborious study and carefully planned, sustained experimentation to the end that knowledge and wisdom may match zeal in the effort to solve a basic educational and cultural problem.

DISCUSSION BASED ON DR. JOHNSON'S PAPER

Presiding: ARTHUR S. ADAMS

DR. F. ERNEST JOHNSON (Study Consultant, National Council of the Churches of Christ in the United States of America): Dr. Adams, Ladies and Gentlemen:

It has been a long time since the reports of the Council's Committee on Religion and Education were issued, and I have taken the liberty of giving an interpretation of the committee's position in the light of events and developments during the intervening years. As I have said on the first page of my paper, except where I am directly quoting or interpreting the position of the committee as it appears in the printed reports, I am giving my own opinions.

First, the position of the committee taken in its earlier report, *The Relation of Religion to Public Education* (1947), was that religion should find a place in the curriculum of the public school when and as religious subject matter is intrinsic to the general subject under consideration.

We wanted to direct attention to the *study* of religion rather than the *teaching* of religion. We wanted religion to be studied as an aspect of culture. We wanted boys and girls to become literate with reference to religion in the life of man and in the conduct of human affairs.

It has sometimes been said that this is a nonsectarian approach to religion. That is quite mistaken. Ours was really a multisectarian approach in that we were not attempting to indoctrinate at all, but trying to make boys and girls, and young people, familiar with religion as empirical fact. Many people thought because we said a good deal about the secularization of life and education that our report was hostile to the secular as such. There could not be a greater mistake than that. We wanted to redeem the secular, if I may put it that way. To the degree that life, human institutions, business and industry, and so on, had become secularized—in the sense that the religious convictions of people, the faith by which people claim to live, had become nonrelevant to the common life—to that same degree the nonrelevance of religion to the common life was a thing that very greatly concerned us. That is what we meant when we spoke of secularism.

Our report called for study *about* religion in the public schools, and it shocked a good many people. Very soon, however, there was a change of mood, and we found the idea being taken up quite widely. We have now come to the point where we have had to recognize that, whereas our position was once thought to be radical, it is now thought by many people to be conservative. It seems to me that the line of demarcation in forensic terms has been redrawn and that

now the chief controversy has to do with the place in public education not merely of study about religion, which seems to be fairly
generally accepted, but rather of something approaching the substantive teaching of religion. At least, this seems to be the chief
point of contention where people assemble to discuss this very controversial issue. Furthermore, I would say that this change in mood
has been greatly fortified by the decision of the Supreme Court in
the Zorach case.

Finally, I would say that regardless of how the new questions may
be answered, the solution of our problem will not come by imposing
or trying to realize any one standard in all types of communities. It
will come as a result of social adjustment, adjustment to community
situations; therefore, our chief resource will be democratic education
and experimentation rather than appeal to legislatures and courts, although the legislatures and the courts must always be accessible for
the redress of the infringement of liberty when it actually happens.

MR. LEO PFEFFER (Director of the Commission on Law and
Social Action, American Jewish Congress): I would like Dr. Johnson to spend a few minutes in telling us what he means by teaching
religion as distinguished from the study of religion.

Dr. Johnson, you indicate that this seems to be the issue to which
you are presently addressing yourself. Specifically, I would like to
know, does this involve the inculcation of religious belief?

DR. JOHNSON: I would say that by *teaching* religion, I mean
inducting growing persons into the experience of a religious community. This is the kind of thing that can be done in the home and
in the church, or in a religious school or a private school. But it is
quite impossible to do that in a public school. I would say that teaching religion, if the term has any substantive significance at all, is
something that cannot be done in a public school.

I have defined teaching religion in terms of what we ordinarily
call religious education. I was impelled personally to shift from the
term "teaching" or even "teaching about" religion to the word
"study," because I found that so many educators, even those who
considered themselves progressive educators and who wanted no indoctrination where religion was involved, took the word "teach" to

mean "indoctrinate." Hence, I thought it was much more accurate to speak about the guided *study* of religion, and thus eliminate any suggestion of indoctrination.

Many educators think indoctrination is a bad word in any case, and I think indoctrination is practiced less and less in public education. But what we are talking about is a study of religion as it bears upon the subject matter in hand, as it is relevant. I refer, for example, to the study of the religious classics in the literature program and of religious institutions in the social studies program. Thus, a social studies teacher should not feel it necessary, when the markets, the labor unions, and the industries of the community are visited, to draw a line around the church and the synagogue and say, "We don't go there." That is what we meant by the study of religion in the context of our reports.

FATHER WILLIAM MCMANUS (Assistant Director, Department of Education, National Catholic Welfare Conference): Dr. Johnson, would you say, then, that the public school should help pupils study Catholicism, Judaism, and Protestantism in their own right? Or would you rather say that it should help them study these subjects only in relation to some other subject or some other series of subjects in the regular public school curriculum?

DR. JOHNSON: I personally feel, though I am not sure I can speak for the committee, that a plan like this should not eliminate the study of religion as a subject if, let us say, a senior high school class were very much interested in an elective course which on a higher level we would call comparative religion but which would really be "religion in our town."

They might want to study the various religious faiths, just as any other subject matter would be studied. This would be similar to studying the platforms of the various political parties represented in the community. I would see no objection to that. But that wasn't what we had in mind.

Monsignor McManus has been active in this committee from the beginning. What we had in mind was rather the anomaly which occurs in the teaching of history when religious movements, the development of religious institutions, and so on are slurred over, because of fear or because of prejudice. All of the social studies tend to veer away from religion because it is a very controversial matter. Nevertheless, the best example, it seems to me, of this objective approach is in the social studies field.

Before our report was published, one of our former students at Teachers College was a social studies teacher at Hunter High School, a public school in New York under the Board of Higher Education. She thought it a shame that these girls were not learning anything about religion in the life of New York. Accordingly, they organized a project and "went to town." They visited synagogues and churches of all faiths, and they asked rabbis, priests, and ministers innumerable questions. They got their information straight, and they did with it whatever they wanted.

MR. HARRISON SASSCER (Assistant Director, Division of Legislation and Federal Relations, National Education Association): Dr. Johnson, although you touched on it, I want to ask this question directly: Why do we use another subject to convey us to the teaching of or about religion? Do we teach American history or about American history? Do we teach American public affairs or about them? Is religion a unique subject so that we can go just so far but cannot treat it as any other subject is treated?

DR. JOHNSON: That is a very fair question, a question that often arises. If I may say so, I think the objection loses its force if you consider that the approach to the study of any subject matter is conditioned by the utility of that approach, by its relation to the entire learning process.

We are having a great deal of discussion throughout the country, are we not, over what the school should do about the subject of communism. Should communism be taught? Well, of course, we don't want the public schools to teach communism in the traditional sense of the word teach. But more and more educators are saying that at the proper level communism should be studied. Young people should learn the nature of communism, how it develops, how it is related to and how it contrasts with democracy, and so on.

I have heard it said that we cannot study *about* something, that study *about* something is not education, because there is no personal involvement. I think that there *is* involvement, even in the study of communism, as there is in the study of crime—a different kind of involvement from what we like to attain in the study of active citizenship, participation in party activities, and so on. But there is involvement because there is a great concern prompted by the motive of responsible citizenship. There is a great concern to understand. So it is with crime.

I feel, therefore, that just as it is necessary to study many different subject matters, with varying degrees and varying kinds of involvement on the part of the learner, so it is possible and necessary, in spite of the very definite limitation occasioned by the separation of church and state, to make a reverent study of religion without indoctrination. I use the word "reverent" because democracy, as I understand it, is normative in our education. Democracy is based fundamentally on reverence for persons, and, if you revere persons, you must revere what men have immemorially held sacred.

DR. EDWARD A. KRUG (Professor of Education, University of Wisconsin): I would like to refer, Dr. Johnson, to the comment in your summary of your paper to the effect that the American Council's position is sometimes challenged for being too conservative, a comment which you also develop in the final section of your paper. I want to ask whether or not this feeling that there are more advanced frontiers to be explored is illustrated adequately by the examples you gave in the final section of your paper, namely, the statements from public school systems holding that belief in God, love of God, or acceptance of God are proper aims of public education. In short, do the quotations from the St. Louis and San Diego public school systems illustrate the kind of challenge with which the American Council committee is confronted?

DR. JOHNSON: Yes. I don't want to speak for the committee here since it has not formulated a statement of its position in the light of all these developments, but I say quite frankly that some of these statements seem to me to be inconsistent with the principle that our committee laid down. However, because some of these views are backed by very strong local sentiment, because we do have a strong tradition of local control, and because we are suspicious of state domination, we probably have to be reconciled to the fact that many communities are going to do things of which we in this room might not approve, but which it would be very arbitrary to stop or prevent.

This is one of the tragic aspects of our problem. It is no simple matter. It isn't a matter to settle by choosing one system over another or one logic over another. The split in our culture is a tragic thing. We are not going to solve the problem simply by making a formula.

FATHER SYLVESTER HOLBEL (Superintendent of Schools, Diocese of Buffalo): I was delighted with your practical approach to the solution of the problem, namely, that it should be worked out on a local level. In your conclusion, however, you said the democratic process should be used. Do you mean that the majority opinion should prevail and that the minority should be disregarded? If the majority in a community should approve a certain program of religious education in the schools, using religious education in the broad sense, do you mean that the program should go into effect irrespective of the minority?

DR. JOHNSON: This is a coincidence, Mr. Chairman. I was writing an editorial today, and I think the last sentence I wrote was: "We must see that democracy means much more than majority rule."

The mere recording of a majority judgment and a policy action based on it do not add up to the democratic process. Now, to be sure, I don't know any other way to settle questions, so far as the next step—the immediate issue—is concerned, than by majority vote if the matter at issue is something that is clearly within the province of the people to decide.

I am one of those who felt that in the Scopes trial in Tennessee, incident to the fight in that state over the teaching of evolution, the people's legislature could not be denied the right to make a determination. We simply have to accept such a decision. But the democratic process involves a continual inquiry into the implications of the process, into all the factors of the situation, and, where religious liberties are being infringed, the leadership in the community ought never to rest until the conscience of the community responds to that situation. I think it is often true that a minority may say, "We wish things were different," yet may be so caught up in the process of policy-making that it will feel that it is already on the way to receiving recognition of its full right.

FATHER NEIL G. McCLUSKEY, S.J. (Education Editor, *America*): Dr. Johnson, I think that no matter what examples we use to describe this problem, we must ultimately recognize that there really are only two choices here.

Traditionally, we are a theistically biased people, whether it be in the form of deism or Christian sectarianism. It seems to me the point is whether or not we should justify our released-time programs, religious holidays, religious program assemblies, our motto "In God We Trust," Thanksgiving Day proclamations, and so on. To make these things meaningful to a student, we must take a position. To the extent that we do, we are inculcating a religious belief.

We have to take one or the other position. I don't think neutrality is anything but a word. Either there is a deistic bias, as several of these statements indicate, or there is not. It is not a case of teaching sectarian religion or any particular form of religion. Neutrality is without meaning. It is a case of accepting a fork in a road when there are only two roads.

I know this is a very delicate point, and I realize we must make full provision for those who have used their full freedom of conscience and their democratic right in not following any traditional interpretation of theism. I still think a decision cannot be avoided.

DR. JOHNSON: I think I cannot appeal at this point to a consensus in the committee, for the committee has not really grappled with that question in the light of developments in recent years. Personally, I feel that the faith of a community which is relatively homogeneous in religious terms naturally seeks some expression in its schools. I think that expression normally takes the form of religious ritual and symbolism. And I have said that it is at the worship level that the secular school is now pressed most strongly to recognize and introduce these theistic elements.

I, for one, think that it is a perfectly proper school exercise in almost any American community to sing, "Our fathers' God, to Thee, Author of liberty" because I think that this does express an authentic communal faith in symbolic terms. Now, we often do, by means of a ritual, bring the pupils in school into an atmosphere of worship which belongs to their culture and to the community. Regardless of what some members of the community may say, I think it is wholly unrealistic and improper to interfere with a clearly manifest desire of the school and of the community to have some such recognition of its faith.

On the other hand, I am very much afraid of committing the school officially to the proposition that all good Americans should believe in God. I am afraid of it because I think that a thoughtful high school senior, for instance, is going to resent being confronted with a proposition that he is not permitted to discuss. An intelligent, inquiring youngster is going to say, "Well, just what does that mean? What is God like? I have heard people talk about God in a great variety of ways, and they have different concepts of God." And the teacher feels obliged to say, "We can't go into that here." So the student says, "Well, at least you can tell me how we know there is a God." Whereupon, the teacher insists, "No, no. We can't go into that here."

It is not good education to propound statements *to be accepted* if they cannot be discussed. But I consider it is a different thing to allow boys and girls to participate, as their parents did, in a ritualistic exercise which does, as Mr. Justice Douglas has said, express the fact that we in America are "a religious people whose institutions presuppose a Supreme Being." That is a very different thing from insisting in the public school that a theistic position must be accepted by all good Americans.

Also, I must say that I think there are some good teachers who find themselves unable to accept a theistic position in any form in which it is ordinarily put forward in our churches. And if we adopt a school creed, then I think we are really setting up a religious test.

MR. W. MARSHON DePOISTER (Administrative Dean, Chapman College): Dr. Johnson, religion is a fact in American culture just like any other fact. Do you feel we will get very far at this or any other conference until we study our own religions, including the major faiths, with the same kind of objectivity we employ in studying other religions, such as Islam and Hinduism? That is, can we expect to get very far in this kind of discussion with a group such as this making statements of purpose unless we grant ourselves the privilege of looking at our own religions objectively, "letting the chips fall where they may"?

DR. JOHNSON: This is a very proper and relevant question, but a difficult one. I worked with Professor William H. Kilpatrick for years. I was a student and later a colleague of his. When I worked on a panel in a course on foundations of education of which Professor Kilpatrick was the chairman, we used to have a good many off-the-record discussions about our program, and I am very sure that he often felt that the educative process is limited by the structure of the community mind, that there were lots of things which he would have liked to discuss more freely. Take the matter of sex education; we felt that an adequate educational program would require more than the community would permit. Communism would serve as another illustration, or the study of socialism where even the most objective approach arouses opposition. Although our goal is objectivity, so far as study is concerned, I don't think that we can always go the full length. In fact, I am quite sure it isn't possible.

But this problem is encountered outside the school. I am quite sure that many a person who wants a passport and who takes an oath to defend the country against its enemies wouldn't get his passport if he were quizzed as to how he would do the defending. I think a good many convinced pacifists have satisfied their consciences that they could say what was expected of them. Furthermore, I am perfectly sure that many a minister, if he were quizzed by a committee of his congregation on particular points of faith or asked to pass a satisfactory examination on the official creed of his church would be in very great trouble. Many an honest, conscientious, and successful minister would be in trouble because he couldn't find thought forms that would be common to him and his congregation. This happens all the time when we deal with our children, although we constantly try to get on a higher level of frank understanding. Nevertheless, I do think that unless we are continually making progress toward frankness, toward uninhibited inquiry, we are stopping short of where we ought to go.

MR. CLYDE VARNER (Supervisor of Social Studies, Department of Instruction, Board of Education, Cleveland, Ohio): Dr. Johnson, in reference to your statement, "Our fathers' God, to Thee," I would like to ask if you would place the new wording of the Pledge of Allegiance to the Flag in the same category? Does that categorize the child's affirmation of faith? He doesn't say, "as Washington or Lincoln said, 'under God.'" He says it in another context.

DR. JOHNSON: That is a difficult question. To answer it you would have to know just what goes on in the average person's mind when he recites that. Personally I think it is a mistake to try to make education religious by arbitrary acts, such as incorporating new phrases in familiar formulas and trying to induce a mood in a purely formal way.

On the other hand, I cannot see anything but good coming from singing, "Oh beautiful, for spacious skies, For amber waves of grain. . . . America, America, God shed His Grace on thee." I just don't see that any violence is being done to anybody's intellectual integrity. However—and this is terribly important—I would lean far backward to avoid coercing anybody to participate in any such exercise.

You remember how the Supreme Court met this issue in a very crucial case when it rendered its final decision about the flag salute—which some people felt was idolatrous and an infringement of religious liberty. The Court, reversing a former decision, didn't say there should be no flag salute. The Court said, no pupil should be required to participate in such salute.

There are many, many cases, I am quite sure, where justice, distributive justice, if you will, is only rough justice. It is not absolute, and it is one of our main tasks to create a democratic mood, a mood of understanding, a mood of empathy, if you like, in which people of different convictions and different backgrounds will learn to share in each other's activities without feeling that they are in any way being imposed upon, being coerced into accepting something that is not real to them.

DR. MILTON R. KONVITZ (Professor, School of Industrial and Labor Relations and Law School, Cornell University): I would like to ask Dr. Johnson if he would elaborate a little bit more on an adverb which he used and which I think may be a key to the whole problem. That adverb is "reverently."

I think he was quite right in saying that, if religion is to be studied, it needs to be studied reverently. A large segment of the people of the world are religious. I would like to speak as a teacher who has attempted to teach some problems reverently for the same reason offered by Dr. Johnson. Let me cite a few examples that may contribute to an elucidation of the problem.

Communism is a "religion." Communism has made an appeal to a very large portion of the population of the world today. Between 35 and 40 percent of the people of the world, I think, are subject to Communist rule. As a teacher at Cornell, it has been my duty to study communism with my students. Moreover, as a teacher I have had to do it reverently. Depending on the tempo in a particular semester, I spend four to five to six weeks on the subject.

Believe me, Dr. Johnson, I often wonder why I didn't undertake some easier way to make a living. One goes through agony day after day and minute after minute because, if one is a teacher and one is going to teach about communism, one must do it first of all from within communism. I must teach it as if I believe what I am teaching. I cannot just stand there and say that communism is wrong for the following reasons, without first telling them why communism makes an appeal to millions of people, why it has been accepted as a religion.

My students have to read the Communist Manifesto and other Communist literature. Of course, when I get all through I become a critic of communism. But I will never know whether or not, subtly, I may not have planted the wrong kind of seeds in the minds of some of my students.

But I haven't any doubt that casting one's self in these roles is an agonizing experience. It is a fearful thing to do. And I don't know that any secondary school teacher ought to be called upon to fill these roles. But mind you, this is a university, where it has to be performed. If I had to do it in a high school, if I had to do it in a lower-grade school, I wouldn't undertake it.

One can think, as do the members of the Florida Legislature and some members of the American Bar Association who are not law teachers like Professor Sutherland, that it is easy to study communism in the schools. That is because they haven't tried it. It is easy enough to stand before a class and tell them why you think communism is anti-American or subversive of American institutions, but that is not studying communism.

I have to do the same thing with religion at Cornell. I spend a couple of months on a discussion of Biblical religion in a course which deals with the roots of American values. Protestant, Catholic, and Jewish students are required to read large parts of both the Old Testament and the New Testament, and again I go through the same kind of agonizing experience. I have to speak as if I am a Christian; I have to speak as if I am a Jew. I am a Jew, but this is entirely irrelevant to my performance as a teacher. My own convictions do not matter. Again, when I get all through, I wonder whether I haven't unsettled some minds. I think I have. I think inevitably I must. Some Jewish students are disturbed by the way I have talked about Christianity. Some Christians are disturbed about the way I have talked about Christianity.

All this is done with reverence. I don't know any other way of teaching that subject. But how are you going to do that in a high school? How are you going to do that in a grammar school?

DR. JOHNSON: In the first place, I think that there is nothing in our proposal that is comparable to that. I have said here that we were concerned chiefly with the secondary level, and we were concerned with guided study, the study of religious art, the reading of religious classics, the close observance of religious institutions, and so on. Of course, that approach capitalizes the interpretation of religious philosophies, institutions, and ways of life by the people themselves, who do not have to put themselves into the mood but who are already there.

The boys and girls go to the synagogue and talk to the rabbi. They don't ask a teacher to tell them what Judaism is. However, it is perfectly right, I think, to suggest that any thoroughgoing educative process will have reverberations. Boys and girls will want to talk and ask questions, and the teacher will be asked for opinions.

But the essence of our proposal is not that the teacher shall undertake to interpret religions other than his or her own. The essence of our proposal is that the pupil be confronted with people who are authorized to speak and, thereby, be encouraged to study reverently.

I was not talking about the teacher trying to interpret some religion other than his or her own. But, as a matter of fact, one of the best teachers I ever had, a professor of psychology, could interpret, as if it were his own, system after system that he thought his students ought to know. I have said, and I repeat it because I feel very strongly about it, that no person is really competent to teach philosophy at any level who cannot or will not learn how to make a reasonably acceptable statement of a philosophical position other than his own when there is nobody else to make it better than he can. Certainly, the teacher of theology in a seminary who is not able to make his students understand what people of various faiths have thought and how they felt is less than a really effective teacher.

Now, on this matter of reverence, let me tell you about this incident. In the Jewish Theological Seminary in New York there is an

Institute for Religious and Social Studies. One feature of this institute is a luncheon course of thirteen weeks during the winter when speakers of different faiths and disciplines participate. There are Christians and Jews and people who are in neither group.

One time, Dr. Finkelstein, the chancellor of the seminary, invited an Episcopalian minister to close the meeting with a word of prayer, and the minister closed it with a Trinitarian benediction.

Afterwards, I said to Dr. Finkelstein, "I am sorry he did that. It wasn't necessary for him to do that. He could have said, 'The Lord bless you and keep you, the Lord make his face to shine upon you.'— the familiar Mosaic blessing."

And the Chancellor said, "Yes, but I am not so sure about it. After all, he is a Christian minister. Knowing that, I asked him to pray, and why shouldn't he do it in his own way?"

I still think the minister would have been wiser to do it the way I suggested, but here was an example of reverence, of real reverence. Louis Finkelstein was able to listen to that Christian benediction as an expression of a devout minister's faith and say, "That is all right. It doesn't irritate me." That is what I mean by reverence.

RABBI SAMUEL SCHAFLER (Department of Education, United Synagogue Commission on Jewish Education): First, let me say that I feel a great empathy with Professor Konvitz because I feel a distress similar to his. As you may gather, I am a religious educator, and I have a great sense of pain that a conference such as this is necessary. If we religious educators were not the failures we have been for so many years, perhaps we would not be here grappling with this very serious problem. So I am prompted to share Professor Konvitz's sense of agony and pain.

But I should like to direct a question to Dr. Johnson on the paper that he prepared, a question pertaining to the following paragraph which I must confess I did not understand and which, I believe, involves an important element:

I have come to believe, as a result of experience during the period here under review, that the effort to construct a national procedural norm with respect to the vital and vexing issue we are here confronting has been a serious mistake. It is one thing to do this in the matter of race segregation, which, in spite of many negative instances, is opposed by the very genius of American institutions; it is something quite other to set arbitrary limits

—important though limits are—to the expression of religious faith and devotion, which is a major characteristic of the American people and deeply embedded in our tradition.

My question concerns the meaning of the phrase "opposed by the very genius of American institutions." The First and the Fourteenth Amendments, as I have been brought up to appreciate and understand them, are also a part of the very genius of American institutions and do set limits. I would like to have this phrase defined so that I can see how it excludes these limits that you feel it would not be possible to set in this instance.

DR. JOHNSON: First, may I say a word about the agony. Ladies and gentlemen, I have increasingly felt that there isn't any other way through this maze of pitfalls except an agonizing way. One cannot do anything that is terribly important without accepting hazards.

Second, let me say that I think it is gratuitous and mistaken to think that the only reason why the public schools are concerned with this problem is that the religious schools have defaulted. The public school's task is very different from that of the religious school.

I have never heard anyone refute the statement that, if the general education program in the public school covers practically everything else that is vital, yet excludes religion entirely, it tends to create the impression that religion is peripheral to education. Nevertheless, the public schools' function is entirely different from that of the religious school.

Now, I think we will all be clear on the rest of the question when Professor Sutherland has finished what he is going to say. I am not proposing at all that we slight the First and Fourteenth Amendments, but I think it is perfectly clear that the judiciary is going through an agonizing appraisal of these to find out exactly what they mean with reference to our subject.

Public Authority and Religious Education: A Brief Survey of Constitutional and Legal Limits

ARTHUR E. SUTHERLAND

Professor Sutherland is Bussey Professor of Law at Harvard University. He practiced law in Rochester, New York, from 1926 to 1941, except during 1927–28 when he was secretary to Mr. Justice Holmes and in 1938 when he served in the New York State Constitutional Convention. Dr. Sutherland was professor of law at Cornell University for five years before joining the Harvard faculty in 1950. In 1956 he was a Fulbright lecturer at Oxford University. His most recent book, The Law and One Man Among Many, *contains some observations pertinent to the subject of the paper here presented.*

THE ANTINOMIES of government sometimes bemuse an observer. The President in his inaugural oath calls on God to help him preserve, protect, and defend the Constitution of the United States—that fundamental law which, the Supreme Court once held, forbids religious instruction in a public grade school.[1] A recurrent theme of social criticism is the decadence of the younger generation: like younger generations since time began, it has forsaken the ancient ways and, for want of the wholesome godliness of the fathers, is bound for perdition. Public schools, where the ideas of the younger generation are largely shaped, must self-consciously shun advocacy of godliness, we are concurrently told, lest fundamental freedoms of

33

the pupils be invaded. One reads of a deep malaise in society, of a wide yearning to return to ancient faith. One also reads that to permit private distribution of the King James Bible after school in a public classroom, to those children whose parents want it, is unconstitutional in New Jersey.[2] The lay reader may well be puzzled by assertions that religious content is proscribed in public education, and may wonder how this comes about in a nation whose free schools derive from theocratic New England and in a republic whose coinage proclaims trust in God. This paper proposes some examination of these contradictions.

Some Necessary Distinctions

At the outset one is conscious of a confusion of terms. Public education means many things.[3] It is available to people of different ages, from the tot in kindergarten to the philosophy student in a state university. Nothing compels government to treat all these alike. Religious content may well be legally tolerable in college teaching where it would not be in the fifth grade. The first lesson in constitutional law is that equality is required only when there is no good reason for inequality. To a certain extent constitutional limitations follow popular sentiment; one seems to sense an opinion that the objectionable character of religious manifestations in public education diminishes in inverse relation to the increasing intellectual resistance of the maturing student. It may be tolerated, that is to say, provided it is ineffectual and therefore awakens no resentment—tolerance and indifference being first cousins, whose relationship is often decorously ignored.

Then, too, religious education is a term which may apply to many different kinds of classroom exercises. It is conceivable that if I were teaching in a public high school I might assure my young charges that they were about to receive the ultimate truth, and require them for that purpose to memorize the thirty-nine "Articles of Religion as established by the Bishops, the Clergy, and the Laity of the Protestant Episcopal Church in the United States of America, in Convention, on the twelfth day of September in the Year of our Lord 1801." This would probably get me in trouble with some pupils and parents, with the principal, the board of education, the state superintendent of education, and perhaps with the state and federal courts.

Or I might be trusted to teach high school seniors modern history, and I might use in class the admirable high school text of the late Carl L. Becker of Cornell.[4] When we came to page 39, we should have to discuss "The Reformation or Protestant Revolt." I could not explain this part of the current of thought in the Western World without explaining a number of the same ideas set out in the Thirty-nine Articles. I am confident that there would be little chance that my instruction would be censored by any public authority.

There is, that is to say, a great difference between the advocacy of religious dogma, and on the other hand the exposition of the history of man's ideas. I concede at once that these two meet, and merge at the point of meeting. A historical lecturer might discuss the ideas of the Reformation with expressions of satisfaction, or with evident abhorrence.

Every idea is an incitement. It offers itself for belief, and, if believed, it is acted on unless some other belief outweighs it, or some failure of energy stifles the movement at its birth. The only difference between the expression of an opinion and an incitement in the narrower sense is the speaker's enthusiasm for the result. Eloquence may set fire to reason.[5]

Nevertheless the distinction between doctrine and exposition is fairly clear. I can teach history unhampered by the law where I would be stopped if I started to preach sermons.

Thus, standards of constitutional tolerance seem different for students at different stages of maturity, and for instruction with differing emphasis. Furthermore, standards vary with levels of government. The Federal Constitution has restricted comparatively little religious schooling. Only once in its history has the Supreme Court of the United States ever adjudged any religious instruction in a public school to be barred by the national Constitution. State constitutions are more explicit in their inhibitions, and religious manifestations which might escape the impact of the Fourteenth Amendment are apt to conflict with a state clause. Local government may be more restrictive than either. The trustees of a school district have to respond quite sensitively to local sentiment, and a teacher or school principal who wished to introduce some religious instruction against the wishes of his trustees would be in trouble at once. On the other hand, much religious teaching may continue in response to community desires, unhampered in actual practice by restrictions in the state or federal

constitutions, which would stop the program if the somewhat ponderous constitutional machinery of inhibiting procedure were set in motion. Most educational policy is locally determined, and perhaps this
is just as well.

The Federal Constitution and the United States Supreme Court

The First Amendment to the Federal Constitution, which took
effect in 1791, put certain limits on the government of the United
States, but imposed no limits whatever on the several states. Its first
clause, which concerns the subject of this paper reads: "Congress
shall make no law respecting an establishment of religion, or prohibiting the free exercise thereof; . . . ." The reason for this insertion seems
quite obvious. The people of the several states had somewhat reluct-
antly accepted the new Federal Constitution of 1789. They were
suspicious of the powers entrusted to the "federal colossus," and their
ratifying conventions in many cases expressed the hope that a series
of limitations might be placed on the central government. A state like
Massachusetts, which during the first third of the nineteenth century
continued, through its town governments, to give tax support for
chosen churches, mainly Congregational, could very well have looked
with hostility at the prospect of a Federal Government establishing
an Episcopal regime, or restricting by act of Congress the exercise of
religions in the several states. The First Amendment ended these
worries.

There was no suggestion, in 1791, that the Federal Government
should be given a general mandate to protect the people of any state
against its own state government. Only after eighty years and a civil
war, in 1868, was the Fourteenth Amendment adopted imposing on
the Federal Government the general duty to protect the people of each
state against outrage by their own state governments. The Fourteenth
Amendment is expressed in vague terms. It says nothing about religious freedom or religious establishments. Its language germane to
the subject of this paper is: ". . . Nor shall any state deprive any
person of life, liberty, or property, without due process of law; nor
deny to any person within its jurisdiction the equal protection of the
laws."

Much of the study of constitutional law turns upon the meaning of
these words. In one case (and only in one) has the Supreme Court

of the United States held that the conduct of a compulsory public school concerning religious instruction attained such a degree of unreasonableness that it fell within the proscription of the Fourteenth Amendment.

The case in question is *McCollum* v. *Board of Education,*[6] in which the Supreme Court declared unconstitutional an arrangement in force in the public schools of Champaign, Illinois, which permitted the school buildings to be used for short periods during the week for instruction given by religious teachers of various denominations having no other connection with the school system. The mother of a boy named Terry McCollum, who was a convinced atheist, objected to the religious instruction of her son. Accordingly the boy, in order to avoid the instruction in question, was obliged to ask permission (readily granted) to go to some other place in the school building to pursue secular studies while the religious class was being held. The United States Supreme Court, in an opinion by Mr. Justice Black, said:

The operation of the state's compulsory education thus assists and is integrated with the program of religious instruction carried on by separate religious sects. Pupils compelled by law to go to school for secular education are released in part from their legal duty upon the condition that they attend the religious classes. This is beyond all question a utilization of the tax-established tax-supported public school system to aid religious groups to spread their faith. And it falls squarely under the ban of the First Amendment (made applicable to the States by the Fourteenth). . . .

The language of Mr. Justice Black is particularly interesting in its suggestion that the general terms of the Fourteenth Amendment, by a sort of shorthand, expressed in brief the more specific and detailed restrictions of the First Amendment, and forbade the states to do what the Federal Government had previously been forbidden to do. Mr. Justice Frankfurter delivered a separate opinion in which Justices Jackson, Rutledge, and Burton joined. His opinion seems to stress more the hardship imposed upon the individual child, and is more suggestive of the reasoning in cases of racial discrimination. It points out, respecting children like Terry:

The children belonging to these non-participating sects will thus have inculcated in them a feeling of separatism when the school should be the training ground for habits of community, or they will have their religious instruction in a faith which is not that of their parents.

One of the most difficult things to remember about constitutional law is that the opinions of the justices often express ideas much more sweeping than the actual matter decided. For example, in 1947 the Supreme Court of the United States, in *Everson* v. *Board of Education*,[7] actually decided the rather narrow point that a New Jersey taxpayer had no grievance under the Fourteenth Amendment when public funds, to which as a taxpayer he was obliged to contribute, were used to pay the transportation of some children in the community to Catholic parochial schools. The Supreme Court held this local school arrangement constitutional. But the language of the Court goes far beyond the holding. Mr. Justice Black, having stated that the Fourteenth Amendment forbids the state to do what the First Amendment forbids the Federal Government to do, goes on to say:

The "establishment of religion" clause of the First Amendment means at least this: Neither a state nor the Federal Government can set up a church. Neither can pass laws which aid one religion, aid all religions, or prefer one religion over another. Neither can force nor influence a person to go to or to remain away from church against his will or force him to profess a belief or disbelief in any religion. No person can be punished for entertaining or professing religious beliefs or disbeliefs, for church attendance or non-attendance. No tax in any amount, large or small, can be levied to support any religious activities or institutions, whatever they may be called, or whatever form they may adopt to teach or practice religion. Neither a state nor the Federal Government can, openly or secretly, participate in the affairs of any religious organizations or groups and vice versa. In the words of Jefferson, the clause against establishment of religion by law was intended to erect "a wall of separation between Church and State."[8]

This eloquent and sweeping dictum scarcely corresponds with the actual decision in the New Jersey bus case, and the latest word by the Supreme Court on schools seems to have cut down the authority of the McCollum case which held unconstitutional the Champaign plan of religious instruction. This was *Zorach* v. *Clauson*,[9] decided in 1952. At issue here was the propriety under the Fourteenth Amendment of releasing children from New York public schools, during normal hours of classroom work, for instruction at various religious centers, while nonparticipating children were compelled to stay on the school premises engaged in secular studies. Mr. Justice Jackson, whose words were likely to be pungent, said that under these circumstances the public school "serves as a temporary jail for a pupil who will not go to Church."

The only difference between the Zorach and McCollum cases seems to be that in the latter the instruction was carried on in the school-house; how this imposes more hardship on the dissenting child than that in the Zorach case is not easy to see. And indeed, the degree of the spiritual duress imposed on Terry McCollum, when he was obliged to leave the schoolroom and read a book somewhere else while his schoolmates had religious instruction, scarcely seems to rise to the same level as the compulsory segregation of Negroes or the extraction of evidence from a prisoner by forcible administration of an emetic. The Zorach case may be taken to suggest that the Supreme Court will not undertake to protect the people of a state against every chemical trace of spiritual embarrassment from public authority.

The Supreme Court of the United States during its 167 years, has considered only ten cases involving the religious problems of publicly maintained schools.[10] The brevity of this list (considered in the light of the observances in many hundreds of schools in many states) suggests that the Federal Constitution as actually applied may not have seriously hampered moderate religious manifestations in the public schools of the nation. The specific facts in the Champaign, Illinois, case, should be remembered: the children, unless excused, were present under compulsion; the instruction was given on public school premises; the children were of grade school age; the teaching was done by outside sectarian religious instructors not in the public school system. What restrictions the Fourteenth Amendment may place upon instruction by regular members of the school staff, or upon instruction of high school or college students, or instruction in the philosophy of religion rather than in the advocacy of its doctrines, all these questions remain to be tested in the federal courts. And the Supreme Court has indicated that it will listen only to a complaintant with some discernible personal grievance. That Court is not maintained to judge debates on abstract questions, even when these concern the separation of church and state.

State Constitutions and State Courts

Public education is almost entirely carried on by the states; if private, it is regulated by them. Federal officers have business with educational functions in the states only when the states look to the United States for aid, or, what is more relevant here, where an individual feels that the state has done him some harm which, under the Fourteenth Amendment, the Federal Government should correct. Because these latter circumstances are infrequent, the great majority of regulations of all sorts covering education emanate from the states alone. The senior state law—the state constitution—ordinarily provides in some way for an absence of sectarian manifestations in public instruction. Thus the constitution of New York, after a preamble which recites that the people of the state are "grateful to Almighty God for our freedom," by its eleventh article, on education, provides:

Neither the state nor any subdivision thereof shall use its property or credit or any public money, or authorize or permit either to be used, directly or indirectly, in aid or maintenance, other than for examination or inspection, of any school or institution of learning wholly or in part under the control or direction of any religious denomination, or in which any denominational tenet or doctrine is taught, but the legislature may provide for the transportation of children to and from any school or institution of learning.[11]

The New Jersey constitution, after an expression of gratitude similar to that of New York, provides: "There shall be no establishment of one religious sect in preference to another; . . . ."[12] Kentucky, after a similar preamble, provides that:

No preference shall ever be given by law to any religious sect, society or denomination; nor to any particular creed, mode of worship or system of ecclesiastical polity; nor shall any person be compelled to attend any place of worship, to contribute to the erection or maintenance of any such place, or to the salary or support of any minister of religion; nor shall any man be compelled to send his child to any school to which he may be conscientiously opposed; and the civil rights, privileges or capacities of no person shall be taken away, or in anywise diminished or enlarged, on account of his belief or disbelief of any religious tenet, dogma or teaching. No human authority shall, in any case whatever, control or interfere with the rights of conscience.[13]

One could continue this inventory to the point of weariness. It becomes apparent, on examination of a few state constitutions, that in general their provisions against the intermixture of the secular and the religious, in any governmentally controlled institutions are much more precise and definite than the due process and equal protection clauses of the Fourteenth Amendment. As one might expect, the number of cases reported from state courts is very much greater than the limited group in the Supreme Court of the United States. To attempt to catalogue all this mass of legal material would tire the eye and extend this paper far beyond its permitted limits. A wiser procedure seems to be to select a few conspicuous features common to much state litigation and discuss these as symptomatic of others.

"Sectarian."—One of the surprising discoveries of the young lawyer is the relevance and wisdom of a good many observations not found in law books. He may well find truth in Humpty-Dumpty's saying, "When I use a word it means just what I choose it to mean—neither more nor less."

The constitutions and statutes of a great many states, in one form of words or another, forbid "sectarian" instruction, but this term does not define itself. From time to time in every part of the country, a problem is caused when the members of some local school board feel that it would be wholesome for the young people under their charge to have some religious exercise in school, often a reading from the Bible, sometimes prayers or hymns. State supreme courts are from time to time faced with the question of reconciling this local desire with the provisions of their state constitutions forbidding sectarian teaching. This has recently given rise to an interesting opinion in New Jersey. In 1950, a taxpayer named Doremus carried to the Supreme Court of that state an action against his board of education,[14] and the state itself. Mr. Doremus sought a judgment declaring the unconstitutionality of certain New Jersey statutes requiring the reading of five verses from the Old Testament at the beginning of each classroom day and directing that no religious service or exercise "except the reading of the Bible and the repeating of the Lord's Prayer" should be held in any public school. He predicated his argument on the First and Fourteenth Amendments of the Federal Constitution, and the Supreme Court of New Jersey found these provisions not infringed by the exercises described in the New Jersey statutes. Mr. Doremus does not appear to have based any argument on the provision of Article 1, Paragraph 4 of the New Jersey constitution that "There shall be no establishment of one religious sect in preference to another" nor did the New Jersey Supreme Court in the Doremus case expressly raise this point. The court, however, stated: "We consider that the Old Testament and the Lord's Prayer pronounced without comment are not sectarian, and that the short exercise provided by the statute does not constitute sectarian instruction or sectarian worship. . . ." Mr. Doremus, disappointed, attempted to appeal to the United States Supreme Court from the judgment of the New Jersey Supreme Court, but his appeal was dismissed on the ground that he was not hurt by the New Jersey exercises, as no expense was shown to the taxpayers in consequence of these services.[15]

In 1953, another New Jersey taxpayer named Tudor who was also a parent of a pupil in the public schools of Rutherford in that state, carried a case to the Supreme Court of New Jersey, seeking to enjoin the members of the school board from permitting the distribution after school hours, but on school premises, to children whose parents requested it in writing, of copies of the Gideons Bible, a book containing all of the New Testament, and the Psalms and Proverbs from the Old Testament, all without note or comment, conformable to the edition of 1611, commonly known as the King James Version. The distribution was made by members of the Gideons organization. The Supreme Court of New Jersey held that this was a sectarian manifestation of religion, and that it was intolerable under the First and Fourteenth Amendments of the Federal Constitution, and was also in conflict with the provision of the New Jersey constitution, Article 1, Paragraph 4, forbidding any "establishment of one religious sect in preference to another."[16] This time the Gideons and the board of education were annoyed; they in turn attempted to carry their case to the Supreme Court of the United States. After a delay of some months, however, that Court declined to consider it on the merits.[17] Thus the Old Testament and the Lord's Prayer seem to be nonsectarian in New Jersey, but the Gideons Bible seems to be sectarian and forbidden under the state constitution.

Such puzzling differences of opinion may be observed elsewhere in the United States. The New Jersey Supreme Court in the Doremus opinion mentions twelve states and the District of Columbia as requiring the reading of the Bible in public school classes, and five other states as making its use permissive. Bible-reading has been upheld in a number of state supreme court decisions and has been struck down in others. This diversity is irritating alike to lawyer and layman who wish to prepare a neat summary of the law. Such an undertaking is all the more difficult because decisions vary in time as well as in space; what is law in a given state last year may not be next year. The diversities in space result from the federal structure of the nation. When the Constitution of the United States was devised, the fathers thought wise to permit to the several states a certain amount of local idiosyncracy. Although this is probably diminishing with the passage of years, a portion of it still remains, and in no subject is it more conspicuous than in that of religious education in the public schools.

A Clerical Faculty in a Public School.—One of the most persistent problems in American public education arises out of the presence of religious schools in need of funds for efficient operation, in territories where there are numbers of young people in need of schooling, but not adherents of the religions of the sectarian schools. The local public school authorities, who may not be subtle constitutionalists, are likely to conclude that the facilities of the religious schools should be made available to the children of the district generally, in exchange for some subsidy from public funds. Obviously, this situation may produce schools under various degrees of religious influence. A member of a religious order might, like any other teacher, be employed to teach in a public school, and few people would suggest his disqualification because of his belief alone. At the other extreme, a parochial school may be completely incorporated in the public school system, without change of religious symbols, instructional staff, religious costumes, or any other feature. Most problems of constitutional law are problems of degree, and that which is legally tolerable ends where the religious infusion becomes unreasonably great. Unhappily, a standard of reasonableness is one which cannot be drawn with mathematical certainty in this or any other field of government. Perhaps an examination of some cases of the kind suggested would be useful.

In 1917 such a problem arose in Kentucky in connection with the United Presbyterian Church.[18] The Church owned Stanton College which conducted a grade and high school as well as collegiate instruction. The local public authorities, instead of building a school building of their own, contracted with Stanton College for the education of grade and high school pupils in Stanton's buildings. In a suit by certain taxpayers, the Kentucky Court of Appeals held that the Kentucky constitution was violated when any part of the common school fund was appropriated "in aid of any church, sectarian or denominational school;" and further held it unconstitutional for the trustees of any public educational corporation to enter into a contract by which their institutions were brought directly or indirectly under the influence or control of any denominational institution.

The difficulty of laying down general rules applicable to specific cases is pointed up by the result of a case decided by the Kentucky Court of Appeals in 1956, this time involving the conduct of public schools in buildings owned by the Catholic Church, rented or furnished rent free to the school board, in which classes were taught, in some instances by members of religious orders, wearing the religious costume and symbols of their orders.[19] The majority of the Court of Appeals held the arrangement constitutional, pointing out that if the nuns were prevented from teaching in the public schools because of their religious beliefs they would be denied the equal protection of the law guaranteed by the Fourteenth Amendment. The Court of Appeals distinguished a Missouri case which in 1953 arrived at an opposite result.[20] There the facts were far different. In the Missouri case, the nuns lived in schools surmounted by crosses; religious holidays were observed, religious instruction was given in some of the schools, acolytes or older boys were excused during school hours to attend weddings and funerals in the adjoining church. In effect, said the Kentucky Court of Appeals, several of the schools involved in the Missouri case were really Catholic schools, instead of public schools with Catholic sisters teaching in them.

However, the Kentucky Court of Appeals in June 1956 indicated that it was maintaining a vigilant watch over constitutional issues in the public schools.[21] In a taxpayers' suit the court found that substantially all the periodicals in a high school library were Catholic publications, which violated Kentucky Revised Statutes 158.190— "No book or other publication of a sectarian, infidel or immoral character, or that reflects on any religious denomination, shall be used or distributed in any common school. No sectarian, infidel or immoral doctrine shall be taught in any common school." The court found that on certain occasions sectarian literature had been distributed. It enjoined these practices.

The importance of these minor controversies is probably not very great. State constitutional provisions vary considerably from state to state; they are supplemented by statutes which vary even more; and a decision within one state can rarely be carried authoritatively into another. The significant lesson to be drawn from the Kentucky cases and the decisions in other states discussed in the Kentucky opinions, is only this; that a great deal of local variation appears in state constitutions and laws governing religious education; and that the presence of frequent judicial opinions indicating controversies on the subject shows a continual impulse in local communities to introduce religious elements in public education.

Some Benefits of Legal Imperfection

Institutions of public education disclose a considerable amount of religious influence at all levels. No matter what the constitutional theory, a good deal of religious doctrine finds its way into public school curricula. The Regents of the University of New York recommend prayer to start the school day, and scores of New York school districts take up the practice.[22] In January 1957 four residents of Nassau County were urging the New York State education commission to prohibit the New York Hyde Park School board from displaying an "interdenominational" version of the Ten Commandments in classrooms.[23] Bible reading is mandatory in the schools of many states, and is permissive in others. When the student reaches junior college or university level he comes by his own choice. No law compels him to go to college, as it compelled Terry McCollum to go to grade school. He may very possibly find himself studying the theory of many religions in courses called Philosophy I, History of Western Thought, Christian Living, or Life's Problems. In no case, as far as I know, has any court interfered with religious instruction on a college level. The only reported case that I can find where this was attempted[24] resulted in dismissal on procedural grounds before the court ever reached a study of the merits.

The Federal Constitution, as interpreted in the McCollum case, and the state constitutions in all their variety impose on public teaching limits more formidable in theory than they may be in practice. The great multitude of comparatively minor religious manifestations which obtain in many grade and high schools probably thrive on local public approval. Most of them escape official interference because of the sheer inertia of the legal machinery, which tends to discourage prosecution, by disgruntled taxpayers and parents, of more than a few cases. No one should welcome judicial delay, expense, and uncertainty. Nevertheless, the difficulties met by citizens who start lawsuits on constitutional grounds to enjoin local authorities from conducting some minor religious observances in the public schools may have some good aspects. The practical impossibility of consistent and doctrinaire constitutional literalism in matters of church and state throughout our federal nation may be one of the curious benefits of the system. It seems to be one of those benign paradoxes which permit an adjustment of localism to national policy, and so make life reasonably tolerable in our widespread and diverse nation.

Conclusions

The due-process and equal-protection clauses of the Federal Fourteenth Amendment, as construed in one case by the Supreme Court, prohibit instruction in religion in grade schools by professional churchmen. What restrictions, if any, beyond these specific limits the national Constitution imposes remain undecided. The language, though not the actual judgments, of the Supreme Court Justices has been somewhat more sweeping in restrictive expression.

State constitutions and statutes differ widely in their restrictions of religious content in public school curricula; but a generalization might be this: sectarian instruction is forbidden in public schools, and public funds may not be used to promote sectarian ends.

State courts and administrators are surprisingly loose in construing "sectarian." The theory seems to be that an average of Christian doctrine, or perhaps of Judaeo-Christian doctrine, is permissible as not sectarian, because it is not identifiable as Baptist, Catholic, Congregational, Jewish, Mormon, and so on.

As a practical matter much Bible-reading, interdenominational religious instruction, and even devotional exercise is conducted without legal interference in public grade schools by direction of local school authorities. This immunity in practice may be accounted for by the somewhat ponderous character of constitutional and legal machinery, which is set in motion only in rare cases.

There is a distinction between devotional exercises and indoctrination on the one hand and instruction in the history of human thought about religion on the other. The latter is free from constitutional restriction, though it may be mistaken for the former in some cases, particularly when attempted with young children.

There is a distinction between young children and mature students. The constitutional cases generally arise from suspicion, felt by parents, that their impressionable small children are being influenced by public school teachers against the parental faith.

There is a distinction between compulsory and voluntary attendance at an educational institution. Because no one is compelled to go to college, even public college instruction is much less likely to run into legal difficulty than religious instruction in lower schools.

DISCUSSION BASED ON PROFESSOR SUTHERLAND'S PAPER

Presiding: ARTHUR S. ADAMS

PROF. ARTHUR E. SUTHERLAND (Professor of Law, Harvard University): Mr. President, Ladies and Gentlemen: It is very flattering to be asked to come down here to talk to you educators, very nice for a country lawyer to be among men and women of learning.

Our discussion at this session chiefly concerns young children. If one examines the occasional court proceedings of American schools in connection with religious programs, he discovers that an overwhelming percentage involve cases of young children. One finds comparatively few high school cases. An example is the Selma District case in California where some gentleman objected unsuccessfully to twelve copies of the King James Bible in the school library. The acute problem arises in the case of the younger child whose parents feel that he is being weaned away from the parental faith by some exercises in the classroom. This is the typical question which the lawyer in this field has to face.

I have done my homework very conscientiously. I have read all the papers, and I wish I could have written them. Among other papers, I greatly admired that of Sister Nona, because I think she tackles the hardest problem of all: What is the function of religious instruction for the child of about ten years, the child of grade school years?

There is very little *federal* interference with instruction in the schools on religious matters. To appreciate this, we need to understand the difference between what courts say in judicial opinions and what courts decide.

I mean no disrespect to the judiciary when I say that judges are not different from other men; they experience a certain verbal *élan* when they write an opinion. For example, in the New Jersey bus opinion about which we have heard so much, Justice Black tells us that the religious clause of the First Amendment means at least this: Neither a state nor the Federal Government can set up a church; neither can pass laws which aid one religion, aid all religions, or prefer one religion to another. But when he got all through, he had actually adjudged, in effect, that there is nothing wrong with a Catholic child going to parochial school in a bus at public expense. That was all that the court decided. The other matter is what Mr. Justice Black wrote for the majority of the court.

I do not mean the slightest disrespect to majority or minority opinions. I simply mean that one should not take the language of any judicial opinion as one would a statute, each word of which presumably has a cutting edge in the enforcement of law. The opinion is an essay in political theory—and quite rightly so. In the broadest sense, it gives the reasons of the Justices in arriving at their conclusions. It should be so read.

In the steel seizure case, the opinions ranged from discussions of the order given by President Jefferson to the American Navy to attack the Barbary pirates down to a final resounding quotation of the great words of Lord Coke one Sunday morning in 1607, when he said to James I, in the words of Bracton, "The King is not only under man, but under God and law." These are noble expressions of general theory. What the court actually held was that when the Congress has said the President must do thus and so, he had better do it.

I want you to approach these cases in that way. I say then we don't have to worry about high schools. And as far as grade schools are concerned, I have never seen a case in any reported opinion that criticized a program of instruction showing the impact of religion on the early history of the United States, such as Sister Nona describes.

When I was eight or ten years old, I was put to reading a little book of stories of the Thirteen Colonies, in Public School No. 6 in

Rochester, New York. This book pictured the Puritans with their colonial hats and blunderbusses marching through the woods, and told how they came to New England to establish religious freedom. It contained stories of Jesuit fathers exploring Canada. It never occurred to me or to anyone else at the time that there could be any criticism of Public School No. 6 for telling us that Roman Catholic missionaries evangelized in part of the United States and that Puritans left England to escape one type of governmental domination of religion and that they established another within limits in New England. It never occurred to me that this was a wrong done to me; I have read about it since.

The chance of interference from the Supreme Court with such a program as is here discussed is minimal. One should remember that the McCollum case dealt with a child of ten years, with doctrinal religious instruction on publicly maintained school premises by clergy or quasi-clergy who came in from outside to teach the particular doctrines of different faiths. And the McCollum case, as nearly as I can see, is predicated upon hardship on little Terry McCollum, because he had to stand up and go out of the room or be exposed to doctrines which were unacceptable to his parents.

This, I take it, is the only holding in the McCollum case, and one may expect that if an attack is made upon such a program of instruction including the story of the Puritans, the story of Jesuit fathers, the story of La Salle, and the rest of them, a clear distinction will appear between the circumstances of the McCollum matter and such a program as that. I surely hope so.

The difficulty arises not in teaching history, but in prayer, Bible-reading, and Bible distribution in the schoolroom, as in the New Jersey case. And here I think the obstacles that one is likely to meet are on the local level rather than on the level of the Federal Government. In general, state constitutional restrictions are much more precise, much more rigorous than those of the Federal Constitution. After all, the Fourteenth Amendment says that no state shall deprive any person of life, liberty, or property, without due process of law. That is what a state cannot do to a school child.

Supreme Court opinions have suggested that this incorporates the language of the First Amendment, "Congress shall make no law respecting an establishment of religion, or prohibiting the free exercise thereof." But that is not what the words of the Fourteenth Amendment say.

The greatest obstacle impeding a program of religious instruction in the public schools comes from the local authorities. Opposition from local school boards is greater than from the state authorities. Local school authorities are sometimes understandably timid because they do not want to get into a row. I have sat on a school board in the town of Ithaca, New York, and I sympathize. Local timidity is the major hazard, and is something to which your serious thought in any deliberation such as this must be devoted.

MR. HENRY BRAGDON (History Department, Phillips Exeter Academy) : I have a question which ties together Dr. Johnson's discussion with that of Professor Sutherland. I am worried about the fact that when there is a division of opinion, the only apparent recourse for the minority is to appeal somehow to the moderation of the dominant majority, which is already violating the minority rights. Perhaps that is an unfair statement, but last year I was at a high school assembly where the students sang, not a patriotic hymn, but a Christian hymn. While I didn't object to the hymn, I thought others might. Furthermore, the reading was from the New Testament, and some people may have objected to that.

Is there no redress? Is it simply that one must accept this situation? If children and parents are embarrassed, can nothing be done? One cannot easily appeal to the Federal Government, and the state courts are rather timid, are they not?

PROFESSOR SUTHERLAND: Sir, the question that you ask is extraordinarily troublesome, of course. I think of this problem in terms of an expanding set of concentric majorities from the school district to the Supreme Court of the United States, and I approach it with a prejudice in favor of the majority of people getting what they want in the United States, unless there is some pretty strong reason why they should not. I have a prejudice in favor of majority rule. Of course, there are things that a minority ought not to have to put up with.

There are things that you cannot do to the minority, but constitutional law is not an exact science. In a world in which government does more and more things for us, in a world in which each of us as an individual differs somewhat from all his neighbors, equality of treatment is impossible as a practical matter. Some of us have to tolerate some differences.

I feel that the McCollum case in Illinois was a mistake because it attempted the impossible. In my opinion, some degree of spiritual hardihood is necessary for existence in a world in which government must be general although individuals are inescapably different. Hence, it seems to me that the embarrassment felt by Terry when he had to get up and go read a book in a different room was perhaps not in the same class as the hardship imposed upon the Negro child who is forced to attend a separate and inferior school. It seems to me that to listen to a hymn in a high school auditorium against one's wish is perhaps not a major hardship and is a sacrifice which a minority might well make to a majority. There has to be some live-and-let-live in our society.

People have been burned to death for their religion. I spent last fall in a city where over three hundred years ago a bishop, being burned for his faith, thrust a hand into the fire and let it burn because he said he had recanted and wanted first to burn the hand which had written his heresies.

After all, a rather small sacrifice would have been required of Terry McCollum. And it seems to me that all the ponderous machinery of the Federal Government is a little bit out of place when it goes down to Champaign, Illinois, and prevents the people of Champaign from having their way because Terry's feelings are hurt. I think this is a disproportionate use of the great power of the Supreme Court of the United States. That is why I think they backed away from it in the Zorach case.

MR. PFEFFER: May I express a minor dissent, Professor Sutherland? I think it requires a certain degree of detachment to make judgments as to what is important and what is not important. It may very well be unimportant to you, Professor Sutherland. Perhaps to me the presence of a child as a captive audience is important because the child has no choice. He must go to school; otherwise, his father is put in jail.

I grant that even though he is a captive audience and his presence is required by law, by the force of fear of jail, no great harm will befall him if, in order to avoid isolation and embarrassment, he hears and says those words which he might on free choice not hear and say.

On the other hand, I wonder whether it is really proper for us to make that judgment for him. When the Constitution protects the individual in certain rights, it protects him against what others consider to be idiosyncrasies. Tolerance means a recognition of the fact that what may be trivia or *de minimus* to us may be the very essence of life to another.

It may be irrational for a child to feel that, if he hears the words "Jesus Christ, Our Lord" or if he is compelled by the force of the whole momentum of the school to sing those words, "Jesus Christ, Our Lord," he will suffer loss of salvation, eternal damnation, and punishment beyond anything this world can offer. To us that may seem absurd and ridiculously irrational, but can we say that it is so irrational, so completely beyond the realm of reason that we have a right to disregard his minority point of view?

I would like to point out to you a little bit of American history, the history of the evolution of some of these decisions which seem to disagree with the view expressed by you, such as the Gideons Bible case, which I must defend, as I was the attorney. It happens, Professor Sutherland, that seven mature, intelligent, and reasonable judges of the New Jersey Supreme Court—headed by no less a personage than Arthur Vanderbilt, and including Justice Brennan, who went on to the United States Supreme Court—did feel that the rights of the Jewish and Catholic children whom I represented were infringed upon by this "small" matter of distributing the Protestant New Testament.

It is not a wholly irrational kind of judgment. It is a judgment which I think can be sustained, and it is the kind of judgment to which I think the Constitution entitles us. The Constitution is not needed to protect those with whom we agree when they represent the majority.

I want to point out in this development of our educational system a fact which I think is frequently forgotten, namely, that the development of the American secular public school system is in large measure due to the courage and the forthrightness and the refusal of many people, Professor Sutherland, to take the position which you urge. In community after community throughout the nation many Catholic parents and priests braved the wrath, the persecution, and often the physical violence of the Protestant majority by going to court after court to get Protestant teaching out of the public schools.

This is the history of courage on the part of the people to whom it was not a little thing, who felt that they would be hurt or that their conscience would be hurt if they had to participate in or listen to a faith and a religion in which they could not join. We make steady progress toward a more civilized status through the willingness of people to sacrifice. Terry McCollum and the little boy in Boston[25] who was beaten almost to a pulp for refusing to read from the Protestant Bible are examples of that willingness to sacrifice.

These are the facts of the development of the American Constitution as well as of the American public school system.

It is not difficult for me to say that my child would not suffer if he were to participate in the kind of thing we are talking about, such as a Christian prayer. My child is deeply embedded in the Jewish religion. Since he has a deep basic Jewish religion, I have no fear. But that is a judgment which only I can make for my child. Under the Constitution of the United States and any concept of tolerance, I cannot make that judgment for anyone else's child, whether it is McCollum's child or the children of thousands of Catholic parents who went to court.

One of the great pearls of the American constitutional system is that the Constitution allows each person to decide for himself whether he shall avail himself, through judicial procedure, of the right which the Constitution gives him.

There is one further point I should like to make: I think it is true that there are many people who are not satisfied with the McCollum decision. I think it is equally true that there are many people who are not satisfied with the Brown decision[26] and with many other decisions. Nevertheless, I think that there is a moral obligation on the part of public officials in the South to abide by the Court's decision in the Brown case and to integrate the schools with all deliberate speed.

I think there is an equal moral obligation on the part of educators in the North and throughout the country to abide by the decision of the McCollum case until it is changed, wrong as it may appear to them and wrong as other decisions may appear to be to other people, such as the people in the South. Until the Supreme Court reverses itself, we must adhere to the decisions of the Supreme Court whether we agree with them or not. Otherwise, we will have anarchy.

I completely agree with you that there is nothing in the McCollum decision or in any other decision of the Supreme Court which makes illegal or unconstitutional that objective and impartial study of religion which Dr. Johnson was speaking of originally. However, when we step beyond this and inculcate or urge acceptance of the premises of those religions, we are transgressing against the Mc-Collum decision.

PROFESSOR SUTHERLAND: I want to say a word about my old friend Mr. Pfeffer. Those of you who haven't seen his book, which I referred to in a footnote at the end of my paper, should do so. He has written the best book on religious freedom in the United States and has collected all the authorities. And it is always a privilege to hear what he has to say.

I agree with him entirely that we should live within the Supreme Court mandates, and I do not advocate that anyone launch a program in defiance of the McCollum case.

All I say is that until the Supreme Court of the United States broadens its decision, we are well justified in taking the premise that they decided no more than the facts in the case and that their decision need not be extrapolated into the field of the high school or into the field of historic accounts of those things which religion has meant to people.

Let me also say one more thing about my old friend Mr. Pfeffer. His account of Terry's hardship in being obliged to accept the tenets of a religion antithetical to his own is not quite realistic. Terry's hardship was that he had to get up and go out of the room, and this is a spiritual hardship, it seems to me, that one might well learn to undergo. Government by majority requires some adjustment. It is too bad, but one has to get along to some extent with unpleasant things. Mr. Pfeffer says, and I agree, one should live within the McCollum case. However, it doesn't seem to me to have been an awfully great hardship to that lad for him to go out of the room when they were engaged in the religious services which his own commitments led him to believe were not appropriate.

MR. SASSCER: Mr. Sutherland, wouldn't you say that the case would have had an entirely different complexion if Terry had been forced to stay in the room and had been beaten if he refused?

PROFESSOR SUTHERLAND: I agree. In that case, I wouldn't say a word. I will join with Mr. Pfeffer and attack anything within a thousand miles of such an outrageous performance as to beat a child until he reads something that is heretical to him.

DR. EUGENE E. DAWSON (Dean of Administration and Students, Kansas State Teachers College): Mr. Sutherland, would you also agree that the hardship Terry McCollum endured subsequent to that decision might perchance have been much greater than the hardship of leaving the room?

PROFESSOR SUTHERLAND: I don't know. Terry's mother and grandfather are friends of mine. The last I heard, Terry was six feet tall and of sturdy growth. How much embarrassment he suffered by this litigation, I don't know. Life is hard. If one boy or his mother feels strongly about asserting his rights, his name frequently gets into the paper, and the other kids say, "I understand you initiated the lawsuit that stopped us from having the lady minister come and talk to us."

DR. THOMAS P. NEILL (Professor of History, Saint Louis University): As another little Terry McCollum, may I be one to agree with you. I remember being in the sixth grade in Oregon shortly after the Supreme Court decision was rendered and being subjected to something like that. No psychiatrist has yet accused me of suffering the sort of thing Mr. Pfeffer describes. After that decision, a couple of us Catholics and a couple of the Seventh Day Adventists were put in a different room where we learned to keep our faces clean. I don't think anybody experienced any sort of a hardship. I believe it is very important in any kind of discussion like this to realize that government in any kind of democracy will pose difficulties for the minority. There has to be an adjustment in which not only the minority but also the majority must make concessions. That is why I do not think we will have any serious difficulty as long as we stay within the limits of Supreme Court decisions and let the local authorities work out the arrangements that seem best to them.

PROFESSOR SUTHERLAND: I couldn't agree with you more, sir. The problem here is to determine what is injustice. When injustice rises to a certain pitch, the Supreme Court will step in and prevent the state from imposing it on the individual. I do not know what justice is. There is a 2,400-year-old dialogue which tries to define it and which ends up by saying, "We haven't found out."

In the McCollum case, the Supreme Court decided that injustice to Terry rose to a point where the Court had to say to the state, "We will interpose our hand between you and Terry McCollum, and the majority of you people in Illinois cannot do that to an individual."

MISS FLORENCE O. BENJAMIN (Coordinator of Social Studies, Abington Township School District, Pennsylvania): Would you comment on the legality of a Bible club as a cocurricular activity in the secondary school? I am referring to a voluntary school activity with a teacher acting as sponsor? I am thinking of an instance where there was such a group. For the most part it was an evangelical group. Some parents objected on the ground that their youngsters became involved, and they felt it was jeopardizing their security. Although it never assumed the proportions of a court case, I am wondering if there have been any such cases.

PROFESSOR SUTHERLAND: I don't know of a Bible group case. Of course, as soon as you use public property to sponsor or promote a sect or any religious belief, you run into hazards not only of the Fourteenth Amendment but also of your state constitutions and statutes. The latter come in great variety, as you know. They are apt to provide that public property may not be used for a sectarian purpose, and acres of newsprint in calf-bound books have been used to specify what is sectarian.

One would gather from a good many opinions that a reasonable average of Christian doctrine escapes the label of sectarianism. There is the New Jersey opinion on prayers and Bible-reading that suggests they are not sectarian. However, I would say that under most state constitutions the use of the public building for a prayer meeting would run some risk of being banned by the state constitution, if some parent felt strongly enough about it to start a lawsuit and if the state provided a taxpayer's suit to enjoin it.

As you suggest by your example, Miss Benjamin, ninety-nine cases out of a hundred of this kind never get prosecuted. The parents of the dissenting child say, "Willy, don't go. You will learn heresy." Or else they say, "If Willy wants to go, we will let him."

DR. KONVITZ: It is difficult for me to disagree with my friend, Professor Sutherland, but I think I would be derelict in my duty if

I didn't express my opinion. I think that Professor Sutherland construes the McCollum decision much more narrowly than I would be inclined to do. I don't think that the basis for the decision was the fact that Terry McCollum was embarrassed or objected to being sent out of the room.

Assume there is a school in which there is released-time instruction within the building, as there was in the McCollum case, and assume no one wants to leave the building or the room. That practice would still be unconstitutional. It isn't the fact that there must be a student or a pupil who will be embarrassed by the program; it is the fact that the public property, the building, is used for religious purposes. If it is used for religious purposes, there is a constitutional invasion whether anybody objects or not. Is this not the decision of the McCollum case?

On philosophical grounds, Arthur, I would go a little further and say that I cannot conceive of a decision of the Supreme Court, especially in a constitutional case, which is not based on a principle. A decision of the Supreme Court, such as the McCollum decision, cannot be based on just a set of facts. It must be a decision that is established on a principle, a broad principle. If it is derived from a principle or if it originates a principle, then it is comprehensible; if it does not, it reduces the whole judicial process to a positivism which makes discussion impossible except as we wish to find out the facts upon which a decision was made. Without a principle, the decision would be merely the issuance of an injunction or the denial of an injunction, depending on a set of isolated facts.

PROFESSOR SUTHERLAND: Milton Konvitz is another friend of mine. We were old friends at Cornell; hence, we are all on a first-name basis.

Milton, if I were back at School District No. 6 in Ithaca and if all the parents of the nineteen children in the sixth grade were perfectly willing to have the Reverend Mr. Jones come in from the Episcopalian Church and talk about Protestantism from 4:00 to 4:30, I would say, "Don't do it." This would be near enough to the McCollum case to invite trouble. Moreover, according to the Zorach decision, it would be better to take the class across the street and teach them in Mr. Brown's back parlor. I don't know whether this is in the McCollum case because I don't understand it very well; furthermore, I don't think the opinion is very clear. It contains a lot of words, but the grounds on which they proceeded are not clear.

On the proposition that we must go on principle, I quite agree. But let me cite to you a really great statement. I think all that I know about constitutional law, which is not very much, is wrapped up in it. The statement was made by Justice Brandeis in 1932 in a case called *Barnette* v. *Coronado Oil and Gas Company.* He was dissenting, and he said something that is worthy of being read by all men. He wrote that in the cases that come before the Supreme Court there is rarely any problem of constitutional interpretation. The principles are all agreed upon. The questions—and he mentioned the due process clause, questions of state and national balance of powers, and many other questions—are whether the facts in the specific case bring it within the boundaries of the undisputed principle.

I quite agree with you that in this great problem of religious commitment and state outrage, there is an immense question of principle. This was raised when Leo Pfeffer spoke of the little child beaten with rods. I think that the principle is that in our country one should be free to worship as he pleases and that hardship should not be forced upon anyone by the public power because of that man's religion. So it seems to me when the little child was obliged to stand up and salute the flag or forfeit his education, this was hardship that rose to a point that the Supreme Court should and did recognize in the Barnette[27] case. The principle is that the public force shall not outrage a person because of his faith. The problem is to ascertain when embarrassment reaches the point of outrage.

DR. R. LANIER HUNT (Executive Director, Department of Religion and Public Education, National Council of the Churches of Christ in the U.S.A.) : I would like to ask Mr. Sutherland whether any case he recalls has been filed with reference to the second clause in the First Amendment. The question refers to the point raised by Miss Benjamin and was posed by a high school principal in the Midwest.

In a large suburban high school of around two thousand students, there were over ninety extracurricular groups. The standing agreement was to grant permission to any group consisting of twelve students who filed a petition for a club. Thus, there were groups in dancing, tennis, card-playing, and so on.

Finally, a petition was submitted for the formation of a Bible-reading club. Now, the state law prohibits sectarian instruction. The Zorach decision confirmed the McCollum decision forbidding the use of public property. On the other hand, the Constitution says we shall not prohibit the free exercise of religion, nor shall we establish a religion.

The principal said to me, "I refused permission to the students to establish the club on the theory that it would be a misuse of public property and that it would be contrary to school rules to have a club without a faculty sponsor. Did I properly refuse it?"

PROFESSOR SUTHERLAND: This is the jam that one gets into. The withholding of action is as much a choice as the imposing of action. This is one of the troublesome things about government. It is this: If one does nothing, one makes a choice as significant as if one does act.

Concerning this particular club, this question arises: Suppose that permission had been granted to read the Bible on the school premises. Since no federal decision exists on this, one is thrown back to his state Supreme Court. In general, merely having Bibles on the premises or reading them, according to my guess, would be condemned by a few supreme courts, even the California Supreme Court, which has stringent restrictions but which upheld the right of a school to keep twelve Bibles in the school library at public expense.

When the child is deprived of religious freedom, when the state power says one may not use the school premises for a Bible-reading club, the specific question is this: Has that state, acting through its agency, the school board, deprived these twelve children of life, liberty, or property without the due process of law or denied them the equal protection of the law? This is the specific question under the Constitution, because we are talking about the Fourteenth Amendment. My guess is not. Although I would have let them do it, I doubt that the outrage imposed rises to the point where the Fourteenth Amendment would send the Supreme Court in to stop them. I am sorry, but I think the decision would have been better if they had let the students read the Bible.

MR. PFEFFER: There is a decision on that. In the State of Washington a suit was brought to allow the teaching of the Bible in the schools, and the Supreme Court of Washington held that it was against the state constitution of Washington to allow Bible-reading in the schools. An appeal was made to the United States Supreme Court, which dismissed the case for want of a substantial federal issue. That is, the Court held that it does not violate a constitutional right to prevent Bible-reading.

PROFESSOR SUTHERLAND: Was this Bible-reading in a class?

MR. PFEFFER: In a class.

PROFESSOR SUTHERLAND: That is different. If twelve youngsters want to go out in a seminar in Room No. 6 on Friday afternoons and read the English Bible, I would let them.

MR. ISAAC FRANCK (Executive Director, Jewish Community Council of Greater Washington, D.C.): I want to return to your idea that the process of government by majority requires adjustments, and I would like to work my way to it by using an illustration.

When my little girl was about eleven, she was in a class in the public school of Montgomery County in Maryland where the teacher began the day's classroom work with the salute to the flag, the pledge of allegiance, the singing of "America," and the singing of "Jesus Loves Me, This I Know." Ours is a religious home, I hope a serious and deeply religious home. My girl and my son have been trained as devout Jews. We have taken quite seriously, both in our practices and in our discussions around the dinner table, the second commandment, "Thou shalt have no other Gods before thee."

This experience posed a serious dilemma for us as a family and, especially, for our little daughter. She came and talked to her mother and me about it. I suppose there were several alternatives before us. Perhaps we could have sought advice and tried to institute a suit to enjoin the school from doing this. I am not a constitutional lawyer; so I don't know. Another alternative was to urge the child to tell the teacher that she did not want to sing this Christian hymn, which asserts beliefs that are not acceptable to us. The last alternative was the one which was actually chosen. She did not remonstrate against it. She did not raise any objections with her teacher. She simply "half" sang and "half" didn't sing the song, and so on. This was a case of making an adjustment to the majority, making an adjustment at the cost of some reasonably serious religious sacrifices.

What you said, sir, suggests to me the elevation of this matter of adjustment almost to a governmental and constitutional principle. I get to the constitutional question now. I have, in my naïvete, as a non-lawyer, somehow assumed throughout these years that the very language of the First Amendment, which says that Congress shall make no law respecting an establishment of religion, and so on, was intended to single out and pinpoint in the total gamut of American life one area which is unique and that the statement in that amendment removed this area from the realm of majority-minority thinking and decisions.

I thought that this was an area in which Congress could not legislate, and that this was one area in American life in which we would not subscribe to the principle that majority rules and the minority has to make adjustments. My daughter made an adjustment. It was something of a traumatic religious experience. She made an adjustment because we, in fact, did what you were here stating as a principle, but we made that choice.

What I am troubled about is your elevating this personal adjustment of ours to the level of a principle. It contradicts my impression that this is one area in American life where the Founding Fathers, when they wrote the First Amendment, said the very category of thinking in majority and minority terms does not apply as it does in other areas.

PROFESSOR SUTHERLAND: You have properly and eloquently raised a question that interests me very much, and you will find many learned men who will bear you out.

My own view of the reasons for the religion clause in the First Amendment is slightly different. It was written at the time when seven states each had to some degree an established church. In my own State of Massachusetts the townships were at that time maintaining Congregational Churches. A great row occurred in the 1820's when the highest court of that state held that if the people of a town were prepared to give their temporal support to the Unitarian Church, the Congregationalists would have to give way.

People did not want the federal colossus, which it was sometimes called and which at the state level was greatly suspected of becoming a new great power, forcing things upon them. It seemed to some to be a danger as great as George III had been across the sea. They didn't want to have a federal church set up in Washington and rammed down their throats. They wanted to have their own churches the way they always had. This is the reason why the state insisted that the Federal Government stay out of the religious business entirely.

I believe that in Massachusetts, for example, when the ratifying convention urged the Bill of Rights, they had no idea that there was to be no interconnection between the organized public and the different religious areas. I doubt that the people of Massachusetts were saying there was to be no interconnection between the town of Weymouth or the town of Cambridge and religion. I think what they were saying was that there should be no intervention by those fellows in Philadelphia who set up a strange, new, and powerful government. They didn't want this government to interfere in their local affairs.

In 1868 we adopted the Fourteenth Amendment. This was a new concept. Then we said, we don't trust our states. We want the Federal Government to come in and put its fostering hand between the individual and his own state. And what do we want the Federal Government to stop the state from doing? From depriving any person of life, liberty or property without due process of law, or denying him the equal protection of the law. What does this mean? In the Everson case the Supreme Court in the majority opinion said (but did not adjudge) that the Fourteenth Amendment is shorthand for the First.

I find this interpretation difficult, because it is not spelled out either in the Fourteenth Amendment or anywhere else. I cling to the fact that, as a common-law lawyer, I was told, from the time I was old enough to listen to anything about the law, that the thing one has to look for is what has actually been decided. The only thing that has actually been decided about religious instruction in the public schools is the McCollum case.

I sympathize very deeply with the position of this little child of yours, and I think, had you cared to push the matter to a legal conclusion, the child would undoubtedly have been exempted from engaging in this exercise. Quite possibly the whole exercise would have been forbidden. But, mark you, this also would involve some adjustment because then the greater majority of the United States speaking through its courts would have prevented the rest of the children from having their way.

So there is no escape from some majority enforcement of its will on some minority. Isn't this so?

MR. MARVIN G. PURSINGER (Chairman, Department of Social Studies, Willamette High School, Eugene, Oregon): One thing that the McCollum case has meant to me has not even been touched upon save once quite indirectly, and that is that it gives me hope.

I have no hesitance in telling my class each year that I go to church every Sunday, that I get there on time, and that, even though we are Protestants, we practice the Jewish tradition of tithing because the church has to have funds on which to grow.

Various persons in our sect have sought to bring groups to the schools, and my wife and I have had many a chat about this matter. We are in favor of what the American Council stood for ten years ago when it was considered liberal. We still favor this position today, although it is now considered conservative, and we would risk everything we have to keep inculcation of any religious belief out of the public schools, even though we belong to the majority. I suppose Protestants are really rather encouraged to find a good deal that they agree with in the McCollum case. They know that, although one can get hurt in the courts, he can get justice. That is encouraging.

PROFESSOR SUTHERLAND: That is a good and proper evaluation, I think, of the Supreme Court's function in these cases. The difficulty is that we need to distinguish case from case.

I would look at a high school program quite differently from the way I would at a grade school program. In my paper I mentioned Carl Becker's account of the Reformation, the teaching of which in the public schools is quite different from the holding of devotional exercises, to which I am allergic.

But even there, mark you, I make a choice. If one self-consciously turns his back on manifestations of religion, he is making a choice. I am not now talking as a lawyer, but as a parent, who faced this thing in both religious and in lay schools. If one is self-conscious about this, if his schoolteacher tells the child in the classroom that religion is different, that it ought not to be mentioned, he makes a choice there, too. There is no escape from choice in government. That is the only thing I know about government. The only free man who ever existed was Robinson Crusoe, and, as soon as he saw the footprint in the sand, he had to start compromising.

MR. VARNER: I am bothered by the word "hurt," which you used in a legal sense and which comes to me when I think about this problem. I like to see children get religious instruction, preferably at home and in the church, but I would like to have them get religious instruction. Isn't it true of any faith that it enjoins hurting a child? Whether or not the hardship was good for Terry, I think all faiths teach us not to hurt him. Can one urge the teaching about religion or the teaching of religion and at the same time violate the tenets of religion?

PROFESSOR SUTHERLAND: I will say something painful. I think government cannot be carried on without pain. Government is not a painless process. Government consists of coercion. Government consists of obliging the minority to do what the majority wishes. That is a cruel statement. This coercion takes place every day in a multitude of ways.

When does this use of force by majority to make a minority comply—and that is government—become such an outrage perpetrated by the state that the Supreme Court will prevent it? Here you have one of those inescapable problems of degree. The Court has said it became outrageous in the case of Terry McCollum.

MR. VARNER: But I want my conscience satisfied on this. If government can hurt, and I agree it can, should I as a schoolteacher take part in helping to get something into the school which will cause some child to be hurt when the government decides it needs to step in? Doesn't my religion enjoin me from taking the step which would do that?

PROFESSOR SUTHERLAND: If I were a school administrator, I would not institute a program like that involved in the McCollum case. Having read the testimony in the McCollum case, I am impressed with the futility of this minuscular injection of a self-conscious and rather stilted type of instruction for a half hour or an hour or so a week. I think this was a wasteful program, and I think it should have been done better or given up. It was given up.

On the other hand, if one says we can have no mention of religious elements whatever in the school, he too makes a choice that hurts some people. We hurt somebody no matter which way we turn. We cannot escape hurting people if we govern at all.

FATHER McCLUSKEY: I think the only reason that this problem is not two hundred years old is that the history of the common school in America is only one hundred years old. I think the trend of the discussion, the remarks that Professor Sutherland is making, bring out very pointedly the intrinsic limitations of the common school. Although we use the words "public schools" freely today, originally it was called and meant to be a common school.

What we are trying to do is find some *common* philosophy of values with or without sanctions, with or without some religious form or sectarianism, to govern a part of the educative process in those common schools. A hundred years ago the problem was a little simpler, because there were two assumptions that were substantially operative in society. One of them was a unified Protestant Christianity, and the second was the natural law, theistic tradition. I think that neither one of those assumptions or premises is equally operative today. This is said with no intent to pass judgment. It is simply fact. We are fragmentized. We are divided roughly into three large interfaith groups, as well as a large group that is not affiliated with any of the traditional religious groups.

Granted that there is need for some common denominator, some common philosophy of values, the acceptance of certain premises or assumptions, how can we teach for commitment or teach to inculcate values?

I think the common school cannot directly do this. I think it is impossible. It is an intrinsic limitation. What I think God is, someone else thinks is a cloud. Is God absolute, transcendant, or triad? Interpretations of these words give rise to a multitude of sects, each enjoying an intrinsic right to believe and follow its own beliefs. So, granted this intrinsic limitation, we go into this majority-minority counterplay.

Basically, the problem is whether the theistic bias in our tradition can still have an implicit or intrinsic place. I am not talking about teaching trinitarianism or unitarianism. I am simply asking whether or not we can continue to follow that theistic, natural law assumption to which we pay at least lip service in coinage, proclamations, holidays, and so forth. That is the nub of the problem. It isn't a question of whether we can teach that there was a Protestant Reformation, that there was a bad Pope, or anything else. The nub of the problem is merely this: Is there a theistic tradition that we can continue while safeguarding the right of everyone to dissent from that tradition?

Dr. Johnson spelled out the answer very elaborately and very carefully, and he is correct. It would be wrong for the common school to force values down the throats of children whose homes do not ascribe to any theistic belief. But these homes still constitute a minority in this country. At present the democratic process would seem to require that we consider some sort of acceptance or nonacceptance of this theistic natural law, whatever you want to call it, as part of the problem.

PROFESSOR SUTHERLAND: Father, I couldn't agree with you more. It seems to me that if we say we are going to teach only about the Puritans in New England and the Jesuit fathers paddling canoes down the Mississippi, we are avoiding entirely the question which a great many good, conscientious people are asking. Some say that our children do not spend their lives at home, that they spend their lives in school, and that they are going to grow up godless unless somebody in school teaches them that there is a God and that he has regard for man.

I also think you are right in saying that we will run into trouble if we tackle this problem in the tax-supported public schools. I am sorry about this. There has to be some sacrifice somewhere. I think if I were back in District No. 6 and it were proposed to our board that we institute a service each morning in which the teacher would say to the children, "Children, throughout the day in your goings and comings you must remember there is a God who watches you and cares for you," I would be against it because I think the policy underlying the public school is against it.

Most of the debate we have had here might be said to have turned on this specific point. You are quite right.

With respect to Sister Nona's paper, I have never seen any dispute about teaching historical accounts, such as stories of religious matters in the Thirteen Colonies in America. I agree with what you say. But there is trouble in the wind when you try public encouragement of religious belief. The litigation that has arisen in New Jersey, California, and elsewhere has turned about the question of doctrinal instruction in the classroom.

FATHER MCMANUS: I hope it is appropriate to address a question to Mr. Pfeffer. Several times Sister Nona's paper has been mentioned as an outline of what we might try to do in this controversial area of the grade school. My question to Dr. Pfeffer is a rather simple one. Would he think a priori that the general plan outlined in Sister Nona's paper would be constitutional under the laws of the United States as interpreted by the Supreme Court.

MR. PFEFFER: I must confess embarrassment, because I have not read Sister Nona's paper. I cannot give you a sensible answer without having read it; however, I will say this which I said before. I do think there is no constitutional lawyer who would dispute the proposition that there is nothing in the Constitution or the McCollum case or in any decision, either of the Supreme Court or of any court that I know of, which requires the public school to disregard the facts of life. There is nothing which prohibits the teaching that a lot of people came to explore part of the country for the purpose of spreading the word of Jesus Christ. There is nothing in the Constitution which prohibits the teacher from telling the children that many people believed in the divinity of Jesus Christ. There is nothing which prohibits the teacher from explaining what is meant by Mass.

I am not saying that this should be done. There are practical problems here. I am talking about constitutional law. We are talking about when the Constitution is transgressed. The Constitution is transgressed when you drop out the words "many people believe." If you say "many people believe Jesus is divine," you are within the Constitution. If you say, "Jesus is divine," you are transgressing the Constitution. You are not teaching or educating; you are inculcating religious belief. I think that is violative of the Constitution.

There is one problem which was raised today which has certain difficulties. The question of visiting churches and synagogues by public school children as part of the study of the community. That is a very difficult problem because I think the difference between the Barnette case and the McCollum case and the reason why the same rules are not applicable has not been fully explained. The Barnette case said that if one's religious conscience forbids him to salute the flag and there is no paramount interest of society that requires that he salute so the community will not be hurt, he is protected by the Constitution from being compelled to salute the flag. On the other hand, one cannot stop others from saluting the flag. That is what the Barnette case says.

In the McCollum case the court did not say, if you do not want to attend, Terry, you do not have to attend, but you cannot stop others from attending. What is the difference?

The difference is fundamental in our Constitution. In the Barnette case the act was a secular act, and, thus, within the scope of a secular state and its secular agencies. Although secular acts sometimes cannot be compelled against some people in violation of their conscience, it is within the competence of the state institution to prescribe those secu-

lar acts for those whose religious conscience permits them to participate in these acts.

The McCollum case involved a religious act, not a secular act.
Terry McCollum did not make that situation unconstitutional. He
played a part in it because under the Constitution the Supreme Court
cannot act except in a case or controversy. In order to trigger the
Supreme Court action, someone has to say, "I am aggrieved."

The presence or absence of the persons aggrieved does not in any
way affect the constitutionality of the act. As I interpret the First
Amendment, it is without the competence of a secular agency to
prescribe religious conduct even for those who would not object to
taking it. The same thing is involved in the problem of visiting the
churches. Actually, in the context in which it is ordinarily viewed,
visiting the churches, like visiting the post offices and the museums,
is a secular not a religious act. You are not bringing pupils there to
inculcate them in religious beliefs. You are bringing them there because you are teaching them the secular account of the facts, the
realistic facts of the community.

As I said before, the Constitution does not compel the public
school to be ignorant of the facts of the community.

The only question here is the question of the Barnette case.[27] Suppose the child's religious beliefs prohibited him from entering the
house of worship of another faith, as some religious faiths do. If this
is so, the same principle is involved as was involved in the Barnette
case. The child cannot be compelled to enter, nor can he stop those
who have no objections from going in there, because they are engaging in a secular act.

That is the difference. Of course, you may still have a problem.
Once you decide the constitutionality of the act, you have only solved
half of the problem. The second part of the problem is whether it is
wise as a policy.

DR. PAUL VIETH (Professor of Christian Nurture, Divinity School,
Yale University): The point I was trying to make is so far down-
stream that I cannot recover it, but the last statement made by Mr.
Pfeffer raises a question in my mind. Did I understand correctly that
a teacher may take a group of pupils to visit a synagogue or a church,
which in this case is similar to visiting a museum, because they are
going to a place to see something which is of interest and value to
their studies? If this happened to be a historical museum, the teacher

could say, "You must go in. This is part of our job." But if the child at the church says, "I cannot go in," you cannot compel him?

MR. PFEFFER: Yes. There are cases where the courts have held that children belonging to fundamentalist faiths that do not allow their children to learn social dancing, which was a prescribed part of the curriculum in some places, cannot be compelled to take social dancing where it violates religious conscience, although other children may take it. The same thing would apply to a museum.

The test is whether or not it can be shown that the needs of society are such that the religious conscience of the individual must be over-ridden in order to protect society, as in the case of the draft for military service. One's religious conscience cannot excuse him from the draft. In this case, the need of the state to defend itself, to defend the community, is a superior and paramount societal need which overrides the individual's conscience. Except for this consideration, the state cannot compel a person to do something that is violative of his religion. In the other instance, everybody will admit that society won't be hurt if my child doesn't learn how to tango.

DR. VIETH: I can understand that. But that doesn't isolate the church that they may visit as an individual case. The same situation might prevail if a group of children were taken to the Peabody Museum in New Haven, which seems to support the theory of evolution. A child might say, "I don't believe in it, and I won't look at is because that will contaminate my mind." Then the teacher would have to excuse that child. That is a religious objection.

MR. PFEFFER: I would think so. It is no trick to be tolerant of idiosyncrasies with which you agree. The purpose of constitutional liberties is to protect those who have these absurd ideas which to us seem to be irrational. For those who have rational ideas, you need no Constitution or Bill of Rights.

DR. VIETH: Let me press this a little further. In the case of exemption for military service, it is not sufficient for a person to say, "I don't believe in war." He has to prove he has religious objections.

MR. PFEFFER: Even then he has no constitutional right to be exempt.

DR. VIETH: Maybe he hasn't. In the case of the entrance into the church, he would have to be able to say, "I have a religious objection as a Protestant to go into a synagogue." Therefore, he has to be excused because there is a religious basis for his conscientious objection.

Mr. Pfeffer: I think so.

Miss Eleanor Thompson (Vice-Principal, Philadelphia High School for Girls): What puzzles me is that we seem to be losing sight of the value of the common law in the whole thing—the custom. I come from Pennsylvania where we have a good deal of latitude because it has been the custom for more than a hundred years. Our public schools are far more than a hundred years old. And I would like to ask Mr. Sutherland to tell us something about custom in regard to this law.

Professor Sutherland: That is a very interesting question. I suppose custom is the basis of all law. Actually, when you have a thing as general as the Fourteenth Amendment, which says, and I repeat this for pedagogical reasons, "no state shall deprive any person of life, liberty, or property without due process of law, nor deny to any person the equal protection of the laws," some of those phrases do not define themselves. These are a charter to the Supreme Court to prevent the state from working outrage upon the individual within its powers. Here custom has an immense force. I will say a shocking thing: What you are pretty used to is probably constitutional. Custom is a very powerful factor. You made an excellent point.

Sister Mary Nona, O.P. (President, Edgewood College of the Sacred Heart): I believe all educators will bear me out that the courts will never have to try a case of going to a church or a synagogue because I understand that schools must always have parental permission for any kind of study tour or trip off the school grounds. So there is a regular procedure which precludes embarrassment and takes care of that matter. It would not be a special case. There is no trip at all, as I understand it, which is taken without the written permission of the parents. So I don't believe we will have to worry about that going to the Supreme Court.

Sister Mary Janet, S.C. (Consultant, Commission on American Citizenship, Catholic University): I am going to change the subject slightly. I find myself concerned about how we are going to teach about the establishment of American democracy. It was established upon certain principles which we find in the Declaration of Independence and which acknowledge immediately that we recognize man's inalienable rights came from the Creator. Our whole system has been built upon that principle.

When we teach children about the establishment of American democracy, how can we do it unless we make some mention of the Creator and of man's obligation to accept sanctions from the Creator? I am not saying that we need to tell children that they must believe in a Creator, but if we are going to tell them about our American democratic ideal, I think we have to tell them that it was actually built upon that belief.

PROFESSOR SUTHERLAND: I think you are completely right, and I see no escape from this. Nor would Mr. Pfeffer think there was anything unconstitutional in any such undertaking. You know, I couldn't get a license to teach in the public schools, but, if I could wangle a license to teach in the public schools, I wouldn't feel it was unconstitutional if I said, "Now, children, the people in the eighteenth century who got up the Constitution were, in general, profoundly religious people. Even Mr. Jefferson was a man of profoundly religious impulse, although he differed from many of his friends as to how that impulse should be carried out."

MR. PFEFFER: There is nothing unconstitutional about it, but I will not agree that it is historically accurate.

PROFESSOR SUTHERLAND: I told you I couldn't get a license to teach.

As a matter of fact, in our life and in our government we are so enmeshed in religious concepts that the effort to disassociate completely religious observances and governmental functions is doomed to failure. It cannot be done. It is like trying to produce chemically pure water. You can distill it and redistill it and redistill it again, and there will still be a trace of calcium in it.

MR. DEPOISTER: Out in my part of the country recently the Pasadena school board passed a resolution forbidding from now on any observance of religious rites at Christmas time. No reference can be made to it as the celebration of the birth of Christ. One can keep Christmas trees and holly but not refer to its religious significance. They are having quite a hassle over that.

FATHER MCCLUSKEY: Do they still call it "Christ-mas"? What do they call it?

MR. DEPOISTER: I guess they will call it "Yuletide."

I would like to ask your opinion as to what the outcome will be, because I think this will eventually come before the Court.

PROFESSOR SUTHERLAND: This is a matter on which I went into print once. In School District No. 6 in Ithaca right after the McCollum case I went to a trustee meeting just before Christmas. The kids were pasting camels and stars on the windows and engaging in the usual activities of Christmastime. I said this was obviously a case of using the force of government to inculcate sectarianism. I wondered whether a United States marshal, such as we see on television with a ten-gallon hat, a badge, and guns in holsters ready for use at either hand, would come down with a putty knife and scrape those things off the windows. I hope nobody would be foolish enough to interfere with this, on-the-whole, not very large intrusion of a religious concept in the schools. What of intrusion of the opposite?

Let's suppose our board had said at this time, "We can't have this. We will get the janitor up here, and we will scrape that off the windows, because we will not have any intermingling of the religious with the secular in our schools." Would our action, thus asserting a sort of secularism, have been unconstitutional in any way? I don't think so. It is within the power of government to attempt this impossible process of sorting out the religious from the secular down to the last chemical trace. If we choose to try this and if we scrape the youngsters' stars and camels off the window, I don't think anybody can take us into court successfully for it.

This is a matter of *discretion* for the school board, and rightly so. We have to allow a lot of opportunity for local autonomy in running schools. I think it is a mistake to intervene in a folk festival.

MISS BENJAMIN: Here is a related problem which I have heard discussed by groups of teachers but never from a legal standpoint: Most school calendars are set up for the observance of Christian holidays; therefore, teachers who are of Christian faith have time off to observe their holidays without loss of pay, whereas teachers of other faiths lose their pay if they take their holidays off.

PROFESSOR SUTHERLAND: I believe it is unconstitutional. I think it is bad government, and, if one of these teachers were to litigate, I think she might succeed. There is no case on this that I know of. After all, the government has to treat people equally; it cannot treat them differently because of their religious beliefs. To treat one woman differently from another because she has a different religious belief is a discrimination. I think they ought to equalize it. But it is immensely difficult to administer, isn't it? They cannot put a teacher to work during the Christmas holidays to make up for the time that she took off.

CHAIRMAN ADAMS: May I make a small contribution to this discussion. In the federal service, holidays of other sects are observed precisely as they are for the Christian calendar. There is no penalty of loss of pay if Civil Service or Armed Forces personnel observe religious holidays other than those in the Christian calendar. The Federal Government has already taken care of this. As to the local or state government, it is another question, of course.

FATHER JOHN HARDON, S.J. (Professor of Theology, West Baden University): I would like to ask Dr. Sutherland about a point that was originally raised by Father McCluskey. It concerns the difficulty of securing or implementing a theistic commitment and not just teaching *about* theism. Instead of saying that many believe in a theistic form of life, the teacher actually would say, "I believe, and I think you ought to believe, in God, in a personal God." Is the difficulty inherent in teaching this something which we would also say should not be overridden?

PROFESSOR SUTHERLAND: In New Jersey, Father, there are, I believe, five verses read from the Old Testament without comment. The Lord's Prayer is optional. This sometimes makes it difficult for the student compelled to go to the class. I think they excuse him in New Jersey if he feels this is a bad thing for his conscience. He can get up and go out.

From the Floor: Yes. I worked for fourteen years for New Jersey, and I never had a student who asked to be excused.

PROFESSOR SUTHERLAND: I am sure of this. In the McCollum case, however, the Court said that, if the child has to go out and has raised the question of constitutionality, he is so imposed upon by the state that the observance becomes unconstitutional. That is why I am troubled with your proposal, Father.

FATHER HARDON: I can see the difficulty. I raised the same basic issue in St. Louis in 1955 at a meeting of the National Council of Churches. There never has been any real difficulty, constitutionally or otherwise, about teaching the religious heritage of our nation. However, in referring to the origins of our government and in describing the Declaration of Independence, one must note that it is founded on a belief in God, a personal Deity to whom man is responsible. This is not merely a historical detail or a past memory about which we want to inform the student. It is a fact concerning the Declaration of Independence and the Constitution on which he, right here and now in 1957, is to submit himself to the authority of the American government.

Frankly, I believe that this three-day meeting will be successful to the degree that we deal realistically with this fundamental issue. I realize there are those who share different interpretations of theism, for example, the Unitarian and the Jew and, for that matter, the Catholic and the Protestant. They might hesitate the moment we begin to speak about a personal Deity, thinking that we must necessarily commit ourselves to a sectarian concept of religion. But, as a matter of fact, there is a corpus of doctrine which is not based on revelation, the Bible, or even religious authority. It is based on what man himself, using his God-given reason, can arrive at.

The Jesuits have a large mission in northern India. Ninety percent of their students are Moslems and Hindus. I have brought with me two textbooks that are used there. There is no difficulty in a pagan nation like India in teaching about a personal God to whom man is responsible and in following a basic moral code which involves obedience to the law of God and avoidance of what might be called sin.

I believe that the fear of infringement on sectarian interest in teaching a theistic concept of life in the public schools results from a misconception. Really there is a fundamental belief among all of us, regardless of what our religious beliefs may be, which involves much more than is presently being taught in the public school system. It comprehends the moral law or the natural law which is derived from a belief in a personal God to whom man is responsible.

In short, Professor Sutherland, I feel that although there are legal, political, and social difficulties, we have not begun to discuss the question which many of us have traveled several thousand miles to consider. We have not begun to discuss the question except in a superficial way. We have to come to grips with this fundamental issue: Are we willing to have our public schools commit themselves to a theistic view of life?

PROFESSOR SUTHERLAND: I think you are quite right. This is the essential question. No doubt it will be discussed at length tomorrow when we take up the specific problem of teaching American history.

A Specific Problem:

How and When Should References to Religion Be Made in the Teaching of American History at Various Levels?

Religion in the History of American Ideas

BERT JAMES LOEWENBERG

Dr. Loewenberg has taught American history at Sarah Lawrence College since 1942. He has also taught at the Universities of South Dakota, Missouri, and Rochester, and at Cornell and Northwestern Universities. He has served as visiting professor in Mexican universities, Ruskin College in Oxford, England, Hebrew University in Jerusalem, and at the Salzburg Seminar for American Studies in Austria. He is coauthor of The United States: American Democracy in World Perspective: 1492-1947 *and* The Making of American Democracy. *He is contributing author of* Essays in Teaching *and is author of* Darwin, Wallace and the Theory of Natural Selection *and* Darwinism: Reform or Reaction.

RELIGIOUS IDEAS and religious forces parallel American life at every significant stage of development. If the New World emerged out of revolution, it was a religious as well as a social and economic revolution. Discovery, exploration, and settlement were not the outcome of economic drives alone. Ideas, attitudes, and values other than economic merged in subtle and ever-changing combination to spur men to action. Columbus set sail from Palos under the patronage of Their Most Catholic Majesties Ferdinand and Isabella of Spain. The Admiral of the Ocean Sea spilled out his life to test a theory and to fulfill a dream. While he was dedicated to the enhancement of the fortunes of Spain and of Columbus, he was also dedicated to the service of his Catholic God.

Portuguese, Dutch, French, and English empire builders were no less eager to singe the beard of the King of Spain than to checkmate each other. Royal queens and regal bishops vied with merchant adventurers and bold pilots to capture fame and treasure. In the process the Catholic Cross and the Protestant Bible were planted deep in the soil of the Western Hemisphere from the Arctic Circle to the Straits of Magellan. For purposes of the present discussion the circumstances under which this cultural transmission was accomplished are less important than the historical fact. Proud Cortez vanquished Montezuma and while he despoiled the Aztecs of their gold, he destroyed their temples and the symbols of their faith. Pizzaro humbled the Incas and filled the holds of Spanish galleons with their precious silver. But Franciscans and Dominicans brought the Spanish version of European culture to the southern section of the New World.

The French yearned for a shorter route to fabled Cathay and later planned to carve out colonial fiefs reared on fish and furs. But the French missionaries were the advance agents of European ideas as well as the pathfinders for trappers and traders who followed them into the western country and southward along the waters of the Mississippi. The Pilgrims carried the Reformation to Plymouth and the Puritans built a Bible Commonwealth in the New England wilderness. Hardly an exception can be cited to the pervasiveness of religious influence in the history of Colonial America. The Dutch, the Swedes, the Quakers, the Mennonites, the Jews, and representatives of virtually every post-Reformation group added their special contributions to the ethnic and spiritual variety which became the United States. The wonder is not that the cultural strands of old Europe supplied the threads for the new design of the New World. The wonder is that the religious thread in the evolving national pattern is so faintly traced. The dye of influence colors the American texture whenever the influence is apparent. But the more subtle the train of consequences, the more pallid the awareness of religious forces. Once the cultural bases of institutions were altered and once ideas acquired added and different meanings, the religious antecedents frequently faded into a mystifying past.

The most startling omission in American historiography is the absence of a synthesis of religious ideas. Equally startling is the inadequate treatment accorded religious factors in existing syntheses of American meanings. Between the commercial revolutions and the Reformation, the religious component in the upheaval of Europe could scarcely be avoided. The expansion of Europe and the trans-plantation of Western culture in Africa, India, China, Russia, and the Americas had a palpable religious dimension. The New World's first fruits were outgrowths of the planting of European civilization on Western soil. None can assess the impact of Europe without con-sidering religious thought during an era when the Catholic Church was universal in Christendom. None can ignore the differing intel-lectual contours of religious ideas in the years following the revolt of Luther. Yet the accounts of American historical scholars have generally been episodic, fragmentary, and limited. Economic inter-pretations of the background of colonization exist in profusion. There are institutional histories, literary histories, diplomatic histories, and histories of ideas. But no integrated philosophical analysis of religion has yet appeared. Historical accounts of denominations, churches, sects, and religious leaders continue to gather dust on library shelves. They are materials out of which a full-scale analysis has still to be written.

W. W. Sweet's volumes[1] most nearly approach completeness of coverage; yet they are narrative and descriptive rather than analytical. The bibliography of American history is conclusive. Perry Miller's classic studies[2] of the New England mind are unique. They are, how-ever, confined to New England and there are no comparable studies of the Southern mind, the Western mind, or of the mind of the Middle Colonies. More importantly, there is no conceptual treatment of the ideas of Quakerism nor of Catholicism, Protestantism, and Judaism. There is no philosophical account of the Judaeo-Christian tradition in America, no analysis of the role of religion in American thought or of the role of religion in the development of American attitudes and institutions. There is but one Parkman in the whole record of American historical literature, and his work has never been matched in scope or brilliance. Henry Adams' *Chartres* stands alone, the single mark of genius in symbolic interpretation. When we speak of religious ideas in American history, we are speaking in terms of partial knowledge.

The portents for the future are less bright than dark. The New American Nation Series,[3] like the old, makes history the slave of a rigid chronology, thus rendering synthesis almost impossible. Topical treatments, despite their fullness, are no substitutes for essays in meaning. Even the *History of American Life,*[4] devoted to a broader conception of culture, produced episodic rather than synthetic evaluations of ideas and institutions. We have been living in the age of the monograph since the decades following the Civil War. As monographs become longer and more detailed, syntheses become shorter and more general.

Such deficiences in our knowledge deprive understanding of fullness. The deficiencies are the more serious as the force of religious ideas, far from diminishing in the so-called era of secularism, continue to influence American thought and action. During the decades succeeding the American Revolution religious assumptions permeated American thought although appearing in different verbal guises and operating through different institutions. Indeed, we need to explore the hypothesis that precisely when religious ideas and institutions seem to lose their conventional forms, they acquire renewed vitality under different auspices. We are implicated in what might be called the fallacy of the suppressed comparative. We cannot avoid the quest for synthesis and we cannot fail to recognize the import of the religious factor. Yet, except for given periods and specific movements, we are insufficiently informed regarding the logical and social interrelations of religion with other forces in American life.

Secularism is a word which continues to delude us. We use it with unconscionable looseness and we apparently believe that its connotations provide immediate understanding. Actually its connotations are freighted with confusion, for secularism as a sociological and psychological process has not been seriously studied by historians. And for the history of religion in the United States secularism is one of the key words. We are repeatedly confronted with such concepts as the "age of secularism" and the "secularization" of ideas and institutions. At no point in American history can secularism be avoided because secularism as a historical process predates the discovery of America. If we seek to unravel the meanings of the expansion of Europe, secularism pursues us. Whether we attempt to explain the disintegration of Puritanism, the movement for independence, the formation of the Constitution, or the emergence of American nationalism, secularism becomes an inescapable part of the analysis. Secularism is a correlate of the industrial revolution in all its phases—the machine, the city, values, attitudes, and ideas.

A dramatic and vital aspect of the history of religion in America is the separation of church and state. The doctrine of separation implies the secularization of the state. Religious historians—those identified with a particular faith—have often deplored separation as hurtful to religion, to morality, and to spiritual values. In fact, the entire trend toward secularism has been lamented. To secularize the state does not denude the state of values. The state is not on that account deprived of spiritual duties or stripped of religious functions. On the contrary, the secularized state may serve religion as creatively as any conventional religious institution. The doctrine of separation was designed to create a greater freedom and a greater equality, concepts which, notwithstanding their ancient philosophical lineage, are concepts with religious overtones.

The most successful and brilliant monographs involved in dealing with secularization present a uniform sequence of interpretation. The problem, as in Puritanism, begins with a body of religious ideas which are really philosophical assumptions. These religious ideas are then evaluated in a larger historical context and related to each other and to contemporary ways of behaving and doing things. Puritan ideas, institutions, and folkways are described in the process of change in relation to internal cultural solvents and to the impact of novelty, contingency, and change from without. Changes result in new attitudes, new values, and new institutions almost invariably described as a dissolution of previously balanced cultural adjustments. Since, as in Puritanism, the ideas, albeit severed from their ecclesiastical and theological moorings, continue to persist, the ideas are said to have been secularized. But how? With what residues, by what cultural processes, with what consequences? As the ideas have been divorced from a given religious dispensation, it is easy to conclude that the underlying assumptions are no longer the same.

The revolutionary ferment in eighteenth-century America represented in one of its phases the secularization of religious ideas. The age of reason, significantly coincident with the rise of evangelicalism, rested in one of its aspects on a body of doctrine denominated natural religion. Eighteenth-century conceptions of natural law reflected a greater change in emphasis, in the perspectives of time and causation, than they reflected a fundamental change in basic assumptions. God may have been respectfully bowed out at the boundaries of the universe, but he remained nevertheless poised at its frontiers. God remained the Supreme Architect, the Great Designer, the Prime Mover whose fiat initiated the secondary laws by which the world was governed. The change was one of degree, not one of kind. It was a change in the conception of the manner in which the world was governed, not a change in the origin and source of its government. There was no real conflict between religion and science among the Puritans nor among Americans during the pre-Civil War period. Science actually advanced as deism waned, for ultimate scientific assumptions were the ultimate religious assumptions. The very notion of order, of a rational order, of a universe instituted by reason and understandable through the processes of reason was a theological conception. In the beginning there was the *Logos,* and the *Logos* was reason. The most unreflective deism was theological, as the word itself suggests. And the most uncompromising secularism was a reaction *from* something. It was partly a reaction from supernaturalism and a tightly organized community composed of the elect of God. The evangelicalism of the frontier, beginning with Jonathan Edwards, was a revolt against formalism and an attack upon prescribed methods of salvation. Evangelicalism made for individualism and equality to the extent that its followers insisted upon the personal equality of believers in the sight of God. However violent the reaction to evangelicalism or to deism on the part of the exponents of the old order, however deep the apparent cleavage, both represented a conflict within religious thought, not a break with it. The crucial break came later with Darwin and evolution, a crisis in thought which historians thus far have hardly done more than describe in narrative terms.

The importance of the specific interrelations between religion and particular aspects of American history cannot be overstressed. Unitarianism and transcendentalism were religious formulations with profound effects upon reform, democracy, and the continuing American tradition. The Home Missionary Movement supplied a carrier for New England culture in the West and gave higher education a denominational framework with results which have merged in our contemporary dilemmas. Antislavery impulses are now viewed as values emanating from a religious base. And the answer of proslavery dialectics spoke out of other varieties of religious experience.

The Protestant crusade against popery was more than simply nativist and anti-Catholic; it reflected malignant tendencies in the functioning of democratic institutions. Connections between the idea of progress, rationalizations of the *status quo,* the gospel of wealth, and the doctrine of stewardship have not escaped historians if only for the reason that historians could not escape them.

Far more important than specific influences are the religious ideas which envelop whole aspects of American culture. The idea of democracy is the central concept of American civilization. Democracy is the American spirit, and the fulfillment of democratic aspirations is the American dream. The cluster of ideas which make up American democracy are not only indebted to Judaeo-Christian sources but these sources are supernatural in historical origin. Basic to a belief in democracy is the concept of a fundamental law and a moral order, a fundamental law not made by man, but an eternal law made by God. Although the roots of this assumption may be traced to Hebraic sources and to Plato, Americans entertained it as a religious doctrine. God created the moral law. He also created the human conscience, and it was through the agency of the human conscience that man was able to grasp it. It was the moral law which, in Ralph Waldo Emerson's phrase, supplied the "constitution of the universe" and it was this universe which Margaret Fuller enjoined him to accept. When William H. Seward spoke of a law higher than the Constitution, he referred to the same divine dispensation. He meant what his contemporaries and many of his successors still mean—the reflection on earth of the divine law of heaven. The inscription on hundreds of courthouse porticos across the nation testify to a belief in law, obedience to which is liberty. But if liberty is the reward of obedience to eternal law, it is not the liberty of democratic equalitarianism. It is the liberty to which the inherent nature of each man entitles him and mirrors the Platonic image of men of gold, of silver, and of iron. To devout believers in religious orthodoxy, the moral order was a divine order, and human striving to attain it yielded an approximation of ultimate reality. To skeptics and deviants, it was natural law. But in either case the underlying premises, although suppressed, were the same.

The concept of individual freedom flowed from the concept of the moral law. Society advanced as man grew in moral stature, and man grew in moral insight as society progressed. A law of progress shaped man's ends, and the law, not man himself, made for righteousness. The progress of society, in other words, supplied evidence for the progress of man as society advanced in proportion to man's comprehension of the immutable principles of existence. As man learned the ways of the universe and learned to conduct himself in harmony with those ways, he matured as a free individual. The ultimate truth alone could thus make him truly free, just as he was free to grow in wisdom and virtue. But do we mean the same thing when we use the same words today? The doctrine of the free individual has been secularized, but has secularization changed its meanings?

Nineteenth-century versions of liberty implied conformity to a fundamental law once the fundamental law was apprehended. And once apprehended, man was liberated from moral astigmatism and freed from the restraints of ignorance. The maxim "the less government, the better" lies behind such convictions, and these convictions are still regnant in powerful sectors of American society. Emerson expressed this belief with characteristic succinctness. "To educate the wise man the state exists, and with the appearance of the wise man the state expires." If the state was destined to wither away, government and the state were transitional. They were transitional institutions designed for the progressive improvement of man and society. Under the dictates of this theory man was envisioned, not as doing what he could, but as doing what he must. Here indeed was a theory of freedom, of liberty, and of progress, but how did the secularization of the later nineteenth century transform it?

To establish relations between concepts which are themselves imprecise is to commit the fallacy of the suppressed correlative. If there are secular ideas, there must be religious ideas with which to compare them. There must be such ideas if it is insisted that secular ideas are without religious content. While there is no real agreement concerning the content of American history, there is a general consensus concerning its scope. But the scope of religion is something less than clear. What exactly do we mean when we speak of religion in relation to American life? At what precise point in cultural analysis does an institution or an idea acquire a discrete and independent character? When is a concept or a fact utterly without relations? Is religion to be understood as a philosophical approach to the ultimate meanings of the universe? If so, it is simply a "candidate for truth" and therefore in conflict with other and different philosophies which are also candidates for truth. All must submit to the rigor of logical analysis and to the scrutiny of public examination. Only private views, privately held, can evade analysis and examination. Are religions traditional ways of looking at existence? If so, they must submit to the tests of history, philosophy, and psychology. Is religion a symbolic interpretation of cosmic and human history? If so, it must submit to the tests of total experience. Are religions varied efforts to devise ways of life for human guidance? If so, they must submit to the same tests.

When we speak of religion in America, what do we mean? Do we mean the religions of the world, or do we simply mean the three major Western religious movements? Is the viewpoint we are asked to adopt secular or spiritual? Is it one of personal identification or one of sympathetic but detached analysis? Is it institutional or intellectual, objective or subjective, inclusive or exclusive, personal or social? Any reasonable approach demands recognition of all possible viewpoints. Emphasis of one to the exclusion of others is partial and warps perspective. The historical task is to encompass every variety of religious thought and expression and to incorporate them in an all-inclusive synthesis.

The content of religion must be systematically appraised and the meanings of religion rigorously defined before religion can be accorded serious historical treatment. Before religion in America can be properly treated, we need to know a great deal more about it. We are not so much in need of the minute data of ecclesiastical evolution as we are in need of evaluations of speculative religious thought. Comparative and critical studies of broad scope are required, studies of the development of religious conceptions merged with other manifestations of the human spirit. The most pressing gap in American scholarship is a thorough-going examination of the Judaeo-Christian tradition. What Francis Cornford and Jane Harrison[5] did for ancient religious ideas is required for the comprehension of American religious ideas. Sterling Lamprecht's essay, *Our Religious Traditions,*[6] is suggestive, but a treatment in less than a hundred pages cannot accomplish a result which demands a many-volumed series. There is also need for a historical examination of theological speculation in America, for a sociological history of denominationalism, and for a cultural study of church organization broadly related to the evolving patterns of American life.

Until such work is undertaken, little progress can be made in solving the problems of religion and public education. There must first be clear understanding and agreement concerning the values common to all religions before there can be any agreement upon which religious values should be taught in public, tax-supported schools. Without such agreement, the values we teach are likely to be our own. Religious elements in American history should of course be presented. But they should be presented as integrated parts of the total culture and as objective manifestations of the total historical process. This is not to say that they should not be taught sympathetically. The historian must strive to identify with the historical subject matter. If he does not do so, he cannot hope to understand it. If he hopes to understand views alien to his own, he must first be able to impersonate them histrionically. He cannot properly criticize such beliefs in terms of his own convictions before he has succeeded in doing so. He must, however, be careful not to mistake religiosity for religion or to confound symbols with truth. Words, after all, are only the surrogates for things, and the historian as teacher must be as certain as human beings are permitted to be that the words he employs represent living meanings or meanings which once have lived.

DISCUSSION BASED ON DR. LOEWENBERG'S PAPER

Presiding: F. ERNEST JOHNSON

CHAIRMAN JOHNSON: Last evening we set the general boundaries, so to speak, for a consideration of the theme of this conference in a pluralistic culture and a secular state. This morning we address ourselves to a very specific problem, which was regarded by the committee as perhaps the best way of bringing our discussion to a practical level. We are considering the study and teaching of American history. To get us started, Professor Loewenberg will summarize his paper, "Religion in the History of American Ideas."

DR. BERT J. LOEWENBERG (Professor of History, Sarah Lawrence College): Mr. Chairman, Ladies and Gentlemen: I think I have said in my paper almost all that I have to say, and I will be very glad to answer any questions directed to it.

By way of summary, I will add that what are usually called "religious forces" permeated American history from its beginning to the present. Of this there can be no doubt. But these religious forces were combined movements, both of belief and of faith, words which refer to concepts which I think are distinguishable. However, in examining American history, it seems to me that it is futile, as well as improper, to seek to differentiate these two. To separate them would distort the meanings of American history. So, even though there may be a real and important distinction, as I believe there is, between faith and belief, it would be improper to try to divorce them. I think it would be unwise to exclude, for whatever reasons, religious factors, forces, faith, or belief from a consideration of American history in any real attempt to understand it.

The only contribution I can make to our discussions of last evening is to suggest a distinction between the usage of two verbs. Most of the time, it seems to me, the discussants employed the verb "to teach" rather than the verb "to study." While "to teach" has an ancient and an honorable lineage in which I participate, I think we can only confuse our present purpose by employing the verb "to teach" in this context. I think "to teach" carries with it certain overtones which confuse our basic intent and our basic problem; consequently, I would strongly urge that, in discussing this general topic of religion in public education, we speak of the need, the function, and the purpose of studying religion rather than of teaching it.

I think that one of my purposes here is perfectly clear. I introduced at one point in a different relation the whole problem of secularization, and I did this with intent, because I think that this word in its historical meaning has been confounded; moreover, I think that one of the things we should strive to do is to rescue it from the corrosions to which history and our own usages have subjected it.

This is an area in which we might find some prospect of compromise, because in the consequences of secularization as a process we have what I conceive to be religious factors and forces, and religious sources as well, quite separate from what we have loosely been calling sectarian or religious influences.

Although conventionally we speak about the religious forces in American history, this is a large area which is really uncultivated. Indeed, it is a very surprising fact that in the record of American historiography, a full-scale, inclusive, synthetic analysis of religion has still to be written. This particular gap in scholarship seems to carry with it an assumption that the religious forces in the United States have remained unchanged since their introduction into America. I am sure the specialists here will agree that, contrary to this assumption, there is undoubtedly an American phase to the development of the three major faiths, an American aspect to the evolution of religious attitudes and doctrines. This development must be taken into consideration, unless we are to become involved in what I have called the suppression of the correlative.

Until we understand some of these things and take them into consideration, we had better proceed with considerable caution. We do not have the facts, the concepts, or the interpretations; therefore, we do not have the meanings.

Before we are able intelligently to attempt to reach a compromise on what is certainly, to quote someone last night, "an agonizing problem" and one which can be solved only through the medium of compromise, we should be sure that we are talking the same language, that we mean the same thing.

I am sure we are approaching this problem in the same spirit; yet I am also sure we share the realization that we have to have additional data dealing with the concepts about which we all seem to be concerned.

DR. KRUG: This is a question of clarification, one I would like to relate to the closing statement last night concerning the theistic commitment in American culture. It has to do with the paragraph in which you speak of the belief in God as an important factor in the belief in the moral law and its influence on American political and other ideas.

I am recalling, or trying to recall, the section in Ralph Henry Gabriel's *The Course of American Democratic Thought*[7] in which he deals with the same idea and in which he has a statement that the God appealed to was, in part or for Christians at least, the theistic God that we were talking about last night, whereas for others it was the deistic God of the eighteenth-century philosophers. I would like to ask you to comment on that distinction from the standpoint of both its accuracy and its importance to our present discussion. If we are going to seek this theistic commitment in terms of what the Founding Fathers felt and believed, it is a vital distinction.

DR. LOEWENBERG: I think you are quite right that the Gabriel treatise does make this distinction in language somewhat akin to yours. He says that for traditional Christian believers, those who belonged to what he called at one point the fundamentalists or evangelical sects, this reference to higher law immediately connoted the God of the Bible and that for skeptics and unbelievers, it meant natural law. In the latter case, I think he was referring to the deists and the small group of nontheists in the United States. This meant natural law without any traditional commitment to the earlier formulation.

I think this makes some difference, but not a great difference. I think the main historical point is that there was a so-called higher law, a larger frame of reference to which human beings referred for guidance in their conduct and to which all gave general agreement. I don't know if that answers your question, but that is as far as I can go on the basis of my understanding of it.

DR. KRUG: My question was about the *source* of that commitment, particularly in relation to our discussion of the theistic commitments based on history.

DR. LOEWENBERG: I think the source was, of course, the ancient source in both cases. In the one case it stems back to Plato and the pre-Socratics, and in the other case it stems back to the reformulation of the Greek philosophy in terms of the Christian tradition.

DR. KONVITZ: In the light of the discussion last evening and the question just raised, wouldn't it be well to emphasize what seems to me to be a rather clear proposition that, while the Bible had incalculable influence on the early settlers and on the later generations in the United States, it is equally true that there were non-Biblical sources for some of the ideas that to us are fundamental?

I recall that Captain John Smith brought with him a copy of the *Meditations of Marcus Aurelius*. There are other similar Greek and Roman classics which contributed either to the originating or the strengthening of the idea of a higher law and of a transcendent moral law that must govern man and his institutions. I think perhaps Professor Loewenberg in his paper puts the matter a little more strongly than I would tend to do when he says in the same paragraph: "Although the roots of this assumption may be traced to Plato, Americans entertained it as a religious doctrine."

I think the roots of the assumption could also be traced to the Bible just as easily, perhaps even more easily than to Plato. There are many instances in the Bible, apart from the whole spirit of the Bible, that point to the law of God and the higher law as being fundamental. There are the famous instances of David and Bethsheba and Ahab and Jezebel and the contributions made by Elijah and Nathan, and these are instances where they told the kings off in no uncertain terms to the effect that they must rule under law and that the law must be the law of God.

But, at the same time, there is a somewhat similar idea in Sophocles' *Antigone* and in Plato and, to some degree, in Aristotle; so it seems to me in discussing the theistic roots of our ideas, a historian of ideas would need to bring in the nonreligious and the non-Biblical sources.

I think this is a topic that Professor Loewenberg could profitably spend a few minutes on here, because it seems to be crucial in the minds of many of us here.

DR. LOEWENBERG: I am perfectly willing to talk to that point, but don't know how crucial it is. In my judgment, it is not the sources but the consequences, when forces converge to underwrite ideas, which are more important. I accept what you have said, although I would give more emphasis to the Greek sources than to the Biblical sources. Again, it seems to me that the results in terms of our present historical situation are more vital than the origins of the idea. However, I am in full accord with the view that there were non-Biblical and non-Greek sources which reinforced at many stages the fundamental conceptions.

FATHER MCMANUS: I wonder if you would mind clarifying a statement in which you say: "Are religions traditional ways of looking at existence? If so, they must submit to the tests of history, philosophy, and psychology." Could you amplify that statement for me?

DR. LOEWENBERG: This point raises what to me are very fundamental questions about definition. As I said earlier, if we are to discuss the influences of religion on the rest of American history and the development of American ideas and institutions, we must know what we mean by religion, and I am here stating a number, not all, of questions which should be, if not answered, at least suggested.

I think I can answer your question briefly by saying any private belief does not have to answer to any test. Any belief which is communicated, and therefore becomes public, must submit to tests. If we regard religion in one of its phases as a pattern of human existence and a guide to conduct and if we study or teach it, then it has to be analyzed in terms of all the relevant data which we can bring to bear upon it.

To elucidate, I said in my paper that "Only private views, privately held, can evade analysis and examination." Then I ask, "Are religions traditional ways of looking at existence?" Are they then philosophical formulations of what to groups or individuals are ways of looking at the organization of the world and its implications? If they are such, then they must submit to these tests, among others. If it is an expression of faith, then it is to be accepted as such. If it is a statement of belief, then it has to submit to certain criteria.

CHAIRMAN JOHNSON: That calls for a pretty sharp definition between faith and belief. Belief is based upon reason; faith is something extraneous.

DR. LOEWENBERG: No, I wouldn't make that distinction. At least I wouldn't make the distinction in that way. I would say that a faith which someone holds is a private matter, and, even if it conflicts with reason or any of its formulations, it is an attitude which deserves a reverential approach. It belongs to that individual. He is entitled to hold it. But if it is a belief, if he proposes it as a belief which others should share and accept, then it is no longer private and becomes public, and then it must submit to criteria. This is the distinction.

FATHER TIMOTHY O'LEARY (Superintendent of Schools, Archdiocese of Boston): Professor, do you make any distinction here between theology as a legitimate, scientific study, and religion as such?

DR. LOEWENBERG: That is a question I posed. I would say that theology is a body of data which is testable, which must submit to the canons of knowledge and insight and wisdom. Until we define religion more closely, I would say there is a real and significant difference.

MR. HERMAN E. WORNOM (General Secretary, Religious Education Association): Professor Loewenberg, would you consider all concepts derived from revelation as privately held matters, matters of faith, or do you think concepts derived from revelation provide norms for the testing of religious beliefs and practices?

DR. LOEWENBERG: I would tend for the moment to banish the word "revelation." I would say that concepts, attitudes, ideas, and formulations that are derived from insight and wisdom must be analyzed when they become public. I trust that my distinction is clear on this point. All these are data, but they are data of a different order, and when they are presented for the acceptance or rejection of others, the very words imply that they are presented with a view seriously to be analyzed by all the criteria, insights, wisdom, and knowledge which we can bring to bear upon them. They are not to be accepted necessarily merely because they are presented.

MR. WORNOM: When you say these are data, what does "data" refer to?

DR. LOEWENBERG: What you called "revelation" and what I am calling—for reasons of strategy—wisdom, insight, other varieties of knowledge."

MR. SASSCER: If necessary, we will have to discuss things which involve revelation and private faith. Let's take examples you mentioned several times, such as Jonathan Edwards and the religious ideas he propounded, the transcendentalists and their ideas, and so forth.

In order to discuss these things at all intelligently in an advanced high school class, and perhaps we can't really discuss them too well except in a college class, one will have to have some idea of what is meant by "original sin," or he will just not understand Jonathan Edwards. He will have to have an idea of what is meant by "grace." If one is going to study certain aspects of American life, he will have to know what is meant by "sacraments." One will have to have an idea of what is meant by "revelation," even if it is defined crudely as that part of one's religious belief which cannot be proved by reason.

All these things will have to be discussed as ideas. A teacher cannot say he will not discuss "sacrament" because that involves a private belief and only certain American religions take it seriously. He cannot talk just about something that is common to all religions. If he did, he would fall down on the job rather badly. I wonder if you would comment on this practical problem.

In addition, can you tell us if there are any distinctly American religious ideas or if there are just the religious ideas that were brought over from Europe.

DR. LOEWENBERG: I am very glad to comment on that. I agree with you that these matters cannot be avoided. Although I do not contend that my distinction between studying and teaching is a solvent of all the problems that confront us, I think it does help in this particular instance and in any attempt to evaluate different religious influences in American history.

It seems to me that if we attempt to study these matters rather than to teach them, we assume a different psychological stance, as well as a different kind of pedagogical orientation. Insofar as these things can be explained to teen-agers in high school classes, they should be explained in an effort to evaluate differences, to draw out distinctions, to make clear to young people what these various ideas meant historically.

I think it would be very helpful if we substituted, wherever possible, neutral words for words which have a long historical association and connotation. And I think this is an aspect of the whole issue which we have to face. If we use loaded words, especially with young and impressionable people, we will not avoid the problem which has been mentioned here so frequently in all the efforts we have made to untangle it, namely, the problem of offering unreal solutions. At the moment I am convinced that, if we agree that the religious sources and religious forces in American history should be taught at levels below the college, we will have to work very hard to get our students to study them, and we can get students to study them without difficulty from our associates who hold different views only if we use language which is not rooted in religious, theological, sectarian meaning.

FATHER MCCLUSKEY: Dr. Loewenberg, I like that thought. I think it is rather absurd to pretend that below the university level we can give graduate seminars in comparative religions. I think it is neither proper nor possible in the common school to present a religious smorgasboard and tell the children these are the forty-seven varieties of religion. There is validity in your argument. I agree with your contention that religious beliefs should be examined according to the criteria of history, philosophy, psychology, and so forth. Your paper, of course, is on a general topic, and it is only fair to remember that you are speaking in general terms. You are not attempting necessarily to apply this to the secondary and elementary primary schools.

I think our difficulty is really a procedural one. We have not yet agreed to face a decision on whether or not we wish to recognize the theistic principle. If we hope to advance the discussion any further, I think we must ultimately grapple with this problem. Personally, I feel that much of what Father Hardon presented last night, with the possible modification of his word "should," will be the solution.

I don't think we can turn our backs on either the need for criteria, which you have pointed out, or on the wishes of the majority, which Professor Sutherland emphasized. Both of these are factors in the ultimate solution, though not the only factors nor possibly the controlling ones. Granting the primacy of the individual conscience and the individual's right to protect it, we must somehow provide for the majoritarian principle and the traditional theistic principle.

For forty or fifty years of the last century the theistic tradition was certainly dominant in education. I think that principle must enter into the solution of our present problem; however, I take exception to the idea expressed last night that one *should* believe in a personal God. This requires clarification. There should be a discussion here now of that particular point.

How can we reconcile these conflicting principles? In this connection, I like to think of the structure of an atom, in which there are four or five different forces held in balance. So it must be with opposing principles in our kind of society. We cannot organize everything around any single principle. We would come to all sorts of absurd conclusions, and in practice we would not accomplish a thing.

If we could accept the theistic principle or a modification of it which would protect all minority groups without embarrassment and still preserve the majority wishes, then the problem would become procedural. This question, then, of examining different religions and of presenting them in history and social studies seems to me to hinge on two things: first, the preparation of a textbook, in cooperation with major religious groups, which uses words that are not derogatory to any group and words that are neutral insofar as the nature of the subject permits; second, the preparation of lesson outlines to equip teachers for these courses.

The matter of neutrality, I realize, is a dangerous one. It reminds me of the story during the last great war when someone told an Irishman that Ireland was going to be neutral during the war, whereupon he asked, "I know Ireland will be neutral, but whom are we neutral against?"

DR. LOEWENBERG: I want to make one brief comment which I hope will be quite clear. I think it would be fatuous for us to endorse a proposal which would suggest the usage of words which are so neutral that they mean nothing at all; consequently, I cannot concede to Father McCluskey that we should endorse a theistic principle, if only for the reason that a very great American, who should be better known, when once accused of atheism replied, "Oh, I, too, would say 'God,' but only if you did not immediately assume that you knew exactly what I meant."

Unlike a movement in American history which had for its basis putting God in the Constitution, I would like to have God kept out of the Constitution. I do not believe that any reference to God should be in the Constitution, because—and this is our problem—there are different views of God. There are different philosophical interpretations of God. There are different metaphysical assumptions, either of a theistic or nontheistic view.

I don't see that we gain anything if we agree to something called the theistic principle or God or revelation or commandments or sacraments or original sin or grace or regeneration or any other series of words, all of which have historical, theological, and sectarian meanings, if we merely use them without regard to their content. And, if we must use their content, then I submit that we do not teach them. We study them as objectively as it is given to human beings to study and to present anything, recognizing, as Father McCluskey said, that we do stem from different backgrounds, that we do have different cultural roots, and that we are committed in democratic theory, principle, and practice to preserve those differences.

DR. JORDAN L. LARSON (Superintendent of Schools, Mount Vernon, New York): I am concerned about those here who are students of theology and who are so far advanced beyond the average schoolteacher in semantics that they tend to forget the practical problems of communication. How much does the average schoolteacher need to know about these things to be able to discuss them intelligently and without controversy in a class of typical American boys and girls? I don't see how the average high school teacher can afford to get involved in all these hair-splitting interpretations, and I wish we could discuss some of the words and expressions they might use without fear of getting into deep theological explanations that would be beyond their comprehension.

I don't know much about atomic energy; so I just do not discuss it except in superficial terms; then I run like heck lest somebody ask a meaningful question. I wonder if a teacher isn't so much afraid of the semantics involved in a discussion of religion that he will think and act the same way. How can we arrive at language that enables us to know what we are talking about?

CHAIRMAN JOHNSON: We have only a few more minutes for this period. I am wondering, Dr. Larson, whether that question might better be explored in connection with the paper "A Study of Religion in High School American History."

It seems to me that we ought to make sure that we have absorbed the shock of Professor Loewenberg's paper, which indicates a very definite need for an evaluation of religious concepts based on some synthesis, which would perhaps begin with a definition of religion. This has been one of the most crucial problems that our committee has dealt with: To what extent do we need to start out with a definition of religion and to what extent shall the public school attempt analysis and validation of religious convictions? Professor Loewenberg has challenged us to some very important thinking, and I believe that we shall find that our most difficult problems are in the areas he described.

Religious Matter in the Teaching of American History

JOHN THOMAS FARRELL

Dr. Farrell is professor of American history at the Catholic University of America, where he has taught since 1945. He received his A.B. and Ph.D. degrees from Yale University, where his studies were in the fields of American Colonial and legal history. During 1935-45 he was on the teaching staff of the College of New Rochelle. His professional publications include The Legal Diary of William Samuel Johnson *and articles in the* Catholic Historical Review. *A member of the Catholic Historical Association, he served as its president in 1954.*

As ORIGINALLY proposed the title of this paper was to be "The Reciprocal Relationship between the Teaching of Religion and the Teaching of American History in Teacher Education." This hinted at something in the nature of a speculative tract, whereas it is rather assumed that the interest of the Committee on Religion and Education lies in the practical order. The paper is therefore concerned with possible answers to, "How does religion, or religious history, constitute a necessary element in American history?" and "Does a degree of 'religious literacy' help in training students and prospective teachers of American history?" I hope to answer these questions (1) by discussing in general the relationship observed by myself—over the past twenty years of teaching—between religion and history, and (2) by a brief survey of the incidence of religion, the religious factor, and religious history in American history. There is here no promise of an exhaustive treatment of the first, and no definitive treatment of the latter point, but there should be sufficient material to promote some useful discussion.

There are some few who speak for an extreme form of Protestant thought who have denied the relevance of any history except as a record of sin. They would give us nothing much to talk about. However, Professor E. Harris Harbison has dealt with these in his stimulating essay, *Religious Perspectives of College Teaching in History*,[1] and the point of view taken here necessarily implies a high value for both religion and history, such as was pronounced by Pope Pius XII in his allocution to the Tenth International Congress of Historical Sciences in Rome, September 7, 1955.[2] If only a few religious thinkers have gone on record as seeing no great compatibility in religion and history, I fear that there have been many more historians who have taken such a stand. As we shall have occasion to note later, the first generation of professional historians in the United States were men who were not greatly interested in religion or in religious history. Many more of them, even today, when much more attention is paid to the importance of religious history, and particularly to religious ideas in history, hold a fundamentally secularist position.[3] While these scholars may not be expressly committed to the extreme position of "historism," a notion that change or evolution affects all reality, both spiritual and material, they do have a bias against theology which they consider to have become a discarded approach, something which history replaced. However, there are some indications of a change in this outlook, a willingness to admit that the subject of history is one which involves, inevitably, human beings in their setting, whether in the Ancient World, or in the United States, or in the Far East, and that religion is something like a key to an understanding of man. Also, today historians are more inclined to make judgments, rather than simply put the facts in order, and so they have to take a stand on the nature of man and his purpose in life. This requires that they frequently take account of religious history, to find a place for moral philosophy and theology, even if they are reluctant to recognize these as scientific disciplines.

It is reasonable to find history and religion compatible, which is to say that while each has an autonomous position in education, both subjects serve as paths to knowledge. As regards their autonomy, at least on the levels of college and graduate school teaching (where my experience lies) there is no proper way of teaching history as an aspect of religion, no proper way of teaching religion as an aspect of history. Intellectual curiosity about the one subject may be aroused by the study of the other, but this elementary reciprocity in the study of both disciplines may lead to a warped appreciation of one or the other unless there is a possibility for specialization. On the other hand, where both disciplines have been developed in harmony, each as part of the balanced education of the whole person, I can vouch for the fact that to the history teacher it means something, if only economy in time. I do not refer here to the development of religious conviction, although teaching religion is something like teaching nutrition—there is some effect expected—and certainly I have never found religious conviction a bar to apprehending truth. What is meant rather is that a teacher of a freshman survey of Western civilization will be able to spend more time in teaching history if he can be sure that his students have a religious knowledge to begin with. Who was Saint Paul? What are the seven sacraments? What is the contemplative life?

We could surely take up a considerable space with the incidental advantage of religious knowledge in the teaching of history, but that is not the primary purpose of this essay. There is just one more thing that needs saying. It is not just the student's literacy in religion which can facilitate the learning process in history. The instructor can make some serious errors of interpretation if, where an exact knowledge is called for, he confuses the notion of fate with the idea of predestination in a religious sense, or if he identifies indulgences and the forgiveness of sins, or makes any one of a number of other errors which a weakness of understanding in matters of religion may induce.

The objective in which we are interested is to have history studied and well taught, particularly American history. The story of America is no exception to the general rule that all societies have some religious heritage. It would be readily conceded, I suppose, that we could not compare one of the Mohammedan civilizations and Western Europe's Christendom if we did not refer to certain basic religious comparisons. The scriptures and dogmas of the two civilizations really make a difference which no other "cause" explains. We recognize certain potentialities of the Christian society, for example, in the division of *regnum* and *sacerdotium,* and at the same time certain limitations in Islam to be attributed to an identification of temporal and spiritual government. There is a great contrast between the willingness of the Christian world to appropriate the whole heritage of Greek and Roman learning and the disposition in most of the Mohammedan world to consider only the Koran as trustworthy, everything else being either superfluous or pernicious. One need not be a Toynbee to recognize that religion is decisive in determining a culture, or that history which ignores the basic ideas and ideals of a people in any era is at best a partial thing. The point is not without some importance to the teaching of American history.

A few decades ago the principal authority on American thought and civilization was Vernon L. Parrington's *Main Currents of American Thought*.[4] A determined rationalist, with a prejudice strongly in favor of a secularized socialist society, Parrington was particularly caustic in his evaluation of the seventeenth-century Puritans. In his opinion only the liberalizing enlightenment, and the clarification of democracy by French revolutionary Jacobin influences, rescued America from a sterile tradition of piety and morality that was handed down from Calvinist divines. It was not just that he allowed his hatred of a Calvinist heritage to distort his judgment which makes Parrington so inadequate. It is rather that it got in the way of his understanding what he was talking about. More recent scholarship, notably that of Perry Miller, has served to correct Parrington's view of things. We know now that the origins of both conservative and liberal movements in American thought, the origins of both some Protestant piety and the rationalist solvent of some of the dogmas that underlay that piety, derive from divergent tendencies in a common theology of seventeenth-century New England. The point is not that theology is hereby vindicated; it is just that in order to understand one of the most important aspects of our cultural past, it became necessary for scholars to acquire a certain expertness in reading "divinity" as taught by Puritan theologians. Once the barrier of ignorance was broken, the historian was better prepared to explain what he was talking about.

Before going on, I should admit that there are certain dangers in the purely cultural approach to history. It is possible to overemphasize its advantages. We can pass too readily over other things which need emphasis. So one has to be on guard against conditioning a prospective teacher of history to pass over lightly the material influence of economic activities or motivations. Military history is having a healthy revival, and we seem to be getting away from what one of my acquaintances in the historical profession called the dangerous "escapism" of the thirties when it seemed that military history was to be relegated to the dustbin of history. We have to keep in mind that anyone who teaches history creates an impression of history by what he or she selects for exposition. But these are not the worst dangers from overemphasis on cultural history. The worst that could happen would be to have history cease to be history, if historians should come to think of themselves as more than historians and try to become quasi-divines or prophets. I believe that this is what has happened to Arnold Toynbee.[5] We may have—although I hope not—some American historians who, bitten by the bug of historism, will, out of the different strands of America's religious and cultural heritage, try to construct the ideal eclectic or strictly American religion.

The teaching of American history has been necessarily dependent upon the work of those writers and research workers who, like so many chefs, make the salads. What goes into the bowl in turn depends upon their selection of materials. Ever since we have had a group of professional historians, or salad makers, which is to say since about the last twenty years of the nineteenth century, the range of interests has been broad enough to include most aspects of history. However, until the 1930's these professional historians did not in general devote much attention to religious history. A possible reason for this is to be found in the reaction against the pietistic emphasis which had been characteristic of inspired amateurs ever since the Puritans of New England had begun to narrate the American story back in the seventeenth century. A characteristic seventeenth-century title would be Capt. Edward Johnson's *Wonder Working Providence.* The providential version of the beginnings of American history was also in evidence in the work of George Bancroft in the nineteenth century. His ten-volume *History of the United States,* although it carried the story only to 1789, was devoted to the theme of God's chosen people, the Americans, who were able to work out their destiny of free government and society with divine aid. Furthermore, the beginnings of professional work in American history coincided with an era of confidence in science. Not only did it become bad form to attribute causes in history to wonder-working providences, it was considered more fruitful to investigate temporal and material conditioning elements in explaining the phenomena of history. A whole generation of historiography in the United States was affected by the geographical determinism of Frederick Jackson Turner and his epochal address of 1893 to the American Historical Association, "The Significance of the Frontier in American History." Finally, it seems to me, there was an awareness that America was coming of age in the twentieth century, which was pre-eminently one of competitive economic systems, or rather competitive national economies, so that it was only natural for the historians of America to look back at those material factors which shaped American society and to stress these as significant while they ignored or deprecated the religious aspects of our history. The religious elements in the American story were treated briefly, and any special research in the field was left to the divinity school men. History was at the service of the age of progress.

One prominent figure in American historiography who was not satisfied with a completely secular interpretation of our history was Dr. John Franklin Jameson. Although he was the inspiration for many of the history projects of the time which reflected a preoccupation with other things, he showed on more than one occasion, while he was secretary of the American Historical Association, an interest in religious history. This was not on his part an expression of piety; rather it was a manifestation of his profound understanding of the importance of religion in the American past, a realization that it was a real conditioning influence. Unfortunately he never published very much on the subject. There is only a mention, in the American Historical Association *Annual Report* for 1913,[6] of the paper he read that year at the annual meeting of the association in Charleston, South Carolina, on "Reasons for Studying American Religious History." However, some of those reasons became apparent when he did publish his *American Revolution Considered as a Social Movement*.[7] Dr. Jameson encouraged those who founded the American Catholic Historical Association, and his correspondence as published recently is evidence of his alertness to the importance of any publication which had to do with religious history. One of his main concerns was to get the study going among the historians outside schools of theology, to make it a regular concern of history departments everywhere, and among the reasons he gave in justification, apart from the importance of the subject, was its value as a means toward teaching fairness of mind.

Of course it was not fairness of mind which had characterized the older school of "religious" historians, particularly those who in the nineteenth century had written of America from the New England point of view. But there was, as Jameson knew, a broader view possible, one that was less sectarian or even less national. I suggest that such a point of view would stress the beginnings of American history in the history of Christendom. What the Christian society of Europe was in the Middle Ages constitutes the common past of most Americans; what happened to that society in the age of exploration and discovery, by way of religious development, contributed to the making of America as well as to the making of modern Europe. When America was discovered by Columbus, there had not yet taken place those changes which brought the division of Christian society into Catholicism and various forms of Protestantism. The religious motivation of the early explorers, Portuguese and Spanish, cannot be stressed too much; an excellent treatment of motives can be found in Samuel E. Morison's *Admiral of the Ocean Sea*.[8] Beyond the matter of motivation there are also the beginnings of international law as we know it in modern times. The norms of international law were established on the foundations of medieval jurisprudence, with notable contributions appearing in the work of Francisco de Vitoria in the sixteenth century. Finally, as to the origins of both the rival systems of colonial enterprise in America and the cultural and political characteristics of an evolving Europe, one may say that religious history includes both, for it was in the pattern of religious development that such things as the state system of Europe and the mercantilist empires of the seventeenth century appeared.

Elizabethan England was the source for that vision of empire which led to the establishment of Jamestown and the subsequent history of those colonies out of which was made the United States. From Richard Hakluyt the younger we get the clearest picture of the influences leading to English colonization in the New World, and specifically from his "Discourse on the Western Planting," written for the edification of Queen Elizabeth in 1584 and designed to open the royal purse for support of Sir Walter Raleigh's proposed colony in

Virginia. Although the Discourse is of basic importance to any analysis of trade and commerce in the background of colonization, the religious point of view manifest in this advocacy of a "large policy" is by no means a negligible thing. Hakluyt was very much aware of the role played by Spanish missionaries in America, and he was very anxious to make the point that Protestant England had an obligation to fulfill along the same lines. Very aptly he exploited the writings of the Spanish friar, Las Casas, to show that the treatment of the aborigines was such that it became the duty of England to provide a better missionary activity. There is here a sense of rivalry, not alone for material advantage, with Catholic Spain, a rivalry as well in demonstrating a proper regard for the expansion of what they still considered to be a "common corps of Christendom." Subsequently the settlement of Virginia was supported with a degree of religious enthusiasm, and a propaganda campaign to promote the colony that was established at Jamestown in 1607 enlisted the services of the Anglican clergy. Their church was established in America along with the earliest settlers, and when those who survived the harsh conditions of the first decade were to meet in America's first legislative assembly, the Virginia House of Burgesses, it was a church in Jamestown which afforded the place of meeting. The same program that included the extension of a share in government to the settlers, by grant of the Virginia Company in England, included plans for a missionary school for the Indians, a college "for the training up of the Children of those Infidels in true Religion moral virtue and Civility and for other godly uses." Unfortunately these plans never materialized, and when Virginia got its College of William and Mary in the last decade of the seventeenth century it was not to become a center for missionary work among the Indians.[9]

If Virginia's beginnings cannot be studied without some reference to a religious setting, how much more is the importance of religion in the making of Puritan New England. It would seem that the characteristic preoccupation of most popular accounts of the beginnings of New England with the Pilgrims, those rather inoffensive separatists who settled on Cape Cod in 1620, has served to take some of the significant things and hide them away behind the turkeys and pumpkins of the Thanksgiving story. The character of early New England was made by migrating Puritans who came to Massachusetts Bay, starting about a decade after the Mayflower landed the Pilgrims on a desolate shore. Between 1630 and 1640 about 20,000 people—not all of whom stayed in America—began an enterprise conceived along Old Testament lines, one which was designed to establish a base of operations for "true religion." As Morison says in his *Builders of the Bay Colony*,[10] these men had primarily a religious motive for all that has been recorded of them in political and economic activity. In England they were associated with a parliamentary opposition to King Charles, one which wrested from that monarch the assent to the Petition of Right (1628). In America they were to become the ship-builders, merchants, educators, and statesmen of a vigorous Colonial society. Their achievements have tended to obscure the basic reason for their becoming empire builders, for if Charles I had not had a French Catholic wife, if his religious policy had not been, in Puritan eyes, popish, and if he had not given royal support to "heretical" Arminian doctrines, there might not have been Puritan support for constitutionalism in the England of that time or any Massachusetts Bay Company with a strong religious purpose. Finally, in coming to America, the Puritans showed no desire to leave behind them for good all matters of religious controversy; on the contrary, what they had in mind was the establishment of a base, not too distant from Europe to be wholly removed from the great religious wars that were raging then, and a position to be exploited for the conquest of this hemisphere.

To be sure, their material achievements were considerable, and the lasting results of the Puritan settlement include political and educational achievements of great importance to the history of the United States, but the point is that they did not come over here with just that in mind. Only religious reasons, and the strategy of what we might call the international Protestant revolution, caused them to commit their resources—a large capital investment as well as their personal safety—in a region which, for twenty years previously, had been notoriously unprofitable for economic enterprise. Moreover, in view of the importance of political changes taking place in England in the seventeenth century—changes which were in great measure the work of puritans in the mother country—the actual preservation of those settlements made in and beyond Massachusetts Bay owed a great deal to the religious compatibility of New England's leadership with the military and political rulers of England between 1640 and 1660. If it had been otherwise, if Charles I and Archbishop Laud had been free to take action against those zealots in the New World who had escaped the Court of High Commission in England, there might have been no successful Puritan commonwealths in America. As it happened, even though there developed some significant divergencies between the policies of the English government and those of the authorities in the Bay Colony, the general sympathy of aims and purposes, grounded upon common religious doctrines, enabled the Puritans in America to establish themselves solidly and without interfering controls exercised from abroad.

Please understand that no successful course of study in the Colonial period of American history could be given if only the religious aspects of its history were stressed. We can account for some things in the beginnings of settlement only if we understand the religious motivation involved, but that is not the whole story. Aside from Virginia and Massachusetts already discussed, there is some very interesting religious aspect to the founding of each one of the Colonies. Maryland owed its existence to the combination of colonizing ambition and religious principles in the person of George Calvert, the first Lord Baltimore. Not only does its history depend much upon the record of English policy toward the adherents to the old religion, it is a history which reveals an interesting experiment in toleration. In an age when the principle of *cuius regio eius religio* was coming into general acceptance, it affords an example of a Catholic ruler and a Catholic ruling class risking their own rights and property to a policy of complete toleration of those Protestants who, elsewhere in America as well as back in England, were committed to the rooting out of anything which even resembled popery. That the experiment succeeded on the whole and that the proprietary government of Maryland endured through many vicissitudes with the principle of toleration intact until 1689, when a Protestant revolution overthrew it, must be accounted one of the marvels of the seventeenth century. It must be assumed as well to have had some influence on the subsequent history of religious toleration.

Even the most abbreviated survey of the remainder of Colonial history must admit of a considerable religious emphasis. Continuing settlement of the North American mainland was affected by the fortunes of Quakers in the British Isles, as English, Welsh, and Irish

Friends took an interest in the establishment of overseas settlements in the Jerseys and in Pennsylvania. It was a common radical Protestantism discerned by William Penn in the Low Countries and in the Protestant minorities of the Rhineland, as well as among Quakers of the British Isles, which inspired him with the idea of making his colony of Pennsylvania what we would call a melting-pot society. Penn had gone abroad as a missionary Quaker to establish contacts with these continental sectarians before he got his grant of a rich area in North America from King Charles II. Also, we ought to note that fundamental changes in religious policy in France and England in the last quarter of the seventeenth century had lasting effects upon the American Colonies. The brutal policy of Louis XIV, followed by the revocation of legal toleration of Huguenots in 1685, set loose thousands of French Protestants, some of whom came to the English colonies; then his subsequent wars in the Palatinate uprooted more thousands of Germans. The German Protestants were encouraged by the English authorities to accept settlement, some of them in Ireland and more in New York and Pennsylvania. The story of immigration has never been without some interesting religious aspects, and this is particularly true of the first influx of non-English elements into the Colonies. Following upon Quakers from the various parts of the British Isles and French and German Protestants, the middle of the eighteenth century was to witness a tremendous movement of Irish Presbyterians to this country. These came to America not just because of the economic discrimination against Ireland and its products as practiced by the English rulers of that country, but because their religion was a bar to civil and political liberty in their homeland.

Religious history enters into the story of eighteenth-century America not only on the immigration side—where as a factor it was rivaled only by the contributions of the harsh criminal law and the social conditions in England which produced the indentured servants—it also must be considered as an influence upon Empire government and upon the making of a domestic climate of opinion. The Anglican Church exercised jurisdiction over America through the Bishop of London and his commissaries. A certain amount of tension between the royal government's religious arm and the multiple sects and independent religious establishments here in America provides one of the important bases of estrangement between the Colonies and the mother country. Not that the conservative part of the communities outside New England ever looked upon the established Anglican Church as an alien influence; on the contrary they regarded it as a bulwark of order in society. It was rather that where Anglicanism was not established, there was fear lest it might be introduced to upset existing church orders, as in New England, and where it was established it was kept weak to a degree that was displeasing to church authorities in England. The prospect of Anglican bishops becoming established in this country was a pleasant one from the English point of view but nowhere in America a popular idea. After that popular stirring of religious fervor we call the Great Awakening of the eighteenth century, the work of Jonathan Edwards, of the Tennents, and of George Whitefield, popular religion and free church organization became a bar to any imposed hierarchical organization.[11]

It was in the Great Awakening that scholars have discerned a decisive change in the emotional climate of America. It had broad social and political consequences, *but it was basically a religious movement.* The breaking away of "New Light" congregations resulted in some considerable dissatisfaction with any religious establishment by the state, a disposition which would lead to a formulation of separation of church and state as the American way of doing religion a service. Religion became more widespread as a force, and as a basis for group organization it took on a new significance. Popular preachers showed the way to patriotic orators, like Patrick Henry, and the education of dissenting ministers became the work of new schools and colleges. There was a strong element of democracy in the whole business, a social leveling and a consequent demand for more political rights. From the point of view of religious thought it produced a conservative theological outlook among the masses, while paradoxically it encouraged skepticism among the well-to-do. Jonathan Edwards and George Whitefield left behind them not only the inspired sects which thereafter provided a characteristic American brand of Protestantism, but they were also responsible for a reaction against emotionalism in religion which led to deism and Unitarianism.

A final word on the Colonial period, which came to an end when religion (as much as anything) had helped to bring about that situation noted by John Adams, an attitude of independence in the "hearts and minds of the American people." Our Founding Fathers were an educated elite, drawn from a variety of stations in life but for the most part educated in church-related schools—Harvard, William and Mary, Yale, Princeton, and Kings (afterwards Columbia).[12] They were formed in a tradition that had its beginnings in the trivium and quadrivium of medieval education, and which had as its fruits the cultivation of the mind with particular attention paid to dialectic. The people who founded those institutions were mindful first of all of the religious basis for society. Like many other religious enterprises the by-products have been so spectacular—in this case the education of our first generation of statesmen—as to make us forget that the original purpose was not to serve material interests or even knowledge for its own sake. We are reminded that the right to knowledge was conceived originally as first of all the right to know more about the relation of God to man.

Having devoted so much space to the Colonial period of our history it becomes necessary to become truly summary in a treatment of the religious aspects of later American life. In general the main theme remains valid. It is often a primary religious orientation which affects political and social development. A knowledge of the religious history of any period is indispensable to an understanding of what happened. Of course, there are great movements which are to be described for what they are, like the formation of the Constitution of the United States, our diplomatic history during and after the War of Independence, the great economic development of the nineteenth century, and the expansion of Americans from the frontier of the Allegheny Mountains to the Pacific Coast. However, there are certain vital issues, the resolution of which had much to do with determining the direction of political and social movements wherein the spiritual and moral attitudes taken by the American people had great significance, all of them associated with one or another trend or conflict which we study in the nineteenth and twentieth centuries.[13] If it is the reaction of America to the French Revolution, behind the attitude of frustration in New England at an apparent loss of control over national affairs to the South and West, there is a strong religious discontent expressive of Puritan piety in its reaction to "infidelism." A generation later the same piety, spread through New York and Ohio by a succession of religious revivals would produce the anti-slavery impulse described by Gilbert H. Barnes.[14] Religion was not lacking in the South, and among the causes of the Civil War must be included the divisions of Protestant churches into Northern and Southern branches. The developing conflict of the sections was no mere economic affair but did serve to bring out the dynamite that lay in a conflict of morals between two branches of a religious-minded people. Southern piety reinforced rather than moderated the Southern attitude toward the race question, as it would continue to do until well into the twentieth century. Northern piety as interpreted by the Beechers would make issues over slavery where politicians would prefer to bury them, as in Kansas. Truly, no one may ignore religion as a part of the background of the Civil War.

Before the Civil War there were two great actions, the expansion of the United States motivated by the spirit of manifest destiny, and the peopling of the country by hordes of immigrants from Ireland and Germany. Neither of these actions was without some religious overtones. Expansion and the war with Mexico stirred the American people in a manner reminiscent of Protestant freebooting in the age of Elizabeth. During the same period the coming of the immigrants, many of them Catholics, brought out latent antagonisms toward Rome and the Catholic religion, ending in a social and political movement to save Protestant America which one writer has called *The Protestant Crusade*.[15] One consequence of this period of nativism and anti-Catholic feeling was the shaping of our public school system in such a way as to divorce it from any affiliation with religious groups; another was to reinforce the group consciousness of Irish Catholics, making them less inclined to accept the institutions and social organizations of other Americans because these were considered to be so many snares and booby traps of Protestant origin.

When we arrive at post-Civil War history, there is at least a change in subject matter and a different orientation to justify a different approach. It is not feasible to attempt any religious explanation, or to pose any religious issue, as involved in political reconstruction in the South. Neither is there much point in discussing the financial and agrarian problems of the postwar era as though such problems had their origin in religious causes. A seeming exhaustion of the emotions was one consequence of the Civil War, and the agitators North and South resemble some extinct volcanos. Only when urban development and industrial changes created new problems did there appear to be any restatements of religious purpose in American life. Moreover, this was the time when material preoccupations were such that, both in Europe and in America, there was a tendency as never before experienced to divorce the prevailing culture from its religious foundations. Popular religion continued to be popular, but so were the infidelities of Col. Robert J. Ingersoll. Despite the prevalence of revivalists there was a growing disposition to find the fundamental causes of things and of purpose in life in pseudoscientific theories. Ethics increasingly became divorced from belief; social sanctions were found not in any moral theology but in one or another rationalization of economic science. Not that all this resulted in any immediate or widespread deterioration of ethics on the part of middle-class Americans, but the very conservatism of these Americans in private life seemed to belie the need for organized religion. For a change, reformers who could point to the extending evils of *laissez faire* in the business world were no longer clergymen or even ex-clergymen, but men with no particular religious orientation, like Henry George and Henry Demarest Lloyd. In short, America was rapidly moving toward a condition in which even the historians would show some reluctance to appreciate the religious bases of American life or culture, a phenomenon referred to earlier in this paper.

One has to refer to the resumption of an interest in world affairs, to the revival of manifest destiny in the last decade of the nineteenth century, for some renewal of a sense of religious orientation in American life. Before doing so, it might be well at least to mention that our national labor movement was able to surmount something of a religious crisis. American laborers, many of them Catholics, had joined with enthusiasm the Knights of Labor when there appeared, in the 1880's, a danger that it would be denounced as a secret society and dangerous to faith and morals. The prevailing acceptance of the social order and its inequalities and frequent injustices by representatives of organized religion would very likely have made any such condemnation popular by putting the church on the side of what most middle-class Americans took to be "law and order." The farsighted ecclesiastical statemanship and breadth of understanding shown by Cardinal Gibbons prevented a condemnation of the Knights of Labor by Rome.[16] The appearance of Leo XIII's encyclical *Rerum Novarum*, in 1891, was another indication that the condition of the working classes was not being ignored. Its mixed reception throughout Europe and America was such that this encyclical revealed clearly what should have been obvious before: The church was doctrinally opposed to the two extreme forms of current materialistic social ethics, laissez-faire capitalism and doctrinaire socialism.

The social problem was in competition for public attention with the exciting events of Europe's new imperialist age. Over the decade 1890–1900 the United States became involved in this movement with a surprising renewal of manifest destiny. Professor Pratt, in his *Expansionists of 1898*,[17] has noted the influence of Protestant religious journals in promoting this revival. It was a reversion to type insofar as the old battle cry against Catholic Spain was concerned. The Spanish-American War of 1898 was the last of a series of conflicts which began with the defeat of the Armada of Philip II; but at least one Catholic archbishop, John Ireland of St. Paul, and the Catholic magazine *Ave Maria* joined in support of an expansionist policy and in advocating an imperialist policy in the Philippines. Complementing the idea of a new manifest destiny was a quasi-religious emphasis upon the racial destiny of the Anglo-Saxons and Germanic peoples—otherwise known as the Teutonic people or Aryans. On its domestic side this racial bias was to furnish support for a new nativist movement, the American Protective Association, while at the same time it gave support to the movement for restriction of immigration from the eastern and southern parts of Europe. Long after the enthusiasm for imperialism was gone, this nativist mania was to spread rapidly among the nonurban Protestants and perhaps reach its peak of hysteria in the Ku Klux Klan of the 1920's.

It would make this paper much too long and involve problems of emphasis to carry this survey into the twentieth century. Besides, assessments of religious causes in the past fifty years amount to reflections upon current events. This is not to say, however, that judgments on our own century's religious history may not be of great importance to one's interpretation of other aspects of its history. We are just too much a part of what we are talking about to speak historically with any confidence of the religious background of what has taken place. When it is time for a summing-up, it is quite possible that historians will have to assess the importance of a religious heritage in the Western world to the rousing of opposition to Nazi and Communist totalitarianism. It may be that we have been living through an age when traditional belief has been vindicated against pseudo-religions, like socialism and positivism. It is very obvious already that the accepted versions of human motivation, popular twenty-five years ago, like the economic interpretation of history or the older idea of racial destiny, have had to be discarded. The surprising phenomenon of Christian democracy in Europe and the restoration of religion to a central place in the literature and thought of the age, after an eclipse of a couple of generations, give us some reason for believing that, just as in previous centuries, the hearts and minds of human beings cannot be unaffected by religious belief. In conclusion, it might be remarked that our own age has seen a restoration of theology. After completing the gamut of pseudoreligious exercise, of nationalism, of socialist experiment, and rationalizing man's experience in this world on purely sociological lines, there has been a return to considerations of God and history, man and his conscience, nature and grace. But this is relevant to the future even more than it is relevant to the immediate past.

DISCUSSION BASED ON PROFESSOR FARRELL'S PAPER

Presiding: F. ERNEST JOHNSON

DR. JOHN T. FARRELL (Professor of History, Catholic University of America) : I am grateful to Professor Loewenberg for some of the points that he brought out. His distinction between what is privately held and what can be taught is, I agree, a crucial one. I would like to discuss with him sometime the relationship between secular ideas and religious ideas. I think it is a very interesting notion that the secular traditions and religious traditions are opposite sides of the same coin so to speak.

I had a very simple task, which was to explore the religious content of American history from the point of view of the teacher. The teacher education aspect I didn't take too seriously, perhaps not seriously enough. I just teach American history. A good many of the people who are in my classes, who earn master's degrees or who go on for the Ph.D., are people who will be teaching. I don't always know at what level.

On many occasions I have talks with some of my students about the problem that came up at the end of the last discussion. They ask the questions: What are you going to tell high school students about this? How can you present complex ideas to high school students and, at the same time, avoid oversimplifications? I do not pretend to know all the answers. Although it is a problem, I don't think it is an overwhelming one unless the teacher allows history to become a substitute for philosophy or a substitute for theology. There are some presentations in history that must be made on a mature level and that are perhaps beyond the capacity of a high school student and certainly beyond that of a grade school student. But one doesn't necessarily teach philosophy when he teaches history. Nor does he teach theology when he teaches history. In a university, at least, he can discharge his duty adequately, I think, if he refers certain problems to his students' experience in other departments or to their experience in general education.

My teaching experience has been entirely in Catholic colleges and universities, and I believe some of you here perhaps could have written a better paper on this particular topic. For example, I see Professor Abell, who is a specialist in the influence of religion on social development in the late nineteenth century. If he had been asked to take the last part of American history, I think he could have made a much better summary than I did.

I don't propose to go through the whole paper or to do anything in the way of making a capsule out of it, but I will be glad to try to answer any questions that you want to raise.

MISS THOMPSON: What do you consider the function of the American history teacher in a secondary school to be? Is he an authority on fact and on interpretation, or is he a leader of young people who tries to study a problem and find the facts and the truth?

DR. FARRELL: I am not a high school teacher, and I have never had to take any responsibility for teacher training in that connection or to establish a philosophy for anybody in that connection. All I can do is evoke memories of the better high school teachers I had. If I were to go back over my experience and pick the best high school teachers, I would say that they were people who introduced me to new ideas out of a fund of knowledge that I didn't have and that they were people who made me think. They were authorities to the extent that they had a command of their subjects that I didn't have. They never, so far as I know, tried to impose ideas on me.

MR. FRANCK: Since this is a paper on teacher education, I would like to ask a question in that connection. In my work, both as a community worker and as a college teacher, I have occasion to talk with a great number of teachers, and I have observed a rather noticeable lack of understanding on the part of teachers on this very subject of the separation of church and state, on its genesis, and on its meaning in American history.

Would it not be useful, particularly in that part of teacher training which concerns American history, to make a special effort to interpret this principle of the separation of church and state, so that a teacher will be able to approach this subject calmly and to explain to students rationally the reason why we are forbidden to indoctrinate religious beliefs in the public schools and, thereby, avoid the impression that these things are "touchy" and that we really don't know much about them? In short, do you think a teacher would have a greater degree of freedom in his or her work as a high school teacher if he could explain freely to students in the course of teaching American history why it is at a certain point we stop and don't indoctrinate in the public schools.

You have a sentence somewhere in your paper, Dr. Farrell, about the separation of church and state being a development which was favorable to religion and which made possible the flowering of religion. Would it be useful to get that idea across to teachers for their own peace of mind in the first place and also for the purpose of enabling them to deal with this subject intelligently at the high school level?

DR. FARRELL: In teaching American history, that could be done more conveniently than in teaching civics or some other subject in high school, because the actual story in its historical context is one that does no outrage, it seems to me, to any particular religious belief. I was quite edified last night by the discussion on this subject. It is quite possible that more could have been said in my paper about this angle, but then one writes these papers before he hears the discussion!

MR. DEPOISTER: I think it is fundamental to ask what ideas concerning religion prospective teachers get in their study of American history. In teaching American history, you probably have some ideas of what you teach about religion.

DR. FARRELL: Well, I am sorry, I didn't conceive of my paper in quite those terms. I thought of it simply in terms of the compatibility of religion taught and learned and of history taught and learned. I realize that the title suggests that people are being prepared to teach American history and certain religious ideas. Do you mean how will these ideas affect the way they will teach American history?

MR. DEPOISTER: Yes.

DR. FARRELL: In the first place, I wouldn't take full responsibility in this. It is a broader thing. The students with whom I have been associated over the last twenty years have been students who have been learning religion without my having anything to say about what they were learning, and they have been learning American history with my having practically everything to say about what they learn.

I have assumed that the combination took. Some of them have been successful teachers. I haven't supervised their practice work or anything else. That wasn't part of my job. Sometimes in learning history, however, they suddenly have become aware of things that they were supposed to have learned in religion and didn't get straight; then they go to their religious teachers to get it straight.

FATHER MCMANUS: As a member of the Planning Committee, I think I can make these two comments gracefully. What we had in mind for Professor Farrell's paper was a document that would set forth, from the point of view of the historian, the connections that exist between American history and religion. We thought that with such a paper in hand the members of this conference could then answer the committee's question whether what was proposed could be included in the curriculum of a privately supported or a tax-supported institution that prepares teachers for the secondary schools. I think Dr. Farrell has done this. I think we have a paper that we can discuss along those lines in our table groups. Is what he proposes feasible for inclusion in the training of a teacher who is destined for public education?

The second comment I would like to make is this: There are certainly four divisions, at least, in the preparation of a public school teacher or, indeed, of a teacher for private schools. There is training in the humanities, the social studies, physical sciences, and the professional aspects of the teacher's work. In addition to this general education, which includes a thorough grasp of American history, the teacher must have, of course, certain professional skills, which include practical techniques for dealing with religion as it relates to education. Here, however, we are exploring the relationships rather than the techniques.

DR. RONALD B. THOMPSON (Registrar and University Examiner, The Ohio State University): Professor Farrell, you indicate that, while you find religion and history compatible on the college and graduate school level, you see no proper way of teaching history as an aspect of religion and no proper way of teaching religion as an aspect of history.

How then are we to implement the kind of thing we have been trying to propose in this conference?

DR. FARRELL: I will stick to what I said. On the level of college and graduate teaching there is a great deal of confusion, a great disregard of the disciplines mutually. Sometimes the historian suddenly turns into a theologian, because he has had a good meditation that morning and is unprepared to talk about the subject matter; consequently, he launches into a favorite discourse on the matter of grace.

Suppose he has spent five or six years teaching apologetics somewhere, and he is suddenly called upon to teach a class in history. He cannot get out of the rut. There are actual cases where religion has been discredited in the minds of students for years afterwards as a consequence of this. The same thing is true when teachers of religion make casual references to history which fit very conveniently into their oral discourse.

These are the things that I had in mind when I said that you can discredit history by trying to teach it as a part of religion or discredit religion by teaching it as a part of history.

SISTER MARY JANET: We are very much concerned that the public schools should not just disregard and neglect religion, because that would tend to make religion seem unimportant in the mind of the child. We are also concerned about the relation of religion to the conduct of the child, and we wish very much to see what the public schools can do about it. What connection do these concerns have with the relationship of religion and history in the preparation of the teacher?

Since the whole of American history is closely associated with religious influences, we want our pupils really to understand this aspect of American history, do we not? I would say that it is not teaching theology at all to point out the religious influences that have affected the development of our country. If we cannot do that, we cannot really teach American history. Now from my point of view, we have not sufficiently emphasized the various religious ideas that have exerted a strong influence on our history.

What might be done, then, in the teaching of American history? I think all these religious influences in history need to be shown in clear perspective and felt in their full force, not to teach the tenets of any religion but simply to focus attention on all religious influences that have played such a tremendous part in shaping the country's history.

If a teacher is to go into our elementary and secondary schools and do a fair job, she is going to need a strong foundation in American history, particularly from the point of view of what the religious influences have been. It seems to me that the persons who are teaching teachers have to look into the requirements of teacher education and see whether or not our teachers are being given that kind of background. Now, in elementary and secondary schools, I would not teach the same thing that I would teach to the teacher of elementary and secondary school children. This morning we are supposed to be talking about what to do about the teacher.

I think our teachers should have a very much stronger foundation than they have had in this whole religious development, even concerning the matter of the separation of church and state, as somebody pointed out a little bit earlier. There will be disagreements about this, and, insofar as the teacher education institution can be objective with these matters, I think it should be. I am certain, however, that we will never approach this matter of religion in public education adequately until we have teachers who have a really strong intellectual foundation in all of the developments of American history.

DR. AARON I. ABELL (Professor of American History, University of Notre Dame): My question is directed to Professor Farrell, but I think it has been essentially answered by the Sister's comments. It seems to me that it is possible in institutions that prepare teachers for the elementary and secondary schools to teach a substantial amount of American religious history, either in a separate course or in connection with political or social or intellectual history of the West. Professor Sweet's interpretation of American religious history as essentially a frontier, agrarian, and Western history, makes it very easy for me to teach much of religious history in my history of the West. I think it is possible without getting involved too much in theology or philosophy to teach religious history indirectly in connection with many courses.

There is a tremendous amount of knowledge of American religious history. I think Professor Loewenberg is right. There is no real synthesis, and there is much to be done, but there is a tremendous amount of raw material. The problem is to put this either in textbooks or in the hands of teachers and get it into circulation, so to speak. For instance, the three-volume work by Professor Cannon Stokes[18] is an amazing piece of work. Although some of it is pretty badly digested, it is really a monumental thing. This is the type of material that should be synthesized and digested and presented to teachers.

DR. FARRELL: I agree with Professor Abell's remarks and, to a certain extent, I try to do what he says. The notion that Jameson had is important in this connection: History is a good forum in which to examine what happened without coming to grips, as one must in a class in dogmatic theology, with the question of grace, for example, by showing how arguments about this concept have been of considerable importance in the development of American history.

There is a certain fairness of mind that comes or can come from the study of history. It is something I always try to keep in mind as an objective. I was taught this in my own graduate school experience. We should always make history something which affords enlightenment rather than something which is an engine of somebody's propaganda. We don't have to be pale and colorless. We can all make our own points of view clear, but, if we teach history, we are pledged not to be specific advocates.

DR. DAWSON: I am still interested in the question raised by Dr. Thompson several minutes ago, asking you to clarify your position in the statement in which you say it is hard to justify religion as an aspect of history and history as an aspect of religion, and so on. As I understand you, you are willing to defend that premise. Doesn't that hit pretty hard at the whole teaching-about-religion approach that is being currently advocated? How would you justify your over-all thesis in this paper if at the same time you are defending this position?

DR. FARRELL: I am not being evasive; I am being conscientious in saying that the problems of high school teaching are not things I can deal with and talk about with any authority. I wasn't aware that this was attacking the foundations of the idea of teaching about religion. One cannot help but teach religion if he teaches history fairly. To teach American history, one has to know something about American religion. In teaching American history, I have always felt I was better off rather than worse off for such theology as I know. However, one cannot teach theology effectively with a historical approach.

MR. JULES COHEN (Secretary, Joint Advisory Committee of the Synagogue Council of America and the National Community Relations Advisory Council): Mr. Chairman, I would like to come back to this very troublesome problem of the definition of terms and the meaning of particular words. I am troubled greatly by it, and, from some of the things that have been said, I sense that others are, too.

As the Sister said, if we are talking about the significance, the impact, or the role of religion in American history when it is intrinsic to the subject of American history, fine. I really believe we wouldn't have much, if any, disagreement about that kind of teaching. The trouble comes in the field of teaching religion. The latter carries with it the dangers of getting into theology, which the first doesn't. The first I think is not dangerous. I think it can be done, but I think the latter puts us all in trouble, whether we are teachers, religious people, or those interested in the welfare of the community in general.

DR. FARRELL: I agree with that. I am more or less willing to let the educators come to grips with it rather than have a historian settle it for them absolutely. We can furnish the things that they need to talk about, and they can provide the devices that are supposed to settle such questions.

I would like to add something of a historical nature. The setting in which we find ourselves is one on the side of a watershed which, I think, is divided by the First World War. We have now a pluralistic society to an extent that we didn't have before the First World War.

I can remember that in the twenties it was taken for granted in New England that the public schools were Protestant. Nobody suggested they were neutral, although already they were committed to a certain neutrality. Today, they are not only committed, they darn well better be neutral.

I might ask this question. Is it more feasible to introduce religion in our present era than it was forty or fifty years ago? I went to an old New England town academy that came to serve as a public school, where the teaching staff was predominantly Protestant. Religion came up frequently. In that school I learned a lot about Protestantism which did me a lot of good. It didn't corrupt me in my faith. It wasn't meant to. I think I had a better education than people get in the same town from one of these rather colorless modern high schools. That may be a conceit, I don't know. I share Mr. Bestor's opinion on that.

DR. GERALD READ (Associate Professor of Education, Kent State University): I think we are discussing an issue here which is the chief concern of teacher education today. I think the two ladies were really asking to what extent we should professionalize a course in American history for teachers.

We are faced with the problem of teaching American history to all the students that come to us. This is one of the problems. The college or university professor is teaching a course in American history for everyone, not just for teachers, and he naturally cannot consider these questions of how to handle certain concepts or ideas in a classroom. At the present time teacher education is under attack for professionalizing the courses, and it is just the reverse in practice.

The Study of Religion in High School American History

JACK ALLEN

Professor Allen is president of the National Council for the Social Studies and professor of history and head of the department at George Peabody College for Teachers. After teaching high school social studies in the public schools of Kentucky, he served on the history faculty at Eastern Kentucky State Teachers College from 1940 to 1946. He is the author of textbooks, workbooks, teachers manuals, and other teaching materials for high school and junior high school American history, government and civics and is editor of the professional yearbook The Teacher of the Social Studies. *Dr. Allen is a member of the Council's Committee on Religion and Education.*

For decades high school students have opened their American history textbooks and seen somewhere among the early pages the figure of a man trudging through a snow-covered forest, the collar of his greatcoat pulled closely about his cheeks and ears as protection from the biting cold of the New England winter. The figure is that of Roger Williams. He has been banished from the Massachusetts Bay Colony. Williams' flight, so the reader is told, has resulted from his controversies with the Puritan clergy. "Divers dangerous opinions," this is the charge the Massachusetts General Court has levied against him.

In theological terms Roger Williams' actions might be described as dissent from orthodoxy. Within a historical context, the episode has come to be viewed as one phase in the development of religious freedom in America. And so, rightly or wrongly, the hero of the piece is the intrepid young dissenter who goes to live for a time with his Indian friends and subsequently establishes a new colony. The villians become the Puritan clergy with their rigid orthodox views.

Much more recently—too recently for textbooks in fact—Americans became familiar with yet another picture. The time: December 4, 1956. The place: a street leading down the hill from the Negro section of Clinton, Tennessee. The central figure: the Rev. Paul W. Turner. In the daily press and on television newsreels this young minister was pictured escorting six Negro children to Clinton High School through a crowd of shouting segregationists. Shortly after leaving the students at their school, the Rev. Mr. Turner was attacked and severely beaten by a small group, consisting of seven men and two women. In taking upon himself the responsibility for escorting the young Negroes, the minister was not acting in behalf of his local congregation nor within the framework of broader church policies. He was acting as a private citizen, carrying out what he presumably regarded as his rightful civic responsibility. To the typical citizen of Clinton, however, the attack was more than simply that of a group upon another citizen. It was an attack upon a "man of God." There had, indeed, been other attacks and harassments in the community. But this was different somehow. Public reaction, as expressed in a local election that very day, together with the subsequent course of events in Clinton, amplified the difference. The clergyman was, in fact, personifying another basic element in America's religious tradition, namely, the role of the church in social action.

Here, then, are two incidents separated by more than three-hundred years of history. The first represents an early stage in what has become a continuing effort to define the nature of religious liberty, the second an episode symbolic of the desire of American churches to play a role in social betterment.

Actually these two themes, and numerous other religious concepts as well, could find some application at any level of classroom instruction. The question here, more particularly, involves the nature of such content in American secondary schools: how it can be applied most appropriately in the instruction of boys and girls who have reached that stage of human development called adolescence.

In all areas of social education, one needs to approach the question of selection of content with considerable humility. The truth is there exists no genuinely empirical basis for the selection of such curricular materials, no matter whether the concern is with the study of historical developments or of contemporary social issues. It thus becomes somewhat presumptuous to say with certainty that this or that *shall* be taught. There are, however, helpful guidelines. They are of three broad types. Stated with special reference to the topic under consideration, they are: (1) the nature and needs of the American adolescent; (2) the products of sound scholarship in the area of American religious history; and (3) the system of values which characterizes civilization in America.

Before moving into a consideration of specific historical content with its suggestions as to persistent and emerging value patterns, a reminder concerning certain characteristics of adolescence is in order. This is the time in the life of the young citizen when he is passing through a transition from the status of a child to the responsibilities of an adult. One of his basic psychological needs is to grow in self-understanding, to see himself more clearly as an individual. This calls for the assessment of personal strengths and liabilities to be sure. But it likewise suggests the adolescent's need for help in developing a system of values, values upon which he can base a concept of desirable behavior and with which he can find an appropriate place in society.

Adolescence is also a stage marked by movement beyond the family orbit into a search for satisfying relationships in the larger community. The unity of religious experience, characteristic of simple family organization, finds replacement in a complex of competing spiritual and sociological phenomena. Another characteristic of the adolescent, particularly the young adolescent, furnishes a third helpful guide to the selection of religious content. Most students at this age level show strong interest in the activities of people. They seem particularly interested in the study of personalities with whom they can somehow identify themselves. The typical adolescent is a romantic in the true sense of the word. He enjoys accounts of heroic deeds where evil is ground into defeat, and justice emerges triumphant. In the same vein, he is impressed with accounts depicting loyalty, obedience to the group code.

Inherent in all these traits is the desire of the adolescent to build a more adequate concept of self and improved status with other individuals and social groups. Since religion in some form is so essentially an aspect of American culture, it goes almost without saying that it is a necessary element in the social education of the young citizen.

The content of high school American history is dependent on selected threads from our Western heritage. The religious thread is, for purposes of background, a dominant one. It supplies, for instance, value patterns from our Judaeo-Christian tradition, patterns which stem from such venerable pronouncements as the Ten Commandments and the Sermon on the Mount. The Crusades furnish another element in this Old World background. Embodied in this series of dramatic episodes are strong religious overtones which are a part of the Crusades' general influence on Western history. The Protestant revolt is yet another strand in the religious thread. Its subsequent influence is not only directly associated with our diverse theologies, but it contributed immediately to national religious rivalries which supplied a considerable portion of the impetus to American discovery and settlement.

Religion was a central theme in the life of the American Colonies. So completely did it permeate the thoughts and actions of the people that it becomes difficult to select those emphases which would be most significant to present-day high school students. In the realm of religious thought the high school student has reached a level of sophistication sufficient to enable him to understand the major tenets of different religious groups. Important groups for study in the early Colonial period would be: Calvinism, with such derivatives as Puritanism and Congregationalism; Anglicanism, with its adaptations to New World culture; and Catholicism, with its early missionary activities and subsequent promotion of Colonial settlement. A significant adjunct of the early Colonial religions is the story of the great champions of religious toleration—Roger Williams, the Separatist; William Penn, the Quaker; and Cecil Calvert, the Catholic.

Religion as a social force is another aspect of the Colonial picture. The churches manifested themselves one way in the towns, in a somewhat different way on the frontier. Church groups were a potent force in early efforts to promote universal education. Religious influences were strongly felt in Colonial literature and music. And the social impact of religion exhibited itself in a particularly dramatic fashion in the Great Awakening of the 1730's and 1740's. The history of religion in Colonial America would be incomplete without attention to the role of certain churches and clergy in the development of revolutionary sentiment. Particularly noteworthy were the dissatisfactions with the Anglican Church, the activities of frontier preachers, and such events as the Parson's Cause.

To assess the impact of the Revolution on separate churches might be too limited a task for the typical high school class. The relation of the new states and the national government to religion, however, is another matter. Inexorably, any special position enjoyed by certain church groups was swiftly undermined, and the student of the period finds it necessary to build meaning into such pronouncements as the Virginia Statute for Religious Freedom in 1786. Here he encounters Thomas Jefferson's pen saying that "Almightly God has created the mind free"; or again that all men should be "free to profess, and by argument to maintain, their opinions in matters of religion and that the same shall in nowise diminish, enlarge, or affect their civil capacities." The student notes near the end of the original Constitution of 1789 that "No religious Test shall ever be required as a Qualification to any Office or public Trust under the United States." He notes further in the First Amendment that "Congress shall make no law respecting an establishment of religion, or prohibiting the free exercise thereof. . . ." And, while he may observe in several of the original state constitutions provisions denying the right of public office to such groups as Jews, Catholics, Unitarians, and atheists, he finds that by 1834 the American principle of separation of church and state had been clearly established.

Separating religion from governmental structure is one thing. Keeping religion out of politics is quite another. On numerous occasions the student of American history encounters situations in which religious issues are employed to generate heat, if not light, in a political campaign—attacks on Jefferson in 1800, the "rum, Romanism, and rebellion" issue in 1884, and the Smith candidacy in 1928 are but isolated examples. Subjecting such episodes to the bright lamp of analysis furnishes a useful means for striking at bigotry in political life.

Somewhat contemporaneous with the development of the principle of separation of church and state was the growth of deism, skepticism, and heterodoxy as challenges to traditional religious thought. In reaction, however, swelled a powerful evangelical upsurge, carrying with it shades of Jonathan Edwards and the Great Awakening. This so-called Second Awakening had its principal origins in New England, but it gathered its real force only after making its way across the Appalachian Mountains. The religious fervor and spirit of revivalism, characteristic of this early nineteenth-century movement is of considerable consequence in American history. From it emerged in full stature some of the largest of our present-day Protestant churches. The spirit of individualism so characteristic of the times likewise encouraged the promotion of numerous sectarian groups. It was a religious particularism run rampant, producing everything from Millerites to Shakers to Two-Seed-in-the-Spirit Predestinarians.

Not to be overlooked in the religious upsurge was the rise of Catholicism. There were perhaps 30,000 Catholics in the United States in 1790. By 1860 their number had multiplied to more than 3,000,000. Such rapid growth did not pass unnoticed. To some Protestants, even certain notable ones like the Rev. Lyman Beecher, it was a cause for alarm. From it emerge accounts of mob activity, a taste of nativism, and the rather formidable Know-Nothing movement of the 1850's.

At no point in American history did issues relating to religion and morality come more sharply into focus than in the slavery controversy. Few topics illustrate as well the need for a judicious combination of democratic values and sound scholarship in classroom instruction. To the abolitionist the controversy resolved itself into a simple issue of moral good versus moral evil. By contrast, the slave-holder came to regard his "peculiar institution" as a positive good, in accord with the laws of God and fully defended in the Scriptures.

But the study of religion and morality in relation to Negro slavery is more than an analysis of polemics. Take the slave himself. He had a religious life of his own, sometimes with a Negro congregation and minister, on occasion in the church of his master. The religion of the Negro today owes a debt to this early instruction. Its influence has, in fact, permeated many facets of American culture, the spiritual being one notable example from the area of music.

As for American churches in general, it was inevitable that they would become involved in a moral issue of such magnitude. A formal protest against slavery was issued by the Quakers as early as 1688. There were, likewise, expressions of opposition by Methodists and Presbyterians in 1812 and 1818 respectively. As the controversy grew in intensity, however, the issues became more difficult to compromise, and schisms developed among church groups. So pronounced were the fractures that it required more than a civil conflict to effect a healing.

Looking at the problem of the Negro in American society today, who would say that we have fully rationalized the moral issues? Who would argue that the churches have fully met their social responsibilities relating to questions of racial and social segregation? These, too, are rightful questions for students to explore.

As the study of American history moves beyond the Civil War, one can suggest with some assurance that religion is usually treated less adequately in the classroom than is the case with the Colonial and early national periods. Whatever the reasons for this, and there are many, it would be extremely tenuous to attribute the cause to a weakened moral fiber among the citizenry or to a slackening of interest in spiritual affairs and church organization. There are, nevertheless, religious issues and movements in modern America with which high school students too infrequently have an opportunity to come to grips.

The religion of the pre-Civil War period was predominately the product of rural cultural patterns. To its simplicity was added great zealousness; but it was also inclined to be overly individualistic and to take an excessively narrow approach to moral and spiritual issues. The machine age, which burst into full flower in the United States in the latter years of the nineteenth century, had its impact on traditional religion as on other aspects of American life. And so was added a complexity to religion that complicates its teaching to adolescents. Where deficiencies occur in the classroom, it is easy to blame the teachers. "They should know their history better," we say. It is interesting to note, however, that the textbook writers have not been inclined to attack the religious issues with vigor either.

Religion in the new industrial America was especially influenced by two movements. One was the growth of science, the other the rise of the city. Any mention of the new science immediately brings to mind the specter of Darwinism. But, if a Mark Hopkins denounced the theory of evolution as "atheistic," a Henry Ward Beecher could be happy with it as a substitute for his Calvinism. And, for that matter, if the teacher were sufficiently alert, students' attention might be directed to recent studies which raise serious questions with Darwinian theories, particularly those relating to the essential nature of man and other animals. In any event, the scientific activity of the latter nineteenth century was instrumental in the development of the conflict between modernism and fundamentalism. It is equally appropriate for students to develop an understanding of these differing points of view in religion as to grapple with conflicting issues which arise in the social, political, and economic realms.

Post-Civil War America was enriched and diversified by the influx of millions of immigrants who came to these shores and contributed immensely to the development of an industrialized society. In their baggage was more than latent mechanical skill and a willingness to work. These new arrivals also brought a deep religious heritage. Most of the newcomers were of the Catholic or Jewish faith, although a considerable number of Lutherans did come from the Scandinavian countries. If the typical American of an earlier day could regard himself as Anglo-Saxon and Protestant, the modern American could not be so readily generalized. The new America was richer for it, but, by the same token, its intercultural problems were magnified. Acculturation, nevertheless, proceeded with considerable rapidity. To the special credit of such outstanding churchmen as Cardinal Gibbons and Rabbi Wise, the new arrivals were soon fitted snugly into the main stream of American society.

The Protestant churches were also on the move and growing. W. W. Sweet reminds us of a song the Methodists used to sing in response to the agnostics of the time:

> The infidel, a motley band,
>   In council met and said:
> "The churches die all through the land,
>   The last will soon be dead."
> When suddenly a message came,
>   It filled them with dismay:
> "All hail the power of Jesus's name!
>   We're building two a day."

It might be observed, parenthetically, that the closing lines of the song could well be resurrected and used in the 1950's.

The old-time Protestant evangelism continued to carry a strong appeal even in what was regarded as a more sophisticated age. From Dwight L. Moody to Billy Sunday to Billy Graham evangelism has kept its headliners and has also continued to operate more modestly in the vineyards.

It would scarcely appear within the province of a high school history class to attempt a resolution of the theological dilemma of faith versus works. It would seem sufficient to observe that religious-minded Americans have been inclined to work both sides of this street. In modern America the issue does seem to have been more sharply drawn at times, however, because of the many opportunities for men to be their brothers' keepers. The new social gospel, for instance, did appear to be in conflict with the tenets of traditional Protestantism. But, then, how could the churches afford to ignore the existence of slums, poverty, and other types of social depression? The fact is, of course, that America's social ills did not go unnoticed. The story is one that boys and girls should come to know better. And the account should include in addition to the work of older churches, the activities of the Salvation Army, the YMCA, and other newer welfare groups.

Recent history also includes accounts of groups that have for good or ill, used religion to further their special ends. It might be a Women's Christian Temperance Union or again a Ku Klux Klan. To study and understand such groups and their varied purposes is also a desirable activity for the history student.

The hope of American history in the schools is that, through its study, young Americans will become better democratic citizens. This is the basic purpose. Citizenship and morality are associated ideas. For the young citizen the study of religion as a phase of American history can be one means of developing his own set of moral anchors. True, such study as a phase of the school curriculum is related substantially to secular morality. And, admittedly, there are those who regard this as half a loaf at best. On this point, however, we should perhaps remind ourselves that the family and the church are both major social institutions affecting the lives of young people. They too have significant roles to play in the development of morality, roles that fit their special functions.

Tolerance can be another outcome of the study of religion. This is, in effect, an intercultural purpose for the inclusion of religious study in the history program. Involved in such a purpose is an understanding and appreciation of the rich diversity of religious life in American civilization.

Finally, the study of religion can help the young citizen find clearer paths to an understanding of himself and those with whom he must associate. During the school years, it is a question of his seeing himself in relation to his family and to associates in his immediate community. The ultimate hope is that he is building a body of understandings, social skills, and desirable values that will hold him in good stead as he moves toward more distant horizons.

Conclusions

1. Religion is, by fact and tradition, so essentially an aspect of American culture that its study becomes a necessary element in the social education of the American adolescent.

2. Religious content in high school American history should be selected on the basis of sound historical scholarship, democratic values, and the needs of the adolescent.

3. While cognizant of the lack of a genuinely empirical basis for the selection of curriculum content, the following areas or topics in American religious history would appear to be appropriate at the secondary level:

a) The contributions of Western heritage to religion in America;

b) Religious traditions and institutions that are the product of developments during the Colonial period;

c) Political bases for the establishment of the principle of separation of church and state;

d) Religion as an issue in politics;

e) Religious awakening and church expansion during the first half of the nineteenth century;

f) Religious issues and church policy in the slavery controversy;

g) The growth of science in modern America and its challenge to the doctrine of faith;

h) The increasing diversity of American religion resulting from the new immigration and other influences;

i) The rise of the city and the concomitant development of the social gospel;

j) The growth of church organization in modern America;

k) The use of religion by interest groups to further their special ends;

l) The persistence of evangelism as a phase of religious activity.

4. The study of religion is an aspect of citizenship education. It can help the adolescent build his own set of moral anchors, broaden his perception of tolerance, and develop a more adequate concept of self. Such study, however, is not the special province of the school. Compelling responsibilities for the development of moral and spiritual values, rest with the family, the church, and indeed with the community at large.

DISCUSSION BASED ON PROFESSOR ALLEN'S PAPER

Presiding: F. ERNEST JOHNSON

DR. JACK ALLEN (Professor of History, George Peabody College for Teachers): Mr. Chairman, Ladies and Gentlemen: It seems to me that we have moved rather logically and naturally in the direction which the committee had in mind. During the last hour your questions have obviously moved closer and closer to my topic and that of Sister Nona.

I would like to talk more as an educationist than as an historian this morning because I think this is the kind of topic that requires some practical analysis. As one studies this problem in an American community as a member of the board of education or as a member of a curriculum committee, he is confronted with its practical aspects which call for a down-to-earth approach.

I am reminded of a story that illustrates how we sometimes approach immediate and pressing problems. Perhaps it is relevant enough to throw some light on the problem we are considering here.

Three men were fishing on a fairly sizable lake when a terrific storm blew up all of a sudden. They were in a small skiff. The waves were beginning to lash the boat pretty heavily. Things looked so bad that they really didn't think they were going to make it to shore.

Finally, the fellow at the helm said, "Bill, maybe we better have a word of prayer."

And Bill said, "I am sorry, I can't pray. What about you, Joe?" Joe said, "I can't pray, either."

"Let's sing a hymn, then," one of them suggested.

"Gee, I don't know any hymns either," said the third.

By this time they were getting frantic. At last, in desperation, the first fellow said, "For God's sake, pass the hat. We have to have something here of a religious nature."

Sometimes on the local level where they feel pressures from on high, teachers who are trying to put something into the curriculum get pretty frantic. It is understandable if they occasionally act without reviewing in detail all the philosophical complications of their problem.

I would like to make one other point. Although I would like to think that the school has as much influence on the lives of boys and girls as we are inclined to think it does, I believe we would be wise to remind ourselves that there are other forces in our society that exert tremendous influences, too. I mention this merely as a caution lest we ignore all other influences in community life and fix an overriding responsibility on the school. Youngsters live in a lot of places other than school.

It was natural that the American Council should have chosen a course in high school American history for discussion purposes, because this is the course that one can safely assume almost every boy and girl will take. For just this very reason, every pressure you can think of is exerted on high school teachers of American history. Teachers and textbook writers alike are urged to include in their courses treatments of Canada, Latin America, Asia, and international organizations, to mention only a few. There have also been doctoral studies on the treatment of public education and other matters in American textbooks.

Almost invariably each of these studies concludes that we are not emphasizing enough the particular thing under investigation; consequently, the textbook writer and the teacher are in the position constantly of wondering, not what to include, but what to leave out. At the same time, teachers are admonished that they ought to teach a few things well.

Now, I want to say two things about my paper in addition to what I have said. First, I felt inclined to call your attention to the character of the American adolescent and to cause you to think about the subject matter with reference to the nature of boys and girls at this age level. I consider this to be very important. Second, I would like to call your attention to something I didn't say in the paper, namely, that a good teacher planning a course in American history might approach it in a variety of ways. He might teach the course pretty much in a chronological fashion, in which case the student might study religion as one aspect of culture through successive stages of history. This would be done best if the teacher avoided an episodic approach that would leave the student with the impression that religion was important in the lives of people only at certain times and at certain places.

On the other hand, a good teacher might also approach American history through the study of selected topical units, such as "The Church and Religion in the American Tradition." Or, he might select a unit that would cut across all of American society, a culturally oriented unit that would include consideration of religious influences as well as others. Such a unit might be called "Life in Colonial America." Another might be concerned with contemporaneous life in the twentieth century.

There is still another kind of approach that a teacher might take, namely, the problem-solving approach. A high school history teacher might pose these questions to his class: Are religious influences less important in America today than they were at earlier times? What was the most important reason for the discovery and settlement of America —religion, trade, or politics? If you are fearful of this approach, may I remind you that frequently the problems do not involve controversial issues, but controversial teachers. There is a distinction.

MR. BRAGDON: I must say right away that I wish the revision of my high school text were not in galley proof because this discussion would certainly alter it.

I want to make two points as briefly as I can. One is a cavil, and the other is a conviction. The cavil concerns this statement from your paper: "The typical adolescent is a romantic in the true sense of the word. He enjoys accounts of heroic deeds where evil is ground into defeat, and justice emerges triumphant. In the same vein, he is impressed with accounts depicting loyalty, obedience to the group code."

I don't think that is the real problem. I think we are overcommitted in this country to the notion that the good guy gets the bad guy, that the good guy bumps him off or shoots him in the hand. The problem which faces the citizen and the problem he faces in history is often the conflict of good against good. The statement in Professor Farrell's paper to the effect that the Civil War was a conflict between two branches of religious-minded people is a case in point.

Another example is the conflict between the abolitionists and the Union around 1850. Both groups consisted of highly moral people; nevertheless, the feeling that the abolitionists sought the destruction of the Union was very profound. Also, Lincoln's various statements about what we should do about slavery are very interesting to follow. Hence, I underline the point that a teacher often needs to bring out the conflict of right against right rather than the conflict of right against wrong.

My second point is that I would change my book right away to bring out more of the religious component in American history. I would cite the social gospel as an answer to Marx's notion that religion is the opiate of the people, and I would show that religion here is used to attack the *status quo* rather than to support the *status quo*. I would indicate the religious pros and cons of imperialism, the religious grounds for opposing it. Finally, I would include the role of the Southern clergymen, both black and white, in the segregation movement.

DR. ALLEN: May I answer your first point by saying that I was talking about the nature of the adolescent. The question of how one should adapt subject matter to this nature is something else.

DR. HUNT: I would like to ask the representative of the Hazen Foundation to give us a summary of Professor Philip E. Jacob's recent book, *Changing Values in College*, published by the foundation, on which he reported at the Association for Higher Education in Chicago this week.

DR. PAUL J. BRAISTED (President, Edward W. Hazen Foundation): I am not sure it is relevant to this particular discussion; however, if you insist, I will give you a capsule. Professor Jacob's study was an exploratory survey of all the studies he could find that had undertaken to deal with values in general education and in social science courses. He found and inventoried approximately four-hundred separate studies of all kinds; then, he undertook to relate them and derive some conclusions. He concluded that neither courses nor methods nor teachers made any very great difference in changing students' values so far as any of these studies had thus far detected. On the other hand, he did find that certain kinds of institutions seemed to have a "climate" in which very significant things happened. These changes showed up in the tests.

FATHER McMANUS: Professor Allen, in your reading of high school texts in American history have you encountered examples of distortion of history that could be attributed to a calculated effort to omit religious references?

DR. ALLEN: I would be hard put to name an instance. When one considers all of the critical review and all of the editorial revision a textbook goes through, he realizes one person doesn't write it. As a grizzled editor said to me a few years ago, a textbook isn't written, it is built. When one starts building a modern textbook, a lot of influences play upon it. I cannot quite conceive of a calculated effort to omit religious references. The lack of adequate scholarship, the author's own limitations, and all the limitations of editors and critics prevent the publication of a perfect instrument. In spite of every precaution, one always finds omissions that bother him. However, I don't think that these are deliberate. There are too many forces operating to make a book.

FATHER O'LEARY: Mr. Allen, you make this statement in your paper: "It would scarcely appear within the province of a high school history class to attempt a resolution of the theological dilemma of faith versus works." As I understand your paper, you would have no objection to the history teacher simply stating factually, let us say, the economic implications of Calvin's theology or the social teachings of the Catholic Church in economics, or the social message of the Old Testament prophets. If I understand you correctly, the teacher would not become involved in theology as such, but would simply represent it objectively and indicate implications of a particular theology for the social or economic way of life.

DR. ALLEN: Yes. I thought I was clear on that. Certainly, there is no necessity to introduce theological dilemmas in a high school class at all. I don't see that these dilemmas should muddy the waters in the study of religion. I go along with Mr. Loewenberg here. This is a study of religion. As such, it is not a problem. I think we are asking for trouble the minute we move in a different direction. That is the only reason I was prompted to mention the thing at all. In American history, of course, one learns that some groups put a great deal of emphasis on faith while others stress works. I think we simply have to remind students that we work both sides of the street. Once again, it is simply a matter of pointing out differences as clearly as the spirit and letter of scholarship will permit. For example, we can point out the shift in emphasis from faith to works between the latter half of the nineteenth century and the present, the period so clearly marked in American history by the rise of the social gospel.

FATHER O'LEARY: Excuse me, I do not quite agree with the previous speakers who made a distinction between "to teach" and "to study." I can understand that at the college level and at the research level; however, I think all great teachers have done both. They do the same thing in the elementary school, and they do it in the secondary school, and they do it by way of induction and deduction.

There are different disciplines, and they have their own problems as to objective, content, and method. It seems to me that an excellent teacher will guide youngsters, but at the same time will lead them through his instruction toward a better appreciation of the heritage of our civilization, which would include the Judaeo-Christian way of life.

RABBI SCHAFLER: I should like to direct attention to your first conclusion, which, I must add parenthetically, does not seem to me to follow from the text of the paper. The thing I am puzzled about involves a larger problem: What do persons mean by "Religion" in the singular with a capital R? Although I am a rabbi and a committed believer in a personal God, I don't believe in "Religion." I believe there are historical religions but no "Religion." "Religion" as such, as an idea in itself abstracted from historical religions is an adulterous abstraction to me.

I don't believe there is such a value, and, if there are people who abstract such a value, I believe it is pernicious. I would like to understand clearly what we mean by religion in the singular with a capital R.

DR. ALLEN: The phrase that helps me along here and supports what I had to say is the phrase "social education." We are thinking about the education of the American citizen in his relationships with

138 A SPECIFIC PROBLEM

other citizens. On that basis, it seems to me perfectly natural that the person, in order to develop his citizenship, needs to have an understanding of the American past and to see it in its full outline. I didn't say it was a necessary element in the personal education of American adolescents, but I did say it was necessary in his "social education." There is quite a distinction.

CHAIRMAN JOHNSON: The time has come to consider the next paper.

Some Religious Aspects of Elementary American History

SISTER MARY NONA, O.P.

Sister Mary Nona, a member of the Dominican Sisters of Sinsinawa, Wisconsin, is president of Edgewood College of the Sacred Heart in Madison, Wisconsin. She was a member of the Commission on American Citizenship of the Catholic University of America and a member of the faculty of that institution. Sister is the coauthor of a curriculum for Catholic elementary schools, Guiding Growth in Christian Social Living, *and the author of several other publications on the philosophy of schooling and education. This philosophy is being implemented on a college level at Edgewood College, where students receive a strong liberal arts program combined with professional studies to prepare them for teaching in the public schools. Sister Mary Nona is a member of the Council's Committee on Religion and Education.*

THE FIRST CHILDREN who learned American history, apart from formal study to be sure, must have been those at the Spanish Court who heard firsthand of Columbus' voyages and, later, the boys and girls of London or Plymouth or Jamestown who were actually making that history. For many generations afterward, the twice-told tales of America's beginnings were heard at the family hearth rather than on the hard school benches. It was not until 1787 that a textbook was written by John McCullough of Philadelphia for secondary school "scholars."[1] Over a hundred years later an organized plan for the study of American history in elementary schools was initiated, although it was being taught in most schools by that time.[2]

Since then textbooks and courses of study have been subjected periodically to the scrutiny of teachers, historians, and the public. Their respective recommendations have brought some notable changes, if not improvements, in the study and teaching of American history.[3] Responsibility for the greatest change lies with the growth of history itself. Year by year, volume by volume, the story of our nation has developed in content and interpretation to the distress of the writers of children's texts, the course-makers, and the teachers.

The Content and Characteristics of Elementary American History

In 1944 the American Historical Association, together with associated historical groups, published a succinct report on the teaching of American history from the elementary grades through college.[4] The report included proposals for the grade placement of important topics and a list of minimum requirements at each level. Many public and private school systems have followed the lead of the association and further developed its proposals. There is no place here to analyze current elementary courses of study in American history. A sampling of recent courses on file at the United States Office of Education, however, reveals that in grades one through six there is rather widespread study of the following topics:

In the primary grades (1, 2, and 3), history is introduced through a simple contrast between the present and the past. Topics may include, for example:

> Our Neighborhood Today and Long Ago
> How the Indians Lived
> When People First Came to Our Town

Holidays, such as Thanksgiving, Washington's birthday, and Memorial Day, afford opportunity to introduce major historical figures and the events with which they are linked. Frequently these are studied by younger children through such picture-story books as those by Ingri and Edgar d'Aulaire, on Washington, Lincoln, and other historical figures.

Introductory references to American history are a part of the social studies program of the lower grades, which usually includes a simple study of contemporary living in home, school, neighborhood, and community. This prehistory, as one may call it, deals with the human elements found in all history—the individual's role in society; his obligations to the common good; the place of law and of rules in group living. Emphasis on these elements in the present helps children to seek them in the story of the past. It also helps to avoid the censure of Salzmann: "History, as it is ordinarily taught, lifts the pupil out of the society of the living and places him in the society of the dead."[5]

In the middle grades (4, 5, and 6), children, while developing skill in reading, are given special help in learning how to study, to outline, to organize material, and see simple relationships. A sense of chronology begins to be evident—but not nearly so evident as some ambitious course-makers and examiners would imply. Historical content usually deals with the following:

> Exploration and Settlement of Our Nation
> Life in the Colonies
> The Beginnings of Our Republic
> The Westward Movement and Pioneer Life
> Map Study Related to These Periods
> The Story of Representative Persons in Later American History

Certain school systems add special study of their respective states, and some introduce major events of recent American history. For the most part, however, courses and textbooks agree with the suggestion of the American Historical Association report: "Here the emphasis is to be on the periods of exploration and colonial history and on the simpler patterns of life in the pre-industrial era."[6] In accord with this suggestion, most illustrations of elementary American history in this paper will be drawn from the earlier period of our history.

No matter what variations may occur in the content of American history for children, there are constant factors which relate to childhood and a child's manner of learning. Among them are these:

1. The course must be *selective.* The limits of the child's mind, and of time itself, allow coverage of only the most outstanding features of our history.

2. *People* should be emphasized, against the background of important events and movements.

3. Historical facts and ideas should be related to living in the *present.* "From known to unknown" is a rule in learning.

4. There is no place in children's history for "debunking." One

of the rights of childhood is an *idealism* that history can serve without betraying truth.

5. Historical *accuracy,* sometimes neglected by a false notion of the child's limitations, should be guarded with care.

Each of these factors is pertinent to the study of religious elements in American history, as it is to all phases of the subject. Each one also poses problems which, in relation to the study of religion, are perhaps more difficult than in any other area.

Limitations Applicable to All Subjects

We are reminded by Samson in *Don Quixote* that: "The poet can relate or sing of things not as they really were, but as they ought to have been; and the historian writes things, not as they ought to have been, but as they were, neither adding to the truth nor subtracting from it a single iota." If this is true of any historian, it is far more so of the teacher of history as she presents religious facts, among others, in the public school classroom. Even one who is fully aware of her responsibility to do so objectively, and is fully prepared to do so, meets with discouraging but necessary limitations. First are the restrictions imposed by the policy of the local or state school system, a policy which may or may not be explicitly stated. The board of education, in turn, has its own reasons for defining or leaving ill-defined the place of religious teaching in the school. The principal, being human, will add at least some subjective notes to the policy.

In the class itself the teacher may view the problem statistically. For example, she may know quite certainly of these religious affiliations in her sixth-grade class of 30: 11 children from Lutheran families; 4 who attend the Jewish synagogue school; 5 Italian Catholics, one of them a refugee; 2 Disciples of Christ; 3 Presbyterians, one of whom is the daughter of a minister; 4 of uncertain religious affiliation; 1 whose parents differ openly on religious questions. Each child in this class represents a family; each family has a composite point of view, a degree of religious practice or nonparticipation, a more or less clear idea of the role of the public school and its fixed limits. The parents of each share more or less consciously in that parental authority over education which our nation upholds.

These factors form a maze of limitations upon the teacher's approach to delicate religious issues; but these are not all. Her sound judgment, her choice and presentation of material, will be tried before a severe court: a class of inquiring minds. These inquiring minds present the most severely limiting factor of all, which is actually protected by all the others: each child's freedom of conscience. This is the heart of the problem. In any kind of school whatsoever the teacher must by her profession respect and protect the conscience of each pupil in her care. Here is the limit beyond which the zeal even of an apostle may not go: "We are not able to impose truth. Faith cannot be imposed. . . . Above all, let no one imagine that the Church, in exhorting Christians to become apostles, wishes to start them on the path to oppression of conscience."[7]

The teacher in the public school who, professionally speaking, represents no religion, is bound to refrain scrupulously from imposing any truths which would disturb the conscience of a child. Interference would be an injustice not only to the child but also to parents and religious leaders who rightly retain for themselves the responsibility for helping him form that "pulse of reason," as Coleridge calls it, which we term *conscience*.

Hedged about by these restrictions, is it still possible for the teacher of elementary American history to "provide for the factual study of religion" in an acceptable manner? According to the Committee on Religion and Education of the American Council, religion can and should be studied, ". . . not as something on which the American public school must settle all arguments and say the last word, but as something which is so much a part of the American heritage and so relevant to contemporary values that it cannot be ignored."[8]

Can this be done in the American history class of the public elementary school? Possibilities lie within two dimensions: (1) events or movements in American history, suitable for children's study, which have had unquestioned religious aspects, and (2) persons of historical importance who in some way brought a religious element into the story of our nation.

Examples of the first class, which will be detailed below, include the Puritan influence on New England and the nation; the work of the Spanish missions; the Judaeo-Christian principles evident in the Declaration of Independence. The second type of factual study of religion in American history is more difficult. Who can judge accurately the religious motivation or ideals of a historical character? How can the lay interpreter of history appraise a character about whom historians disagree? Having attempted to do so in broad terms, how can the teacher present this historical person in the clear-cut image of a hero? Some approaches to this problem may be exemplified in Christopher Columbus, Abraham Lincoln, and George Washington Carver.

Examples of both types will be given in chronological order.

Study of Christopher Columbus and the Vanguard
of Western Civilization

The first American history textbook tells its readers that the crew of the *Pinta,* on sighting land, "instantly began the *Te Deum* as a hymn of thanksgiving to God." Landing, they "returned thanks to God for conducting their voyage to such an happy issue."[9] Nearly all public school texts since that time have featured the thanksgiving of Columbus and his men, even though they may not refer by name to the *Te Deum.* Some have mentioned the singing of the *Salve Regina.* Most have emphasized the fact, recorded in the Admiral's Journal, that Columbus and his men prayed while on their voyage, knowing that "their ship depended for safety not only on her staunchness and their own skill, but on the grace of God."[10] For younger children this is the only religious fact that need be given in relation to Columbus Day.

Older children, especially in the fifth and sixth grades where historical ties between Europe and America are studied, can appreciate the significance of the *Te Deum* itself in American history. The first prayer of thanks offered by men from Europe, it was the vanguard of Western culture, the first spiritual gift brought from the Old World to the New. It had been sung in Europe for more than a thousand years before Columbus set sail. Credited to Augustine, a native of Africa, it was written in the Latin language and had its poetic and religious antecedents in Hebrew psalmody. Although these facts are of interest to sixth-graders and are in keeping with their level of understanding, they should not be overemphasized to the detriment of historical balance. Yet, other major events have often been remembered best by words associated with them. Morse's message, "What hath God wrought?" and Patrick Henry's "Give me liberty or give me death!" are two examples. That the ideas of the Old World entered the New with the first public recital of the ancient prayer,

"We praise Thee, Oh God!" is intrinsic to the historic occasion.

Children usually know that Columbus' ships carried cargo to and from Spain, thus inaugurating America's economic history. They know that the Admiral carried in his person the authority to claim new lands for Spain, thus inaugurating the political history of the Americas. But they should know also that the cultural history of the American nations began with Columbus. His ships brought the Spanish language, a share of European knowledge of that day, and a faith and liturgy which have had an uninterrupted role in the history of the Western Hemisphere.

Three religious facts, then, may be taught concerning Columbus: (1) he and his men prayed during the voyage, for protection and as a religious duty; (2) their first act on reaching land was to thank God; and (3) their hymn of thanks, the *Te Deum,* was the first gift of Old World culture brought to our shores.

There need be no laboring of religious motivation, of missionary purposes, of the virtues of Columbus. These are too difficult to judge and present to children.

Study of the Pilgrims and the Puritans and the Idea of Freedom of Conscience

The yearly recurrence of Thanksgiving Day on the school calendar makes the story of the Pilgrims a standard introduction of younger children to English colonization. The story is also inseparable from the factual study of religion. First, there is the principle of freedom of conscience and of worship which, if it was not the sole motive of every Pilgrim, was certainly dominant in the desire to emigrate. Second, there is the fact that on the *Mayflower* the passengers (with noted exceptions among the crew) prayed. Like Columbus' men, they asked God for protection and prayed as a daily duty to their Creator. Finally, the Pilgrims combined in their Thanksgiving feast a very human celebration of the harvest with public thanks to God, not forgetting at the feast those Indians who had befriended them. These are religious facts generally taught in all schools to younger children.

At the middle-grade level, children can understand that whereas the Pilgrims' story is one of a single event and a small colony, that of the Puritans pertains to a whole movement, having as its source religious ideas which influenced certain aspects of New England and American life. History in the middle grades frequently centers about areas of living, describing the home life, work, and culture of a certain segment of our people at a given time. New England Colonial life lends itself admirably to this type of study, through which the religious *motif* may be presented. Concerning the Puritan religion one might select for children the following ideas: (1) the Puritans thought of themselves as a Chosen People, going forth like the people of Israel to carry out God's covenant, or agreement, with them; (2) they aimed to "purify" the religious practices of the Church of England from the "vain worship" which made use of art, music, and sacred signs (the sacramental idea) to convey spiritual truths by means of material things; and (3) the religion of the Puritans urged them to strictness in keeping the law; respect for the dignity of each person (provided he abided by Puritan doctrine); a firm belief that "God gives all things to industry," and that "an idle man is a Burden to himself, to his Family, and to the Publick."[11]

Many concrete examples of Puritan religious culture can be found by children in the daily life of early New England: schooling in the Horn Book and New England Catechism, by which one learned to read in order to know the Scripture; discouragement of frivolity and worldliness in clothing and recreation; the severity of Sunday, with its long sermons and stern rules, as contrasted with Merrie England's dancing on the village green. Yet none of these should be exaggerated.[12] Neither should children fail to see that there were links between New England and Europe, even pre-Reformation Europe, which had not been broken. While worshipping God from the Bay Psalm Book, for example, the Puritans were using the same psalms that had been and were being sung throughout Christendom. The whole Bible, in fact, was their inheritance from the long past.

To the secondary school can be left such facts as the development of Calvinism in England; intolerance and factions of Puritanism; the concept of a theocratic government, or Bible state;[13] the prevalence of a Presbyterian sense of duty and of order in society, together with Congregationalist emphasis upon assemblies and covenants of the people. It is enough that middle-grade children identify the Puritan religion with New England's beginnings, and these in turn with the forming of our national culture and democratic government.

Study of the Spanish Missions

To children it is obvious that the Spanish missions of California and elsewhere in the Southwest represented a type of religious society different from that of the Pilgrims. The latter came to America to preserve what they believed in conscience to be the true way of serving God. Missionaries like Junipero Serra, the Franciscan who founded the missions along El Camino Real, came to share their faith with the Indian natives, working under and with the Spanish Crown.

A number of religious facts which belong to American history may be learned by children concerning the Spanish missions: (1) religious motives—love of God and of fellow men—led the missionaries to accompany Spanish soldiers into California and establish Christian settlements for the Indians; (2) life in the missions was a combination of Spanish and Indian culture, centered about the church; (3) the psalmody that was unadorned and unaccompanied in Massachusetts meeting houses was sung in California amid the liturgical splendor of the Mass and Vespers. The churches themselves, built by the Indians in Spanish style, were ornamented with Indian symbolism and craftsmanship; and (4) education of the Indians was a part of the apostolate. Their schooling included Christian doctrine, the Spanish language and their own, agriculture and other vocational training, singing and art, instrumental music, and even dancing.[14]

Since the motive of the friars was to convert the Indians from paganism to Christianity, their intent was to impose the Spanish language and customs no more than was necessary to the larger purpose, and, further, to keep all Indian customs that were worthy of being a part of Christian living.[15] From this religious fact children can understand, to some degree, the paradox of present-day Indians in the Southwest who, in areas where the missions were discontinued, combine pagan superstitions with some Christian practices and greater or less adherence to Christian teachings.

Without denying the harshness of Spanish conquerors and the imperialism of their rulers, it is possible to show children how these traits were opposed by friars like Junipero Serra. For self-interest they substituted total service to the Indians. They challenged greed by their voluntary poverty. They challenged the extravagant frivolities of certain Spanish colonials by the simplicity of family life in the missions.

Although it is true that the Spanish settlements have influenced our history only in a limited region, the missionary ideal of which they were the first example has never been absent from our nation's story. The idea that the best gift one can bring to others is faith in God led missionaries to accompany, to follow, and sometimes to precede the explorers and settlers. There were missionaries to the Indians, to the first frontier, to the Louisiana Territory, to the Middle Border, to the far Northwest. When the nation reached its last frontier, and began to take increasing interest in world affairs, missionary zeal led Americans to other lands, as it had brought the first missionaries to our own.

*Study of the Declaration of Independence
and God-Given Rights*

From the maze of current interpretations of the Declaration of Independence, of each Founding Father and all of them collectively, we can select for children's study one unchallenged fact: the first Americans determined to be free to govern themselves, and took up arms to gain this freedom. But they justified their actions by religious declarations which they said that reason could not deny, because they were self-evident truths: (1) that all men are created equal, and (2) that all are endowed by their Creator with inalienable rights. These ideas are at once simple enough for children to understand, and at the same time so profound that they influence our entire philosophy of government. They are in effect a declaration of dependence on God, and of human rights, inalienable because they are God-given.

Studying these American principles, children may learn in how many ways our nation acknowledges officially its dependence on God. For example: (1) the motto "In God We Trust"; (2) our custom, since Washington, of taking an oath on entrance to public office; (3) the opening of Congress with prayer; and (4) presidential proclamations of Thanksgiving, and other public references to our reliance on Providence, our need for God's help, our need to pray.

The meaning of rights—and of corresponding duties—is understandable to children, who see them exercised by themselves and others in daily group living. It should not be difficult for them to

realize, as did the first citizens of our Republic, that the only inalienable rights are those which come from God; that rights given by a
state can be taken away by the same. They ought to see that a godless
government will be ruthless of men's rights, which have no divine
source or guarantee in that type of political economy.[16]

In contrast to that totalitarianism which the Declaration of Independence condemns by its philosophy, and to link the Declaration with
present-day Americanism, children might study such recent statements
as the following by President Eisenhower: "We are one nation, gifted
by God with the reason and the will to govern ourselves, and return-
ing thanks to Him by respecting His supreme creation—the free
individual."[17]

The question of exact sources from which the ideas in the Declaration of Independence came is not a subject for children's study. The
claims of Tom Paine, Locke, the Enlightenment, and deism are for
mature students to judge. Thomas Jefferson himself stated that the
ideas in the Declaration were "an expression of the American mind."
Furthermore, the American mind on democracy was formed upon the
concept of man in our Judaeo-Christian heritage:

> What is man that thou art mindful of him
> or the son of man that thou visitest him?
> Thou hast made him a little less than the angels,
> Thou hast crowned him with glory and honor,
> And hast set him over the works of thy hands.
> —Psalm 8

Study of Abraham Lincoln and Public Acknowledgment to God

One way to introduce pertinent religious facts in American history,
as has been said, is through representative men who in some way
brought a religious element into our history. Abraham Lincoln is an
admittedly controversial example. History denies that Lincoln was a
regular church member, or adhered to any creed. Yet he wrote and
spoke some of the most stirring words of our national history in
which God is publicly acknowledged.[18] The words were not empty
or hypocritical. Lincoln's honesty and sincerity were affirmed by both
friends and enemies. His private letters and conversations revealed his
reliance on God, his desire to do His will, a trust in His providence,

his love for the Bible. Men and women of his own time and count-less historians afterward have borne witness to the religious character of Lincoln.

For children, who invariably respond to the moral force in Lincoln's character, selections from his public statements will speak for them-selves:

1. *From the Farewell Speech at Springfield, 1861:* "Without the assistance of that Divine Being who ever attended him [George Washington], I cannot succeed. With that assistance, I cannot fail. . . . To His care commending you, as I hope in your prayers you will com-mend me, I bid you an affectionate farewell."

2. *The opening passage of his first message to Congress, 1861:* "In the midst of unprecedented political troubles, we have cause of great gratitude to God for unusual good health, and most abundant harv-ests."

3. *From the first presidential proclamation of Thanksgiving Day, 1863:* After recounting the blessings of the "ever watchful provi-dence of Almighty God" Lincoln says: "They are the gracious gifts of the Most High God who, while dealing with us in anger for our sins, hath nevertheless remembered mercy. It has seemed to me fit and proper that they should be solemnly, reverently and gratefully acknowledged as with one heart and one voice by the whole of the American People."

4. *To a group who serenaded the President on the evening of a victory:* "God bless the soldiers and seamen, with all their brave com-manders."[19]

Without doubt, the second Inaugural Address is one of the finest examples of a religious man thinking aloud in the presence of the nation. Lincoln himself wrote privately, "Men are not flattered by being shown that there has been a difference of purpose between the Almighty and them. To deny it, however, in this case, is to deny that there is a God governing the world."[20]

Yet, the very profundity of Lincoln's thought in this address makes it difficult to present to children of the middle grades. Also, the military and political ramifications of the address are not usually a part of history at this level. These same factors affect the choice of other quotations from Lincoln. Perhaps it is enough to point out that

Lincoln the President, in both words and action, exemplified in public office the dual principles of the Declaration of Independence: our dependence on God and our belief in the dignity and equality of all men.

The rights and duties deriving from human dignity were defended in practice as well as speech by Lincoln, "as God gave him to see the right." Examples include his life-long condemnation of slavery as a moral evil; his presidential defense, nevertheless, of Southern property rights *as such,* that could only be abrogated by an act of war; his personal sense of duty as the leader of the nation, responsible for the welfare of all citizens; his profession of belief in the divinely given human rights of the Declaration of Independence and the Constitution. Lincoln said that his knowledge of right and wrong was learned from the Bible. He frequently showed that his sharp sense of morality had a religious foundation.

Study of George Washington Carver and Personal Religion as a Source of Public Service

One of the most interesting figures in our history is George Washington Carver. Neither a political nor a military personage, he exemplifies the cultural leadership which is at least as influential in American history as presidential terms and the wars by which we tend to mark its course. Born at a time when science began to walk with secularism, Carver was a scientist "through whose delicate fingers God all but instantly transformed everyday objects into a thousand products."[21] By his careful study of plants, seeking to know "what the Creator made them for," he initiated a revolution in the agriculture of the South. Recognized as a genius by Negro and white alike, he was a symbol of hope to his people. Born in slavery, virtually self-educated until he entered college at the age of thirty, he spent the rest of his life in devoted service of others.

Children of the middle grades will find that the life of George Washington Carver was one of close relationship to God. These are some points that his biographers[22] emphasize: (1) He saw his own life and work as a part of God's plan, and prayed at every step to know the details of this plan, and carry them out. (2) His reverence for the Creator extended to all creatures, ranging from man to the humblest weed. (3) He looked upon time, and all creatures, as gifts that had a definite use and should not be wasted. On this principle he worked untiringly with lowly plants and discarded objects to produce "over half a hundred creations, any one of which would have honored the most elaborately equipped laboratory of our greatest universities."[23] (4) In his attachment to God and His creation, he was detached from a desire for money or men's gifts. (5) In his understanding of the greatness of God he saw his own smallness, and at the same time his own powers to "work hand in hand with the Creator." (6) He overcame bigotry, with which he was frequently confronted since childhood, by an all-embracing charity.

George Washington Carver should be known first for his scientific contributions to our nation, and secondly because, as Henry Wallace said of him, "To the world he was known as a scientist. Those who knew him best, however, realize his outstanding characteristic was a strong feeling of the eminence of God."[24]

Religious facts are so integral a part of Carver's life that a children's biography of him (of which there are several excellent titles) needs no teacher's commentary. Its readers cannot fail to see, in addition to the religious character of Carver, that the unjust treatment of the Negro, while it may occasion his practice of patience and other virtues, is itself inexcusable on the part of anyone who calls himself religious.

The examples given in this paper were chosen from among many possible ones: persons like George Washington, Isaac Jogues, William Penn, Marcus Whitman, Robert E. Lee; movements like the Quaker impetus to reform, and the religious background of the anti-slavery movement. Yet any examples would illustrate the fact that the best setting for the factual study of religion is cultural history, with its emphasis upon the American people and their ideas and ideals. When military, political, or economic history is overstressed, it is difficult to introduce religious facts suitable for children's study.

In the classroom where religious facts are to be learned, one inescapable condition must prevail. This is the habit of *reverence* in both teacher and pupil. "Reverence is the mother of all virtues." Certainly, it is the mother of all learning unto wisdom. The reverent mind sees beauty and potentiality in material things. It sees "the measure of man" in all persons. It gives homage to God as Creator and Father of all. Religious facts will be learned well in a class where reverence is cultivated. And this habit of mind will discover a sacredness in all truth and all learning.

Conclusions

Assuming the thorough preparation of the teacher of American history, and her use of good teaching materials, the following conclusions are offered:

1. Teaching religious facts in American history to public school pupils is admittedly difficult, but it can be done. In fact, it must be done to teach history validly, for certain religious facts are inseparable from it.

2. The difficulties are chiefly these:

a) The content of American history in grades 1-6 is restricted, for the most part, to discovery, exploration, Colonial life, the birth of the nation, the westward movement. Some representative persons of the entire span of our history are studied.

b) In public schools, religious teaching must be limited. These limitations are imposed by law, by policy of the system and school, by parental convictions; but most important, by each pupil's freedom of conscience, which must be respected.

c) History for children must be accurate, yet uphold ideals. It should be selective, but balanced. It should relate the past to the present. These requirements apply to teachers of religious facts as well as of others.

3. The possibilities are chiefly two:

a) Events or movements in American history which have had unquestioned religious aspects: for example, the Puritans, Spanish missions, Declaration of Independence.

b) Persons of historical importance who in some way brought a religious element into the story of our nation: for example, Columbus, Lincoln, George Washington Carver.

4. Cultural history forms a natural setting for the teaching of religious facts which are an integral part of the nation's story. Overemphasis on military and political aspects ought to be avoided.

5. A prerequisite for both teacher and pupils in the teaching of religious facts is reverence for God, for all persons, for things.

DISCUSSION BASED ON SISTER MARY NONA'S PAPER

Presiding: F. ERNEST JOHNSON

SISTER MARY NONA (President, Edgewood College of the Sacred Heart) : To make some of my points clear here, I should tell you immediately that, through a liberal arts and professional studies program, our college prepares a number of elementary teachers each year for the public schools. Our graduates teach from New York to California, and we are happy to perform this service for our country.

Although we give our Catholic students religion courses for personal development, we have never essayed to give them any kind of help to teach religion in the public schools, because we took it for granted that they could not do so. We teach them that they must obey not only the laws of the state in which they will teach but also the regulations of the board of education, the principal, and the school system. Furthermore, in a course called "The American Public School," we teach them the principle of separation of church and state. In doing so, we do not go into all the legal aspects; we simply emphasize the conclusion.

I was amazed to discover that there are possibilities of doing some very significant things in this field. I learned a very great deal in reading about it in the American Council books, and I learned a great deal from hearing you. I think it has been a wonderful opportunity.

I have only three points to make. The first is that my paper is not about either the study or the teaching of religion. It is about the teaching of *history* and of certain religious aspects which are inherent in that history and which are already in the textbooks used in the public schools. Some of the illustrations I gave are in all of the textbooks. All of them are in some of the textbooks. So I am dealing with recorded facts in our history. It is up to you to judge the way in which they were used.

My second point is that, if we cannot teach the religious aspects of history, we cannot teach history adequately. I once had a shocking experience while seeing a motion picture on the geography of a certain region in the United States. The movie ended in a rather romantic and glamorous way with the statement that "We hold these truths to be self-evident, that all men are created equal and are endowed with inalienable rights." Someone had deliberately left out three words, "by their Creator." Here was a deliberate eclipse of a fact in American history. As an American, I would certainly oppose this omission to the last breath because the omitted phrase was a religious fact and a religious source. No matter what we know of Tom Paine and all the other influences that figured in the writing of the Declaration of Independence, the words are that "men are endowed *by their Creator* with inalienable rights"; consequently, such a deletion as was made in the movie constitutes a distortion of history.

My third point is that there are only two possible ways in which we can teach the religious aspects of history. One is to report those events which, *without any question,* had religious aspects. Now, there are teachers who will tell you blandly in the classroom that Lincoln opposed slavery because of a religious motive. Historians know much more about it than that. There are teachers who will refer to religious motives that did not exist or that were very mixed. In teaching children we have to be especially careful because we are giving them a distilled history that must have simplicity. Therefore, first, we can give them a knowledge of events which are *inescapably* related to religious influences. One cannot teach about the Puritans without teaching about the Puritan religion.

The second way in which we can reveal the religious aspects of history is through persons. It became a kind of game to me to try to figure out who was a religious person in American history, but I gave up. Who knows which motives were religious? However, we can identify persons who *introduced a religious element* into American history by their words or actions.

The religious aspects of American history fall into place as we teach cultural history, and we should teach cultural history more than we do to elementary school children, because it is the history of people and their ideas. Most important, however, the teacher must be a person of intellectual honesty, one who knows her history, one who can exercise sound judgment in making selections, and one who can preserve historical perspective in placing emphasis without bias.

At the University of Wisconsin, which is our great neighbor, there is a plaque which was known for years as the "Winnowing and Sifting Plaque," and which refers, of course, to the winnowing and sifting of the truth. I think that phrase is the best one to use here, for there must be much winnowing and sifting of facts if we are to present to children the religious aspects of American history and still respect the conscience of each child, as well as the convictions of his parents and the group from which he comes.

DR. VIETH: I have two comments on Sister Nona's presentation. The first one is in relation to her story and the matter of semantics, about which we were talking earlier.

Back in 1947–48 I spent a little stint as adviser on religious education with the occupation forces in Japan. One of my duties was to visit schools and observe them. I visited a number of Catholic schools, and, if this were the place to do so, I could speak with very high regard for the splendid way in which they were run.

In particular instances I tried to be smart and show these children in the elementary school my ability in the Japanese language, of which I knew about a dozen words. One day as I stepped into the classroom and the children all rose as is customary there, I said, "Good morning, children," exercising great care to use the appropriate form. They answered in excellent English, "Good morning, Sister."

My second comment deals with an uneasiness I have had creeping up on me, as a member of the committee that drafted the original statement on policy, that in much of our discussion we seem to be concerned with teaching religion *per se* and using history and other subjects as a vehicle to get everything in we can.

Now, my view of it has been that we need to include religion in the teaching of history because history demands it. To be fair with history, as Sister Nona pointed out, we are forced to include the religious words concerning inalienable rights.

Now, it may be that we are getting radical enough to move in the other direction and to say that, in spite of the fact that home and church are the principal teachers of religion, they are not doing an adequate job. Perhaps, the situation in America now demands that we do teach more religion than we are and that the public school do more of it. If this is the case and if we still expect other subjects to carry their fair load, then in fairness to the proper presentation of those subjects perhaps we ought to go a step further and include a new subject of religion.

SISTER MARY NONA: I think all that has been said and all that we know indicates that we cannot include the subject of religion, particularly at the elementary level. Because of all the philosophical derivations that bewilder even us as we discuss them here, it would be impossible to present the facts of religion to children at this age in public school.

MR. PFEFFER: First, I would like to match Sister Nona's story with another concerning a more recent omission of words. This is an omission that may show the reverse side of the coin.

Several weeks ago I appeared in Albany before Commissioner Allen arguing, among other things, against the resolution of a certain Long Island community to place in the public schools the so-called inter-denominational or nonsectarian commandments which had been drafted and framed by the public school authorities. An interesting aspect of those Ten Commandments is that they started out, "I am the Lord, Thy God, who brought thee forth from the house of bondage."

When I looked in both the Douay and the Authorized Versions, besides my own Hebrew Bible, I found that is not the way the Commandment read. It read: "I am the Lord, Thy God, who brought thee forth from the Land of Egypt, from the House of Bondage." Somehow or other, the words "from the Land of Egypt" had been dropped out. While it may have been bad history to omit "by their Creator" from the Declaration of Independence, it was bad religion to omit "from the Land of Egypt" from the Ten Commandments if, unfortunately, through imperfection, it was in the original. That is the religion that we are committed to, not to a different type of religion. Although this is not completely relevant, I thought I would contribute it for what it was worth.

I would like to comment on Sister Nona's paper, which I have now read. I am sorry I didn't do my homework before, but I did do it last night. I would like to reiterate the somewhat improvident judgment I gave last night as to my views of its constitutionality. I think I can say now that what I said last night is correct with one reservation which I will come to shortly. I have no doubt that the program suggested and outlined by Sister Nona is completely within the bounds of American constitutional law and of the various laws and constitutions of the states. Except for one point which I will come to later, the difficulties which Sister Nona's paper raises for me are not constitutional and legal difficulties. They are difficulties in a somewhat different area.

I am making these comments with the full realization that there are many here who will not agree with me, and I am not necessarily committed to them myself; however, I think they are comments which must be borne in mind if we are to maintain that intellectual honesty and integrity which Sister Nona has so eloquently stressed.

First, I think that we are proceeding on a number of presuppositions. I think we are proceeding on a presupposition that religion is important in American history. Now, I am fairly certain that no one would deny or dispute that presupposition; nevertheless, I think we must recognize that it is a presupposition. Of course, "important" is a very relative term. Yet I wonder if it does not merit as objective an examination as can be made. How important, really, is religion in American history? Is it really true that there is a major religious aspect to American history? Perhaps there is; perhaps there is not. I am raising a question which I think intellectual integrity requires us to raise. I am not giving an answer. Is it really important, for example, that the first things that the sailors on Christopher Columbus' ships did was to say a *Te Deum?* In the over-all picture of American history, in the historian's scale of values, is that really an important fact?

Is it important that the first words that Samuel Morse typed out on the new invention were "What hath God wrought?" Would it be more or less significant if he had used the type of words Bell first used on the telephone, completely neutral words? Is there any great historical significance in these facts? Is it possible that we may be overemphasizing or trying artificially to create an importance which does not exist in the same degree as we are assuming it does?

Secondly, is it not also true that historical omissions of religion may likewise be important? Sister Nona points out—how many times I have heard it—the references to God in various forms in the Declaration of Independence. Perhaps that is an important fact. Undoubtedly it is an important fact that God is mentioned four or six times, I don't remember how many times, in the Declaration of Independence. But, is it historically fair to cite this fact unless we also say at the same time that in the Constitution of the United States, which is many times longer than the Declaration of Independence, and which is the basic charter of the American Government, God is not mentioned once at all? Is not the omission of this fact equally a distortion of history? And is it not a distortion of history to fail to point out that the omission of the mention of God in the Constitution was not inadvertent but the result of careful argument and consideration? It seems to me that it is a tremendously important fact that, after careful consideration with the precedent of the Declaration of Independence before them, the people at Philadelphia decided not to mention God in the Constitution.

We are also proceeding on the notion, although it has been implicit rather than expressed, that the word "important" is a synonym for good. Is that necessarily so? Perhaps most of us would feel it is. But is that not also a presupposition? Has the influence of religion on history been all to the good? Examine American and European history. Has religious influence not had a checkered career, sometimes good and sometimes not so good? Can we just assume that the over-all influence of religion has been uniformly good?

Now let me comment on the question of the constitutionality of Sister Nona's paper. I read it from beginning to end, and until I got to the end I was confident that it was constitutional. The last sentence disturbed me. The last sentence says, if I remember correctly, that there is a prerequisite that the teacher shall be committed to or have a reverence for God. If I understand it, this statement means that the teacher must be committed theistically, that the teacher must believe in God. That troubles me. It troubles me because I think it is contrary to a deliberate choice made by the founders of our Republic. When our Constitution was being debated and discussed, there was a strong feeling on the part of a number of clergymen that the very least that should be required of any person serving under the American Government was that he should believe in God. It was not a question of whether he should believe in the trinitarian God or the unitarian God or the Christian God or the Jewish God, but it was at least a question of whether he should believe in God.

The outcome of that debate resulted in the last words of the Constitution before the enacting clause to the effect that no religious test shall ever be imposed for service in the United States Government. It was asked: Does that mean that an infidel and an atheist may be President of the United States? As the men in Philadelphia deliberately made the choice, yes, it does mean that an infidel and an atheist may be President of the United States, and it is more consistent with our principles that the people should have the opportunity to elect to the presidency an infidel and an atheist than it would be that, because a man is an infidel and an atheist, he should be barred.

Inasmuch as the high office of the President of the United States, undoubtedly the most important office in the whole world today, was deliberately kept open for the infidel and the atheist, I would question, if not the constitutionality, then certainly the wisdom of a prerequisite that prevents that same infidel or atheist from becoming a teacher.

SISTER MARY NONA: I should like to comment, first, on the last point. Since I wrote the statement, I think I can interpret it. As I think of it in this context, reverence for God, for persons, and for things involves the subjective quality of standing back, so to speak, before any reality. I do not say here that this person must believe in God. I simply mean that, when a person is a teacher and comes to those words in the Declaration of Independence, she will treat God reverently as the entity which is found in that Declaration. But I do not mean that the teacher has to express a personal belief.

In many cases, we ourselves ought to show reverence for certain things in which we do not believe and respect for certain persons whose beliefs we do not share. I do not mean that a teacher must pass a religious test and must believe in God, but I do believe that I must treat God with reverence in the classroom. Even a woodcarver has to treat wood with reverence. Starting with the lowest things, there is a reverence in the handling or in the approach to reality which is demanded of every person.

Now, I would like to speak to the question of the importance of religion. I don't know why we are here if that is not a first prerequisite of our thinking. Taking it exactly as you have, Mr. Pfeffer, we could substitute the word "democracy" and ask: Is democracy important to us? And we would say, yes, absolutely. Or we could follow your thinking and say that, since we cannot be really sure that democracy is important, then we must be careful not to use such words as "Give me liberty or give me death," or the many wonderful historical statements that we have. So I certainly have assumed that it was important.

The inclusion of the *Te Deum* was only a selective item. I would not say at all that it was an absolutely necessary choice. I chose it because the earliest American history textbooks brought it in, and I thought it would be interesting in terms of a textbook of 1787 to see what religious points were introduced by McCullough, the author; so I chose that particular one. As I said at the end of my paper, it could be many other ones.

DR. KONVITZ: I have had the feeling throughout the entire morning, that history has been pitched at a factual level. This disturbs me. There is a factual type of history, the type we are talking about, that seems to me to be relatively unimportant. As a teacher and a parent, I do feel this is a relatively unimportant aspect of history. What is meaningful to my child is not the event. The meaningful thing is what is distinctly human, the idea behind the event, the value of the event, the motivation of people acting in such a way as to create the event. These are the important things. The accumulation of facts can only come to be a history of monuments. Even though the monuments may be events rather than stones, this kind of history can be deadly. It is insignificant. It isn't going to be read. It doesn't excite.

Once you broaden the concept of history so that it deals with the distinctly human element, it becomes significant. It is not enough to say, for example, that there are 256 denominations in the United States. As a matter of fact, there are a great many more, but we have a record of 256. Why? How can you explain why without going to the roots of the Protestant idea? How are you going to explain the roots of the Protestant idea without becoming involved, for example, in the logic of John Robinson's sermon to the Pilgrims as they left the shores of Europe for the United States? And how can you explain those ideas, whether you accept them or not, unless you explain them in a proper way?

One can be a Catholic or a Jew, but, if he is going to be an honest teacher, he must actually make these ideas exciting. He must talk about them as if he believes them, although he may not believe them and although the next moment he may be talking about ideas contrary to these ideas. Then he is involved, deeply involved, intellectually and emotionally. When students become excited, history becomes significant. They are not going to take away any specific ideas as dogmas, but their minds will have been opened up. If history teaching doesn't open their minds, I think it doesn't illuminate their minds. The facts are deadweights, to begin with.

I am disturbed by our present emphasis, but I want these comments to incite discussion. My intention is not to end the discussion but to encourage it. I would like to hear some discussion.

CHAIRMAN JOHNSON: It is an important contribution, and I hope it will be discussed, as I hope many other questions that have been raised here will be discussed, at the tables.

There is no plan to have a summary as we sometimes have at the end of a session, and I am sure that this is wise. It would hardly be possible to summarize discussions of this sort. However, if you will permit me, I will say a word about the profound significance of what has just been said by Milton Konvitz and what was said a few moments ago by Leo Pfeffer.

I would assume that the more seriously we take the proposition that there should be objective study of history and the other disciplines with respect to their religious content, the readier we will be to include within that study a consideration of the criteria of importance. It would not be a case, then, of taking somebody's word for it. I think the same applies in general to what you were saying, Dr. Konvitz, about the criteria of judgment.

I see our time is up. On your behalf I want to thank the writers for presenting such thoughtful analyses and for so patiently answering our questions.

Table Reports and Discussion

F IVE ELEVEN-PERSON table groups, each an occupational and religious cross-section of the entire conference membership, met separately to consider the following two questions: (1) To what extent does the group agree with the conclusions of the morning's papers? and (2) What modifications would the group like to suggest to improve the conclusions of the morning's papers?

Although it was originally planned to digest the table reports, it was finally decided to publish them without substantive changes since it was felt that duplication would be less objectionable to the serious reader than "distillation." "Distillation," as everyone knows, is a misnomer for "dilution" and invariably involves watering each concentration down to a level at which it will mix with others. The final solution, although inoffensive, is colorless, odorless, and tasteless, as well as unidentifiable.

In spite of the fact that the table reports vary greatly in form and in emphasis, there is a remarkable agreement on matters of essential importance. This consensus is apparent, striking, and, it is hoped, preserved in the following individual table reports.

TABLE I REPORT

Chairman: JAMES L. HANLEY, Superintendent of Schools, Providence, Rhode Island

Recorder: HARRISON SASSCER, Assistant Director, Division of Legislation and Federal Relations, National Education Association

As might be expected, several members of the group felt the need for more precise definitions of terms used in the papers (for example, "religion," "theism," and "correlation" as applied to religion and history). Some felt, for instance, that a substantial majority of the American public agree on such fundamental religious principles as the existence of God, the obligation of man to his Creator, and a theistic basis for moral and natural law. They conceded, however, that although the majority of Americans admit belief in God, the content of this belief would be hard to assess in terms of any consensus or agreement as to the nature of God or the obligations implicit in such belief.

Some members of the group expressed the concern that the public schools were taking attitudes toward religion that might undercut commonly held religious convictions or at least minimize the importance of maintaining such convictions. They felt there has been more reluctance on the part of the public schools to handle touchy and controversial issues than overt hostility to religion as such. On the other hand, one member states that in high school, at least, such statements as are contained in the Declaration of Independence can be discussed quite freely without offending any student's religious sensibilities.

Another member cited his experience in reviewing history textbooks and called attention to the neglect in these texts of all but a few of the topics suggested by Mr. Allen's paper as appropriate for inclusion in high school history courses. It was also his opinion that timidity rather than hostility is responsible for this neglect.

The table agreed that there is now a definite need for an authoritative historical survey of religion in American life and culture. It was felt that such a survey should be prepared under the auspices of a professional historical association, such as the American Historical Association, in consultation with religious authorities, and should be written as a reference work for high school and elementary school teachers of social studies.

The group also felt that interested persons would have a clearer picture of the fairness and adequacy with which religious questions are handled in public school teaching if a cooperative study could be made of textbooks and other curriculum materials used in public schools for teaching English and the social studies. Most of the group felt that this should be a commission-type study in which the conclusions would be subject to review by persons representing different religious faiths, including those representing nontheistic beliefs.

The problem of improving the religious literacy of teachers produced a description from one member of the group of some of the pilot projects under way in teacher-training institutions as a result of stimulation from the American Association of Colleges for Teacher Education. He reported that some of these institutions teach comparative religion; that others are emphasizing history of Western religions; and that one is offering a course on religion on twentieth-century America. The danger of unqualified or biased teachers was pointed out, but most members of the group seemed to express approval of the progress that was being made.

The question of how much of a religious commitment should be sought in public schools elicited these points of view: On the one hand, there were those who were personally convinced that there are naturally understood religious truths to which one can be committed and who believed that the public schools should encourage this kind of commitment without indoctrination. Others, while they admitted the existence of commonly held religious truths, believed that the public schools should not encourage any commitment to these truths since, to do so, would abrogate the rights of those parents and children who regard religious truths as something to which a final commitment cannot be made.

The participants in Table I were all but unanimous in their agreement with the general conclusions of the four papers discussed during the morning; however, there was no member of the group who did not disagree with some of the details of the papers. One member expressed much reservation regarding the advisability of putting into practice at the elementary school level some of the practices suggested by Sister Mary Nona since he felt that experimentation at this grade level should take place in private secular schools.

TABLE II REPORT

Chairman: ROSCOE L. WEST, President, New Jersey State Teachers College, Trenton

Recorder: DUMONT F. KENNY, National Program Director, National Conference of Christians and Jews, Inc.

As it considered the relation of religion to the teaching of American history, Table II selected certain areas or issues as the crucial ones cutting at the heart of the papers dealing with the problems of how and when references in religion should be made in teaching American history.

1. We are in thorough agreement with the approach of the Committee on Religion and Education in advocating the factual study of religion when and where it is intrinsic to general education. We support and favor the study of the role of religion in human affairs in our schools when it is relevant to the subject matter under consideration. We suggest that a better formulation of the phrase "teaching about religion" might be "a full competent treatment of history —in this case American history." We clearly distinguish between "teaching religious factors in history" and "teaching a religious faith." The former is acceptable. We are agreed, moreover, that we should intensify our efforts to equip our teachers in public schools to do this more adequately. We favor "teaching religious factors in history" because this is basically involved in the competent teaching of history.

2. Our group agreed that the teaching of religion in schools, as distinguished from the study of religion, depends on the possibility of prior agreement on basic religious values and sanctions. This concurrence raised the question of whether we *can* teach religious values in our public schools. Inasmuch as the group agreed with Professor Loewenberg that there "must first be clear understanding and agreement concerning the values common to all religions before there can be any agreement upon which religious values should be taught in public, tax-supported schools," and inasmuch as the group was of the opinion that reaching agreement is presently impossible, it concluded that the teaching of a common core of religious values should not be undertaken at this time.

This same problem was dealt with by the American Council committee in its 1947 publication, *The Relation of Religion to Public Education.* We quote the conclusion reached by the committee at that time.

To begin with, we think it objectionable from the religious point of view. Catholics, in particular, will object because of their traditional position that Christ established one true church to which all men are called. The notion of a common core suggests a watering-down of the several faiths to the point where common essentials appear. This might easily lead to a new sect—a public school sect—which would take its place alongside the existing faiths and compete with them. The great religious bodies in

America hold their respective faiths too seriously to admit of such a procedure on the part of the public schools. (P. 15)

We would point out, however, that the school has no monopoly in inculcating moral and spiritual values and that the resources of home and church should be used freely. In addition, we support the teaching of such specific values as are contained in the publication of the Educational Policies Commission, *The Teaching of Moral and Spiritual Values in the Public Schools,* as well as those contained in the Universal Declaration of Human Rights of the United Nations Organization. Because of the intrinsic limitation of the common school, we can agree on the teaching of specific values, but not of ultimate religious sanctions.

3. This latter consideration brought us to a third problem area, the mutual relationships of religion and public education, and the question of whether religion has been neglected in our schools. We deny the charge that our public schools are "godless." We accent that our schools have been and are friendly to religious institutions. We note that this favorable climate is increasing, and we commend all those efforts, such as the work and recommendations of the Committee on Religion and Education, which are fostering this atmosphere. We reaffirm the belief that the school has responsibility for character formation. We agree with the Committee Report that we must create and maintain an atmosphere or climate favorable to religion including, we would add, those religious positions to which the theistic position is not acceptable. One member of the group would reformulate this position to read, "should not create an atmosphere or climate unfavorable to religion, etc." We have, the group felt, an obligation to teach ethical values in our public schools, but not to teach the religious sanctions on which they are based or even the claim for such sanctions. On the other hand, we must be on guard to prevent atheistic and agnostic indoctrination under whatever guise.

4. Finally, our group addressed itself to the question of whether public school teachers can be expected to provide guidance to pupils who are asking questions involving religious problems. We felt that the teachers' role should be one of sympathetic referral to an appropriate religious agency or leader. We hold that the agencies of church, home, and school should cooperate in such matters. In the case of

a child who cannot turn to parent or church for such guidance, we felt that the teacher has a legitimate role to play in trying to help the child solve his problem. We agreed that public school teachers have an obligation to cooperate with religious organizations, and within the limits of law, to create a climate favorable to religion.

TABLE III REPORT

Chairman: PAUL H. VIETH, Professor of Christian Nurture, Divinity School, Yale University

Recorder: ISAAC FRANCK, Executive Director, Jewish Community Council of Greater Washington

The beginning of the group's discussion centered around Professor Loewenberg's paper and, especially, his assertion that the formulation of a synthesis of American beliefs is a prerequisite for the determination of the proper treatment of religious facts in the public schools. Mindful of the principle that there should not be any indoctrination or commitment in the treatment of religious data in the public schools, the group felt that Professor Loewenberg's suggestion of a synthesis implied such commitment, and they expressed the view that the formulation of a synthesis is not a necessary condition for taking cognizance, at least, of religious ideas and facts which are intrinsic to the teaching of American history. Notwithstanding this view, the group agreed that Professor Loewenberg's proposal for a broad, scholarly study of the various religious ideas in American history would be a useful undertaking.

The question was then raised as to whether religious influences as an aspect of American history are actually being taught in American public schools now. Some thought they were, whereas others raised doubts. It was pointed out that many teachers do not have enough training to deal adequately with religious facts; however, there was no clear view as to what knowledge would be required for teachers. One member suggested that a pamphlet on religious elements in American history might be useful for high school teachers, but another felt such a pamphlet would not get much use. Still another member expressed concern lest such a pamphlet be misused for improper, "missionary" purposes by a few teachers who do in fact indoctrinate now. The members agreed that a reduction of indoctrination generally follows the emergence of religiously pluralistic populations in most communities; however, they also pointed out that public schools are subject to constant pressures to teach all kinds of subjects, including religion. The question invariably arises as to how much freight the curriculum can carry, in view of time limitations.

What happens in a public school when pupils ask teachers questions about God or other theological or doctrinal problems? Too often teachers do try to answer and indoctrinate. At other times the teachers refer children who ask such questions to their parents or clergymen in a way that puzzles the child or looks like an evasion. There were three views expressed by the group as to how a teacher should handle questions about God, theology, or religious doctrine: (1) The teacher should be taught to understand and to explain to the student the principles of religious freedom and of church-state separation as part of American history and thus furnish the student the reasons for the teacher's inability to deal with such questions within the framework of the public schools. (2) The teacher should attempt to show the student the various views held in the community on the questions raised by the student. (3) The teacher should do nothing more than refer the student to his parents or his clergyman without further explanation.

Whether or not the negative, as well as the positive, religious facts should be included in the treatment of American history depends partly on the age and maturity level of the pupils. Questions are often raised about the treatment of such historical events as the Crusades, the Know-Nothing movement, and similar events or movements in history and the difficulties involved in their accurate and adequate treatment for children. The group felt that such difficulties must be resolved by the curriculum developers for different age levels and that it should consider only general principles. Since historical accuracy is paramount, the group felt that the treatment at one age level should leave open the possibility for a broader and more detailed treatment of the same subject at a higher age level.

The group next turned to a consideration of Professor Allen's and Sister Mary Nona's papers. The question was raised as to whether these papers seek to use American history as a vehicle to carry the maximum freight of religious information or whether they seek to explore proper ways of teaching *significantly* American history, which inevitably includes religious data.

The consensus was that the two papers present useful examples of some, though not all, religious facts relevant to the teaching of American history. Although there were several points of difference concerning this or that specific item or statement in the two papers, half of the group expressed its general approval of the *conclusions* of Professor Allen's and Sister Mary Nona's papers. The other half of the group expressed a number of reservations, which included the following:

1. That in Sister Nona's paper, the concluding paragraph [see page 153] which now reads "A prerequisite for both teacher and pupils in the teaching of religious facts is reverence for God, for all persons, for things" be rewritten so that it contains no implication of a requirement of a belief in God on the part of the teacher or the pupils.

2. That the use of personalities outstanding in American history, which is suggested in paragraph 3*b* of Sister Nona's conclusions include personalities in American history other than those with theistic commitments.

3. That paragraphs 1 and 2 in Professor Allen's conclusions [see page 131] be rewritten so as not to imply that his paper is designed to describe a course in religion or in American contributions to religion but to make clear that it is designed to describe aspects of a course in American history which includes material on the contributions of religions to American history.

TABLE IV REPORT

Chairman: HERBERT L. SEAMANS, Director, Commission on Educational Organizations, National Conference of Christians and Jews, Inc.

Recorder: MAX BIRNBAUM, Educational Consultant, American Jewish Committee

There was general agreement that the Council's Committee on Religion and Education should focus attention on the study of religious influences in American history as they apply at all three levels: elementary, secondary, and teacher education.

Specific Suggestions

1. There was a revision of Sister Nona's Conclusion 2*b* [see page 153] to read as follows: "In public schools, teaching about religion must be limited. The limitations are imposed by virtue of parental convictions and responsibilities, by each pupil's freedom of conscience, by law, and by policies of the school system."

2. A revision of Sister Nona's Conclusion 5 was approved as follows: "A prerequisite for both teachers and pupils in the teaching of religious facts is respect. This means dealing reverently with references to God and religious symbolisms as they occur in American history."

3. Under the heading "Declaration of Independence" in Sister Nona's paper, the third paragraph [see page 148] was revised to read as follows: "The meaning of rights—and of corresponding duties—is understandable to children, who see them exercised by themselves and others in daily group living. It should not be difficult for them to see in the words of the Declaration of Independence an avowal that rights endowed by the Creator are inalienable and, therefore, different from rights bestowed by the state, which can be taken away by the same."

4. Table IV suggested that the conclusions in Professor Allen's paper [see pages 131–32] be amended to provide for the inclusion of religious factors in high school American history wherever these are relevant and needed for comprehensive treatment with due regard to the appropriate level of maturity of the child and to the integrity of the subject.

General Suggestions

1. Table IV expressed the conviction that the public schools should at all times and in all ways maintain a climate friendly to religion but they should also recognize that religious indoctrination should be left entirely to the home, the church, and the synagogue.

2. In the teaching of American history, Table IV agreed that due care should be taken, with allowances for the maturity level of the child, to assess the influence of both theistic and nontheistic motivations in human behavior and human affairs. To do otherwise would be to provide a distorted framework for the treatment of American history.

3. Table IV suggested that the teaching of religious factors in American history could be more soundly achieved if there were close and effective cooperation between the college or university professor, on the one hand, and the curriculum-maker, on the other. Such cooperation would involve not only an awareness by the professor that many of his students are future secondary and elementary teachers but also an awareness by the curriculum-maker that he needs the history professor's advice on the content of history courses.

4. Finally, Table IV suggested that other aspects of the curriculum and school life should be examined to ascertain and apply wherever appropriate the relevant teaching of the impact of religion.

TABLE V REPORT

Chairman: MSGR. WILLIAM E. MCMANUS, Assistant Director, Department of Education, National Catholic Welfare Conference

Recorder: A. L. SEBALY, National Coordinator, Teacher Education and Religion Project, American Association of Colleges for Teacher Education

Table V discussed papers of this section individually. The members agreed on the following points in relation to Professor Loewenberg's paper [see pages 77–86]:

1. They affirmed his first statement that "Religious ideas and religious forces parallel American life at every significant stage of development."

2. In his statement which reads "The most startling omission in American historiography is the absence of a synthesis of religious ideas," the members felt that the emphasis was too strong and objected to the phrase "startling omission." After some discussion, they agreed to the following statement: "In American historiography religious factors have had inadequate treatment. There is need for further historical examination of theological speculation in America, for a sociological history of denominationalism, and for a cultural study of church organization broadly related to the evolving patterns of American life."

3. The members agreed to Professor Loewenberg's statement that

"Before religion in America can be properly treated, we need to know a great deal more about it." They understood by this agreement that what was wanted was a *scholarly* approach.

4. The members felt that the following sentence should be eliminated: "The content of religion must be systematically appraised and the meanings of religion rigorously defined before religion can be accorded serious historical treatment."

5. There was considerable discussion of Professor Loewenberg's statement that "There must first be clear understanding and agreement concerning the values common to all religions before there can be any agreement upon which religious values should be taught in public, tax-supported schools." The dissent was on the phrase "which religious values." The group tended to scatter its opinions in this manner: (*a*) There was disagreement about the idea of "values common to all religions." (*b*) There was disagreement with the word "before." Some members felt that a start could be made now without a waiting period and that the word "before" seemed to imply a delaying tactic. (*c*) There was disagreement on the implied interpretation that religion and culture are two separate things. (*d*) Finally, there was a feeling that any tendency to equate religion with Americanism should be avoided.

6. The members opposed any artificial or synthetic bringing-together of religion and American history. They took a definite stand against a synthetic approach.

In relation to Professor Farrell's paper, the members of Table V agreed on the following points:

1. They agreed that the Council's Committee on Religion and Education should recommend to Dr. Farrell that he balance his excellent treatment of the reciprocal relationship between the teaching of religion and the teaching of American history of the Colonial period with a treatment of these same relationships as they apply to later American history.

2. They endorsed what can be referred to as "the scholarly approach" to the teaching of American history.

3. The members felt that Dr. Farrell's paper demonstrated that it is possible for a scholarly American history course to benefit equally those students who intend to teach and those who do not intend to teach.

In relation to Professor Allen's paper, the members of Table V recommended that his conclusions [see pages 131–32] be modified in the following manner:

2. Religious aspects of high school American history should be selected on the basis of sound historical scholarship, democratic values, and the needs of the adolescent.

3. While cognizant of the lack of a genuinely empirical basis for the selection of curriculum content, the following areas or topics among others in American religious history would appear to be appropriate at the secondary level.

a) (1) The contributions of Western heritage to religion in America;
  (2) The contributions of religion in America to Western heritage;

. . . . . .

c) Bases for the establishment of the principle of separation of church and state;

d) Religion as a force and issue in politics;

. . . . . .

g) The growth of science in modern America and its challenge to the doctrine of faith, and, conversely, the challenge of faith to science;

h) The increasing diversity of American religion resulting from immigration and other influences.

4. An important aspect of religion is its value in citizenship education. It can help the adolescent build his own set of moral anchors, broaden his perception of tolerance, and develop a more adequate concept of self. Such study, however, is not the province of the public school alone. Even more compelling responsibilities for the development of moral and spiritual values, rest with the family, the church, and indeed with the community at large.

The members of Table V recommended that the conclusions to Sister Mary Nona's paper [see page 153] be modified as follows:

2. The difficulties are chiefly these:

b) In public schools, the teaching of religious facts must be limited. These limitations are imposed by law, by policy of the system and school, by parental convictions, but most important, by each pupil's degree of maturity and freedom of conscience, which must be respected.

. . . . . .

4. Cultural history forms a natural setting for the teaching of religious facts which are an integral part of the nation's story.

5. An important attribute for both teacher and pupils in the teaching of religious facts is that all reference to God, persons, and things, be reverent.

DISCUSSION BASED ON TABLE REPORTS
Presiding: GALEN JONES

CHAIRMAN GALEN JONES: (Director, Study on Economic Education of the Council for Advancement of Secondary Education): We are now ready to discuss the table reports. Are there any questions?

DR. JOHNSON: Mr. Chairman, I was a member of Table I. I had intended to make one suggestion that slipped my mind. This has to do with a very small word, but sometimes small words are important. In reference to the belief in God professed by a majority of the people, the word "admit" was used. I believe it would be more accurate and much more prudent to say "avow belief in God" rather than "admit."

DR. WEST: I wonder what is meant in the last paragraph of the report of Table I that states one member objected to certain elements in Sister Nona's paper with regard to her suggestions concerning elementary schools. He said he thought they ought to be tried out in private secular schools.

DR. SASSCER: Mr. Pfeffer is here to speak for himself. Suppose I let him do that.

MR. PFEFFER: I expressed the view that I would welcome experimentation along the lines of Sister Nona's paper in private secular schools where problems of constitutional law and private conscience are not acute, if they are present at all, before I would want to see them tried out in the public elementary schools.

This is nothing new. I have said this many times in various places and before some of the people present here. I certainly believe in the suggested approach at the college level, and I think I concur with it at the upper secondary school level. The reason is very simple. I am speaking as a parent now, not as an educator. When my child reaches the age of fifteen or sixteen, I have done about all I can to ground him in my religious commitments. Maybe I am timid, but, until he is at that age, I would rather he get his religious commitments exclusively from me. I want a monopoly on that part of the commitment. I do not want that shared with anyone.

When he is fifteen or sixteen, if I have done my job reasonably well, I will take a chance and let him be exposed to others. That may be only my private bias as a parent. On the other hand, I may be wrong. It may be desirable to expose him to competing or different religious commitments at a younger level. However, before I risk my children to that exposure, I would very much like to see how the plan operates in a noncompulsive atmosphere.

I can never forget the basic fact that the children are a captive audience in the public school system. They are not there because they want to be there. They are there because their fathers and mothers will go to jail if they are not there. Before I try Sister Nona's admirable suggestions before a captive audience, I would like to see how they work out with a voluntary group. I specified a secular group because the experiment obviously would have no real meaning in a religious school. I would like to see some honest-to-goodness experimentation along these lines at the elementary level in a secular private school.

At the secondary level, at the junior and high school level, I am willing to risk my children in the public high school. This is the motivation of my reservation contained in the table report.

DR. WEST: From the standpoint of the child, is he less captive in the private school than he is in the public school?

MR. PFEFFER: I don't think it is realistic to speak from the point of view of the child in this sense. The child is a captive when he is called in to eat or called in to sleep or when he is sent to any kind of school. When we say "captive" here, we mean the parent to whom is committed the responsibility for the moral and religious and secular upbringing of the child before the child reaches an age of discretion.

DR. WEST: I don't quite see the distinction you make there. But would you believe, for example, in grades five, six, and seven, the middle grades, in teaching about the Puritans, the Spanish missions, the Revolutionary War, and all these phases of American history? Do you believe references to these religious influences should be omitted?

MR. PFEFFER: Never.

DR. WEST: Those are the things that Sister Nona suggests. I don't see what you object to.

MR. PFEFFER: If, like Molière's would-be gentleman, we have been speaking prose all our life, then I think there is little purpose in a conference such as this and the launching of a campaign to get people to speak prose. Implicit in this conference and in the series of suggestions in Sister Nona's paper is the assumption that we have not been speaking prose all our lives, that we have not been doing these things that Sister Nona would want us to do.

Apparently there is an assumption here. Incidentally, in our table group I challenged that assumption, and I urged that the assumption be considered with detachment. Is it true that we have been unfair? Have we treated religion unfairly or inadequately in the public schools? I certainly am not prepared to accept the assumption that we have been unfair. Have I no business being here if I challenge that assumption? Can I not say perhaps there is nothing wrong, perhaps what we are doing is good practice? Perhaps we should all go back and say, "Fine, this is the way the public education system should be." I am not ready to say that it is wrong.

The assumption is made in the suggestions in Sister Nona's paper, as well as in the discussion that we have had, that we have not been talking prose all the time, that we have been inadequate, that we should do something either more or different. And I say, before we undertake to do anything more or different in the public schools and subject a captive audience to it, I would like to see it tried in the private secular schools first. That is all.

SISTER MARY NONA: I would like to say that I did not write my paper with that assumption. The examples that I took for it came out of the textbooks that are now being used in the public schools. I could cite them in each instance. And it was a new thought to me, as Mr. Pfeffer expressed it, that it was experimentation. In fact, as I told you, when I gathered these ideas together, I found that all these ideas have been taught or are being actually taught in the public school. To put this in another way: Some of these are being taught in all the textbooks, and all of them are being taught in some of the textbooks. So, I didn't think of these ideas as being an experiment; I didn't think of them as being new at all.

MR. SASSCER: I would like to call on Mr. Bragdon to bring out something that we did not find it possible to include in our brief report but that we found very interesting. Most of you seem to have your papers with you. You remember that in his conclusions Professor Allen listed a whole group of topics that could be studied or brought into the course in American history. Mr. Bragdon has had occasion to examine American history textbooks and has compiled a rough check list on how many times these particular topics are mentioned in textbooks. I would like him to present that list to us. I think you will find it very interesting.

MR. BRAGDON: I am prepared to do it with the prefatory understanding that I did this very quickly and that I based it on my recollections as an examiner for the College Entrance Examination Board first in American history and later in social studies. We had to know what was in every textbook because we obviously couldn't test on material which wasn't in all of them. For instance, there was once a question on architecture that involved the name of Frank Lloyd Wright, but, since one textbook didn't mention him, we didn't think we could use that question.

In the conclusions of Mr. Allen's report he has listed twelve possible topics in American religious history, which would appear to be appropriate. According to my recollection, this is the score: "Yes" means the topic is in textbooks in some form. I wouldn't say that it is necessarily well treated, but it is treated. "Slight" means it is treated sometimes and sometimes not treated, or slightly referred to. "No" means it is treated in very few American history textbooks.

a) The contributions of Western heritage to religion in America—*Yes*

b) Religious traditions and institutions that are the product of developments during the Colonial period—*Yes*

c) Political bases for the establishment of the principle of separation of church and state—*Slight*

d) Religion as an issue in politics—*No*

e) Religious awakening and church expansion during the first half of the nineteenth century—*No*

f) Religious issues and church policy in the slavery controversy—*Yes*

g) The growth of science in modern America and its challenge to the doctrine of faith—Although there is reference to the Scopes trial, I might say *"Slight,"* if you insist, but I think *"No"* in terms of any fundamental treatment.

h) The increasing diversity of American religion resulting from the new immigration and other influences—*No*

i) The rise of the city and the concomitant development of the social gospel—*Slight*

j) The growth of church organization in modern America—*Slight*

k) The use of religion by interest groups to further their special ends—*No*. I will challenge anybody ever to get that into a textbook.

l) The persistence of evangelism as a phase of religious activity—*No*

Total: Three "Yes," three "Slight," and six "No."

FATHER McMANUS: Could I ask Mr. Bragdon whether he means to say that textbooks used in public schools do not refer to the Ku Klux Klan or the APA's or such movements as those? These references could be classified, I think, under the heading of the use of religion by interest groups to further their special ends.

MR. BRAGDON: The Ku Klux Klan is referred to, but it is carefully not tied to the Bible Belt as such. In other words, it is not described as a manifestation of the perversion of Protestantism.

MR. VARNER: Are those senior high school textbooks?

MR. BRAGDON: I am talking about senior high school textbooks.

CHAIRMAN JONES: You have now had all five reports and you are free to raise questions on any of them.

DR. SAMUEL M. BLUMENFIELD (Director, Department of Education and Culture, Jewish Agency, Inc.): I want to observe that these five tables, though they did not communicate with one another, have written reports which, by and large, sound to me very harmonious on basic matters. Here and there I detect slight deviations, but, on the basic things, I sense a certain amount of agreement that, frankly, I am surprised and pleased to hear.

CHAIRMAN JONES: I recognize Mr. Pursinger, from the Willamette High School of Eugene, Oregon.

MR. PURSINGER: I want to make this point. A textbook proves absolutely nothing except that the text will sell. Many, many textbooks are written to please the different pressure groups which read them, in order to pass local inspection. There isn't any one of us in the public schools who doesn't skip chapters in textbooks. Frankly, I skip the one on religion in my American history. I might say before I go on that I came here convinced that the study of religion and religious influences in American history is necessary and wise, but I have quite a lot of questions as to how it should be done.

I know—and the superintendent knows—that our reputation as a school, apart from sex education, hinges on what we do in social studies. If I decide to take up a controversial subject like religion in the school, I would make sure that no one would ever find anything about it in my room in print. That is rule number one. I may divide the class into what are commonly called buzz sections, and we may discuss such a thing as: "Is it the responsibility of the church to increase respect for the marriage vows in our state?" We will discuss this together and shuffle our ignorance, but not in print. This is the first law.

To quote the number of times these various topics appear in textbooks honestly does not prove anything. We should not think that, if we succeed in getting our recommendations here into textbooks, we have fulfilled our mission. I don't think that will be the case. Moreover, I'm not convinced that it is safe.

DR. LARSON: I am one of Dr. West's loyal subjects, and I enjoyed the fraternity of those present. While we agreed that the school should create a climate favorable to all religions, we also raised the question of whether or not the schools could expect religious groups to create a climate favorable to the schools. As a school superintendent, I would like to know what kind of attitude toward the schools we may expect in return.

DR. ADAMS: I would like to speak to that point, Mr. Chairman. It fell to my lot a couple of weeks ago to spend a long and very stimulating evening with a group of churchmen who were talking very seriously about developments in education, particularly about this reciprocal relationship of which you speak, Mr. Larson. They asserted that in the period from the end of the depression to the end of World War II the guiding philosophy of the schools and of society at large had been pretty much that of a logical positivism, but they were considerably encouraged with developments which they had heard about since World War II, which I would interpret to mean activities precisely along the lines of some of the things that have been discussed here.

This indicates to me that some progress has been made in cultivating the awareness of certain values which are not reducible to the precise dimensions of logical positivism. I was encouraged by their favorable interest, because usually when I am in the minority in the company of clerical people, all I hear in the course of the long conversation is critical and adverse comments concerning what the schools are not doing. I think there has been a development of a more favorable attitude on the part of clerical people with respect to a corresponding development in the schools.

FATHER McMANUS: I would like to comment immediately on Dr. Adams' remark by suggesting that perhaps he travels with the wrong clergymen most of the time. (Laughter)

I dare say that the clergy are conscious, as are other citizens, of the importance of the public school system in the United States, and I think that they would be the first to inform the lay public of their civic duty to lend not only financial but also moral support to the nation's public schools. And I dare say that their failure to do that in some instances is conspicuous only because it is an exception to a general rule.

There seemed to be an implication, however, in Mr. Larson's remark that perhaps some sort of deal would have to be negotiated whereby, in return for having a little more religion in the teaching of the Crusades, we would have a little more talk in the pulpit about better finances for the public schools. Although that is probably a crude way to interpret his remarks, I don't mean to be crude. I simply want to illustrate forcibly what might be inferred. I certainly do not think that the clergy, and I speak here only for the Catholic clergy, would be willing to enter into that kind of deal.

I think it is unfortunate that during the course of this conference we have not reminded ourselves often enough that this is essentially a conference on public education and religion in which we are trying to discover ways and means of enriching the public school program by bringing into it the riches that religion has to offer. I think that if we had given a little more attention to that approach, some of the evangelistic desire to do something for religion might not have been so prominent, and some of the fears that religion would be short-changed in the bargain might not have materialized.

MR. VARNER: I want to see if I can get something straight out of Mr. Larson's question, Mr. Pursinger's statement, and your remarks, Father McManus. The situation in Oregon, where Mr. Pursinger lives, might be improved if teachers could feel that the community would stand back of them when they teach these things correctly or even when they make a pretty bad boner. If a school system undertakes to carry out the recommendations of the Council's Committee on Religion and Education, can we expect the clergy and laymen of all faiths to stick by the schools and the individual teachers as they attempt this difficult task?

DR. WEST: That's a good question. To what extent can a teacher expect some community understanding of her effort to go along this line even if she makes a mistake? Will somebody jump down the superintendent's throat and say, "What kind of teacher do we have?" Or will the community understand that she is seriously trying to get somewhere with a difficult problem? I would like to hear Mr. Sebaly speak to this question.

MR. SEBALY: The American Association of Colleges for Teacher Education has been concerned with this problem. Our experience has been that teachers, by and large, handle their problems with tact. We have been working with fifteen colleges during the past four years. They have tried different things, and they have made some mistakes. At the same time we have had the cooperation of the various faiths throughout the United States, and I can say that without their support we would not have been able to go ahead.

I think that perhaps we are much further ahead than people think. We don't make any claims because we do not know the answer, but we do know that this problem can be worked on, and we do have a sympathetic audience with which to work. We are at the operational level and that is the place where these problems really confront the classroom teacher and the local community. Gerald Read, Eugene Dawson, and many other people can tell you that the problem is quite different at the operational level than it is at the theoretical level.

DR. DAWSON: I think that all of us would concur on this point that the difficulty seems to be on the operational level. We are sensitive to the gap between the level of insight and the level of actual operation.

I would like to speak to the question that Mr. Larson and Mr. West have raised here. I think rapport between the clergy and local school authorities varies from community to community. Nevertheless, I think it is remarkable that we do so well, nationally speaking. We are prone to be impressed by some of the traumatic experiences which we hear about from time to time but which are usually peculiar to the heterogeneous and heavily populated areas. By and large, however, I insist that the remarkable thing is that we do so exceedingly well.

In those situations where we do have some degree of tension, it is probably because of a multiplicity of factors. I suppose all of us are quite insecure at times emotionally. We are insecure in our respective positions as educators and as clerics. To the extent that we are insecure and withdraw into our own spheres and behave ostrichlike, we become suspicious of other groups. There are occasional misunderstandings between educators and clergymen. Clergymen alone aren't responsible for this. I think educators are inclined at times to be suspicious and egotistical. We have a kind of intellectual egotism, and clergymen at times have a kind of religiosity and piety; so we sometimes have difficulty getting together.

The remarkable thing is that we do so well, and we do well in those situations where both groups are working at the problem together. When we are getting along in this particular area, I think it is symptomatic of the fact that we are getting along pretty well in other areas in the community structure, too.

CHAIRMAN JONES: Any other comments or questions? Father Donovan.

FATHER CHARLES F. DONOVAN (School of Education, Boston College) : I address my question to Table II. The statement was made flatly that you deplore indoctrination in any form. I am sure you mean religious indoctrination. This happens to be an educational dispute also. Can we indoctrinate for democracy, for example?

DR. WEST: We are talking about religious indoctrination.

DR. KONVITZ: On this point, the committee thought, too, that we meant to include antireligious indoctrination. We objected to religious or antireligious indoctrination.

DR. HUNT: I would like to press the question which Father Donovan just raised as to the indoctrination. The word "religion" covers such a wide variety of things—morals, and ethics, and so on. Would that mean the public schools should not permit indoctrination for honesty? I would like to have that point cleared up.

DR. WEST: We made that clear when we pointed out the desirability of teaching the concepts that were approved by the Educational Policies Commission in their publication on the teaching of moral and spiritual values. What we are opposed to, because we think it is now impossible, is the teaching of religious sanctions of those character qualities which I think we would all favor. That was the distinction that we discussed at great length in the committee.

FATHER McMANUS: Dr. West, would the committee agree to the proposition in the NEA booklet that the children may be told that most people find their sanctions for moral behavior in religious beliefs?

DR. WEST: I cannot speak for the entire table. I think we would. I think that would be an accurate statement.

The General Problem:

What Is the Proper Relationship of Religion to Public Education?

The Next Decade of Research and Experimentation Relating to Religion and Public Education

EUGENE E. DAWSON

Dr. Dawson became president of Colorado Woman's College in June 1957. He was formerly dean of administration and students at Kansas State Teachers College, Pittsburg. In 1954–56 he served as national coordinator for the Teacher Education and Religion Project sponsored by the American Association of Colleges for Teacher Education. President Dawson holds degrees from Kansas State Teachers College, Boston University, and Harvard University, and has done postdoctoral work at the University of Chicago. He is a member of the Council's Committee on Religion and Education.

THOSE OF YOU who have been identified with research activities or who have at least become sensitive to the variegated elements of research, must understand something of the hesitancy and concern with which an assignment such as this is approached. This is so much more the case when the subject to be considered is within the context of religion in public education, and when those who have been commissioned to serve as critics are among the most impressive on the current scene. Perhaps the writer should take new courage in this, however, for surely you have cultivated the fine art of being charitable and tolerant and will overlook no opportunity to make substantial modifications when required.

Speaking of research, the writer is reminded of the words of C.

187

F. Kettering, who, as the top research man for General Motors, had this to say:

Research is a high-hat word that scares a lot of people. It needn't. It is rather simple. Essentially, it is nothing but a state of mind, a friendly, welcoming attitude toward change going out to look for change, instead of waiting for it to come. Research, for practical men, is an effort to do things better and not to be caught asleep at the switch. The research state of mind can apply to anything. Personnel affairs or any kind of business, big or little. It is the problem-solving mind as contrasted with the let-well-enough-alone mind. It is the composer mind, instead of the fiddler mind; it is the "tomorrow" mind, instead of the "yesterday" mind.

Would you not agree that one of the heartening inclinations at present is the disposition on the part of a larger number of people, in ventilating the problem of religion in public education, to aspire to the kind of climate depicted in these lines? It would be to underestimate the complexity of the problem to indicate that there are easy answers or simple solutions, but it does appear that people have a readiness to commit themselves to needed and healthy exploration and experimentation in this area. All of us would no doubt agree that there is an urgent need to develop a more critical and evaluative understanding toward the problems and possibilities in relating religion to public education.

To go immediately to the assignment at hand, the writer should like, at the outset, to focus attention on the area frequently described as the "factual study" of religion, or the "teaching about" religion approach, or again what is sometimes referred to as an attempt to teach the reciprocal relationship of religion to other elements in human culture, or still further, as an effort to deal with religious references in the curriculum as and when they are intrinsic to the study of subject matter. It will be recognized that such procedures were, in general, represented in the earlier inquiries and recommendations of the American Council on Education and are currently being given consideration by the American Association of Colleges for Teacher Education as well as by other agencies and school personnel. I would venture to say that during the next decade there should be and will be an extended interest in considering the possibilities and limitations embodied in this particular approach.

In view of this likelihood, I am inclined to think that one of the initial undertakings should be that of ascertaining as conclusively as possible the current status of the factual study of religion and about religion in our public schools. In traveling about the country and in conversing with educators, religious spokesmen, students, and citizens' groups, I am not convinced that one receives definitive answers to this question; but I am certain that no inconsiderable number of people are raising the question. I do not believe it is an overstatement to say that in one form or another it is being posed about as often as any other question, with perhaps one exception, that being, "What do you mean by religion?"

Recently the writer invited a number of scholars over the country, especially perceptive in this particular field of study, to indicate some of the needed research in religion in public education; and the need to study what is now being attempted in this respect was mentioned more than any other one thing. The reader might be interested in some of the representative replies which were related to this point.

Dr. Philip Jacobson of the American Jewish Committee, speaking personally, remarked,

I should like to see a fairly comprehensive study made of the ways in which schools now deal with religious references as and when they are (and should be) intrinsic to the study of subject matter—in the social studies, literature, art, music, etc. We could thus learn how teachers in the public schools now deal with questions of diverse institutional interpretations; the attitudes teachers bring to their discussion of controversial subjects concerning religion; the kinds of questions children ask and the ways in which such questions are treated; how, if at all, children are affected by such classroom discussions; and the extent of children's information about religion conveyed both as a result of textbook treatment of these areas of instruction and as a result of classroom discussion. Such a study might serve several purposes. It would spell out much more clearly than has yet been done what we need to do about providing factual information concerning religion in the public school curriculum; we might have enough information to prepare a suggested guide for teachers in the treatment of religious subject matter, somewhat along the lines of the Educational Policies Commission report on moral and spiritual values;[1] and the controversy over religion and public education would be seen in much clearer perspective.

The Very Rev. Msgr. William E. McManus, assistant director of the Department of Education of the National Catholic Welfare Conference, commented as follows:

I think that there is a great need to make some careful studies of textbooks used in the nation's public schools for the purpose of determining (a) whether they deal with the reciprocal relationship between religion and their particular subject and (b) whether they do so accurately. In other words, I think that some studies comparable to the Hazen Foundation's research on religion and higher education would be extremely valuable in the area of elementary and secondary education.

Dr. J. W. Maucker, president of Iowa State Teachers College, has responded in this way:

In my opinion, the first big job to do is to find out just what is the status of the teaching of religion and about religion in the public schools at the present time. The American Council on Education study was designed to accomplish this, but it received such a meager return on the inquiry forms that it seems to me the study provides an inadequate foundation for further research. All throughout the work of the Teacher Education and Religion Project of the American Association of Colleges for Teacher Education, we have been going on the assumption that teachers were failing to instruct students properly concerning the role of religion in human affairs because they were afraid to do so or because they were incompetent and, consequently, unable to do so, but this is still too much an area of assumption. We have not really demonstrated that point and nailed it down. Then, if the major hypothesis of the American Council study were confirmed, I think the next step would be to make detailed analyses of the factors that hamper teaching about religion, and analyses of the kind of helps that teachers and administrators need in the way of pre-service and in-service training, new instructional materials, the development of community relationships which will support teaching "about religion," etc.

It seems to me that the questions raised in the above paragraphs are substantial and must be considered before we take important "next steps" in the area of research. It is so easy to make assumptions and to engage in loquacity. There may or may not be an unusual degree of religious ignorance and illiteracy among our teachers and pupils. We would probably do well to determine this. Moreover, should we discover a sizable amount of religious illiteracy prevalent among our youngsters, we would want to make certain that it was due primarily to deficiencies in our school programs. There are some observers on the current scene who contend that pressures of recent years to introduce young people to "our religious heritage" have actually furthered rather than eliminated religious illiteracy. This, too, is something that we need to explore. Again, there are those who insist that school administrators and teachers are hesitant and fearful about treating religion in courses of study. All of us have read or have been told of unhappy situations in this respect, but we need a more adequate and extensive picture of such happenings and, in addition, of those instances where discreetly developed and implemented pedagogical efforts have not resulted in such traumata. Such research efforts may or may not indicate that we have been attempting too much, at least too much that is erroneous and unjust; but, at any rate, we need to discover this in a systematic way.

I should like to say that as we take a good look at the current situation, it would appear necessary to focus attention not only upon elementary and secondary schools but also upon schools of teacher education. If we are to face the future intelligently, we need a comprehensive picture of what is going on in each of these areas.

Now, what is it that we shall be searching for if we are to scrutinize the picture as it currently exists? Is it possible to spell out a bit more the concerns in such an effort? This is, indeed, a necessary precursor to any further action.

For one thing, we would be interested in those materials of a religious nature that are now being used for educational purposes—at all levels. What are the concepts that are most meaningful to students at the various levels? What methods have been designed to relate religion to the various disciplines? What textbook and reference materials and tests seem applicable at the various age levels? What outcomes in knowledge and attitudes have been realized through past and current efforts? What kinds of student-teacher and other interpersonal relationships have developed?

It would also be interesting to investigate the ways teachers belonging to different faith groups operate within the classroom, as well as those who belong to no group. Still further, what are the obstacles which are characteristically met in initiating a factual study of religion in the schools and what are the policies and procedures which are most effective in obviating these difficulties?

We would be interested in additional questions relative to the preparation of the teacher for such assignments. To what extent have teachers been given adequate preparation to teach such material with factual accuracy? What role does the factual study of religion seem to occupy in the professional education of teachers? Who appears to be assuming the most responsibility for this in our teacher education institutions?

Actually, I suppose, we have omitted up to this point, some of the basic questions with which the investigator would have to be concerned in grappling with the many questions raised in the preceding paragraphs. Before any appreciable amount of progress could be made in interpreting current conditions, there would have to be a clear understanding as to what is meant by the factual study of religion or the "teaching about" religion. Many will raise these questions and, in addition, will ask questions such as: (*a*) What do you mean by religion? (*b*) Does the teacher need to label subject matter as religious in order to be "teaching about" religion? (*c*) When is religion relevant to the subject matter? These are most important queries, and, of course, it would be of considerable value to determine what great numbers of teachers have to say about these matters and many more similar topics.

All this leads the writer to pose this question: What methods should be employed in obtaining the necessary representation of what has been attempted or is currently under way with respect to the factual study of religion within the context of public education? No attempt will be delineated here as far as any master design is concerned; but the writer is persuaded that if we are to stimulate a climate of scientific inquiry concerning the search for ultimate solutions to the many problems in this area, we must be receptive to the full use of scientific methods and tools of research. This may appear dilatory and tedious but it will prove rewarding. I should like to amplify, at least in a cursory fashion, some of the considerations that seem relevant.

How much do we know of the scholarly studies treating this general problem which have been conducted and developed as dissertations? They would not contain final answers or solutions but I am inclined to agree with J. Edward Dirks of Yale University, when he says, "I have particularly felt that there was undoubtedly material hidden away in doctoral dissertations in various places which deal with issues of religion in public education and which might possibly be brought to light in some coordinated way through a research project or through some type of publication." We are not thinking here, of course, only of doctoral dissertations but of any competent and scholarly research efforts. As we all know, such a procedure is taken seriously in all divisions of education and it would seem that the same should be in order here.

There is probably a place, too, for a careful analysis of existing textbooks at all levels and in all disciplines to determine the manner in which religion is treated. It will be recalled that in about 1950, Brubacher made such a study, the results of which were published in *College Reading and Religion* sponsored by the Hazen Foundation and the American Council on Education.[2] Dr. Herman E. Wornom, general secretary of the Religious Education Association of the United States and Canada, in calling attention to this contribution, has said:

With the great increase in concern about religion and public education since 1950, it would seem to me that a new study in the history and philosophy of education is warranted. It would seem to me, too, that attention should be given to textbooks in literature, history, the social sciences, home economics, etc. The concern should not be to see whether or not religion as a separate body of subject matter is covered in these textbooks, but as to whether religion where it naturally belongs in our cultural and literary heritage is adequately presented, and as to whether the treatment is objective, favorable or unfavorable.

Still further, how familiar are we with some of the recent investigations and projects in which the factual study of religion is given emphasis? One such effort which might be cited is the Teacher Education and Religion Project being sponsored by the American Association of Colleges for Teacher Education. Here again, the point is not that this is a project to end all projects or that definitive answers to our problems are going to be forthcoming from this activity, but it should be emphasized that data from this project, together with other resources, should provide interesting and valuable insights.

I should think, too, that with the cooperative assistance of research specialists, curriculum experts, persons in tests and measurements, and scholars in the behavioral sciences, as well as in religion, we should want to prepare rather elaborate instruments and procedures for widespread observations of classroom situations. Other devices would be interviewing of teachers, pupils, and others; the analysis of textbooks, course syllabi, and curriculum materials; and the compilation of data from case studies which may be available.

I fail to see at the moment how we can neglect any of these measures and still gain proper insight and knowledge of current practices and problems relative to the factual study of religion in public education. To proceed on this basis, would, among other things, require the cooperation of educators and school authorities; but I am inclined to feel that current interest in the problem is at a level which would make this possible on a rather comprehensive scale.

Let us assume, for the moment, that such an exhaustive study is carried out. Let us also speculate that, along with other findings, we should discover an ample need for further experimentation in the specific areas we have previously described. What then?

With the background of experience and study available, it would seem feasible to engage in experimentation in a way approximating the recommendations arising out of the previous study conducted by the Committee on Religion and Education of the American Council on Education.[3] It is the judgment of this writer that it would be difficult to improve on these recommendations for experimentation. I would suggest that not more than three experimental centers be selected, and it would probably be better to have only two. I would assume that at each center there would be cooperation on the part of the school system and the teacher education institution. Speaking of cooperation, I should like to emphasize that institutions selected for such a project should have a sincere desire to participate, and those schools accepting responsibility should pledge complete cooperation. This should not be the mere pledge of an ambitious and publicity-wise administrator, but it should be the pledge of a well-informed and highly motivated faculty. Such a project will need for its success genuine cooperation from school officials and teachers alike, as well as a readiness on the part of community groups. A thorough study of this situation should be made before pilot centers are selected. In concluding my emphasis of this point, I should like to quote from the American Council on Education's report:

In an undertaking of this character it should be understood, of course, that no individual, institution, or community should participate in any aspect of such activities unless or until there is sincere desire to do so. This problem is one which makes peculiarly imperative a scrupulous observance of the constitutional principle of religious liberty. One of the most important aims of such studies and experiments should be to learn how this principle can be applied to all—minorities and majorities alike.[4]

There is still another research possibility which might be cited at this juncture in that it bears some affinity to research consideration of the factual study of religion approach. It should be kept in mind that the factual study on the "teaching about" approach to religion is generally considered within the context of general education courses or regular courses within the various disciplines, and that references to religion are justified only to the extent that they are relevant to the subject matter at any given point. There are some who contend that such an approach accomplishes little in the way of giving youngsters a greater understanding of the role of religion in human affairs or in the preparation of teachers to teach the role of religion in human affairs. What is needed, they believe, are formal courses in religion where the major tenets of all the world's great religions are given emphasis. The proponents of such a position point to certain courses which are being offered over the country on both the secondary and college levels and suggest that these programs be emulated.

There are some educators and instructors who are inclined to be sympathetic with this position, not only because they feel it affords a more exhaustive treatment of the subject but also because they think it enables them to avoid having to consider "explosive" topics within their own courses. They can always say, "This is being treated in the department or course on religion." There are, likewise, some religious spokesmen of the various religious positions who have indicated interest in the possibilities of this plan. On the other hand, it should be pointed out that there are educators who see limited value in such a procedure. On the college level they sense that comparatively small numbers of students would find it possible to elect such courses, and on the secondary level they question if students are sufficiently mature to take such subjects.

Certain religious leaders have serious misgivings on these points, too. They question whether students are sufficiently mature on the secondary level and they are also dubious of the ability of teachers to teach such courses. They also question how "objective" many college instructors would be. They see serious social tensions arising out of any such attempt to teach religion.

We are not arguing the point one way or another—we are simply joining the ranks of a growing number of prominent educators and religious leaders who feel that some carefully developed experimentation and research might be conducted in this area. Admittedly, such a research design would have to be carefully formulated and there must never be any attempt at religious commitment of students. The only consideration should be that of determining if it is possible to teach the religions of the world objectively and what happens when this is undertaken. I should think that if we are willing to undertake a limited amount of research in connection with this problem, we might expect to emerge as somewhat more intelligent individuals regarding the matter than we have been up to this time.

As one gazes into the crystal ball and attempts the difficult assignment of predicting research trends over the next decade, there may be seen problems other than the ones given attention to this point. Delaying reference to them is not to indicate their unimportance. While they may not receive during the next ten years the consideration they merit, they should be included in our present discussion.

One of the areas in which research is needed is that which is frequently referred to as education in moral and spiritual values. Some may wish to raise the question as to the relevance of this matter in a paper dealing with the problem of religion in public education. Among other considerations, I suppose it is a matter of definition of terms. Be this as it may, the topic is included inasmuch as we regard it as one of importance.

As all of you know, procedures embodied in this particular approach have been given considerable attention over the last several years, especially since the report of the Educational Policies Commission. Workshops, conferences, numerous articles, and a variety of projects have developed. The writer is not aware of any comprehensive attempt at evaluating moral and spiritual programs, however, especially at the level which would afford anything approximating convincing results, one way or another. It is always possible that, as some have argued, such a program holds more promise within the context of public education than any other single effort. We need to experiment and evaluate more carefully than we have done thus far to find out. Some of the very questions we have raised relative to the factual study of religion need to be brought forth regarding this program, and the same emphasis needs to be given the importance of employing carefully refined tools of research.

Dr. William Clayton Bower has probably contributed as significantly as anyone else to the rationale and activities in moral and spiritual values, and in recent correspondence with the writer, he suggested the following items on which research and experimentation are urgently needed:

1. A functional, as distinguished from a theological, concept of religion. The school can and should take full account of religion as functionally understood, but should not deal with religion as theologically conceived. What is involved in a functional concept of religion?

2. Experiments in the development of moral and spiritual values, by the schools and churches in cooperation but as separate and autonomous institutions under the principle of the separation of church and state.

3. Analyses of the moral and spiritual value content of: (a) the subject matters of the curriculum and (b) the relations and functions of the school as a community of interacting persons.

4. Criteria and procedures for measuring the growth of persons in the perception and effective realization of moral and spiritual values.

5. Experiments in the incorporation of an emphasis upon moral and spiritual values into the program of teacher education institutions for the preparation of administrators and teachers, as well as the inclusion of this item in the certification of teachers.

I have made reference to these remarks of Dr. Bower, not because I concur with him on each point (particularly on his reference to the certification of teachers) but because he does point up some of the areas in which further research is needed.

Most of those who are actively and, perhaps, effectively engaged in current moral and spiritual values programs would welcome further experimentation and evaluation of their efforts. Certainly all of us need to have a clearer conception of what is meant by moral and spiritual values, the resources and materials available for dealing in such values, and how to resolve some of the thorny problems relative to sanctions.

There is still another problem which I believe deserves someone's responsible research concern during the next few years. I am not sure I know whose job it is, but I do know that if it is to be done, it will have to be assigned to someone who is not biased to begin with and who can thereby approach the assignment with the necessary objectivity. The problem to which I am referring is what is frequently termed "released-time" or "dismissed-time" religious education. While it is true that such programs are not the particular function or responsibility of the public schools, in most situations it cannot be said that school programs remain unaffected by them. Moreover, it is obvious that some of the objectives and activities of released-time projects are objectives and activities in which many of us have an interest. It is certainly not an overstatement to say that a considerable amount of money is being expended on such projects, to say nothing of the time and effort exerted in their behalf.

As we all know, there are some salient points which are being raised regarding this design of religious education, inquiries which merit research attention. I should like to make specific reference to some of the issues which have been recently advanced by certain thoughtful observers.

Dr. George H. Williams of Harvard Divinity School has issued this question:

Can we ascertain the extent to which teachers and the children of parents who are either neutral or negative about religion or who belong to a self-conscious religious minority (this will, of course, depend upon the neighborhood or region) do in fact, as it has often been alleged, suffer academically and socially from the released-time and kindred programs to bring children close to the public school instruction?

Dr. Simon Greenberg, of the University of Judaism, has said,

I believe that an important subject for research in the area of religion and public education at the present time would be that of measuring the effects of the various types of programs, involving the teaching of religion off the public school grounds but during hours usually set aside for the public school program. We should try to determine if there is some reliable way of doing it; the effect that this has had on the religious attitudes of the children and on their attitude to children of other faiths or those who did not participate at all in such religious instruction hours.

Dr. R. L. Hunt, executive director of the Department of Religion and Public Education of the National Council of Churches, sees the need for an inquiry concerning remedial defects which public school teachers see in operating programs of released time. He states,

It seems to work in some places and not in others. We as yet have no objective evidence as to what makes it work in some places and not in others. What can be learned from the experience of the public school teachers as they see these programs in operation?

Jordan L. Larson, superintendent of schools, Mount Vernon, New York, in an article in the *Phi Delta Kappan,* April 1955, made this comment:

Considerable experience is being accumulated in schools having policies of weekday released time. What results in religious literacy can be observed? in institutional loyalties? In objective terms, what differences can be noted between children who have this experience and those who do not? What differences exist in schools which have this policy and in schools which do not? Has not the time arrived when we should make an objective appraisal of the effectiveness of this program?

Many of the above questions now have the ring of familiarity about them. They have been chimed over and over again. The writer does feel, however, that such questions and comments are being heard with greater frequency and that the time has come for some systematic researches in this particular realm of activity, and that they should be conducted by persons free of emotional involvement or bias.

Before the termination of this article there are two points which I should like to underline. In the first place, it should be said that the research items treated in these comments represent only a few of the several that might have been listed. Those of you who have been close to this general problem over the years could easily extend the list. There are legal questions and court decisions, interesting and pertinent questions relative to Bible-reading in the classroom, religious practices and extracurricular programs of a religious nature, intercultural projects of varied forms, and many more fertile and timely research possibilities. However, in the opinion of the writer, the three general areas given emphasis in this presentation represent the more significant research needs as we look ahead for the next ten years, or perhaps much longer. I need not tell you that we are not expecting to see these problems completely resolved; rather, we are hopeful that productive explorations may be started so that we might at least experience some small gains or minor successes. As one views the prolific amount of research under way in all other areas of education—the sciences, the humanities, and the social studies—and in the various phases of teacher education, and the consequent gains in the discovery of new insights and skills in such disciplines, he cannot but speculate over possible outcomes if we were to free ourselves to attempt parallel research efforts in religion in public education. Can we afford to wait much longer?

My final point is this: As we continue to deal with the total problem of religion in teacher education and public education, we need to promote and facilitate a greater amount of communication, not only among representatives of all segments of education, but among educators and religionists, the laity and professionals, students and teachers. We need to converse with one another, to become more trustful, more understanding. I am not advocating tactical maneuvers and artful polemics, for such are not antidotes for substantial problems; rather we need more in the way of humble, honest, mature reasoning together. Let us be realistic, however. Better communication will not resolve all our differences and difficulties, but neither will the absence of such a climate of understanding represent a solution to the problem. If we are interested in this matter of "community," whatever the sanctions which may be related to it, a good place for us to begin is with ourselves. If we are really serious about this matter, and I think we are, then we have a real opportunity to implement our concern in our own personal lives as educators and religious leaders.

From the American Council report, to which I referred earlier, there is a further quotation with which I should like to close my remarks:

It would be a misunderstanding of the character and an underestimation of the complexity of the problem we face to assume that such a solution can be achieved easily or soon. Religion is too basic for human needs, too vital to man's potentialities, and too fundamental to education to yield to special study. To assume that a solution cannot be achieved is to evidence a lack of faith in the resourcefulness of the American people. A major part of the problem, we think, is the achievement of a fuller understanding on the part of the people at large of the inherent limitations with respect to religion, under which the tax-supported educational institutions must operate.[5]

DISCUSSION BASED ON DR. DAWSON'S PAPER

Presiding: GALEN JONES

CHAIRMAN JONES: Today's discussion is a logical continuation and climax to all our previous discussions. In effect, we will take a look into the future and make some recommendations to the Council's Committee on Religion and Education. The last paper focuses our attention on the next decade of research and experimentation relating to religion in public education.

DR. DAWSON: I have endeavored to point up in my paper three general areas of research concern. I do not pretend, of course, that this is an exhaustive list at all.

The first area of concern that I pointed to in this paper is the one that we generally refer to as the "teaching-about-religion" or the "factual study-of-religion" area. It generally involves discovering and developing reciprocal relationships between religion and various disciplines in education. One of the most frequently raised questions in this area is the question: Aren't we doing this at the present time? Haven't we been doing it all along? Inasmuch as this question is asked so often, this seems to be a fertile area for research. One of the initial undertakings should certainly be that of discovering what we are doing currently.

We need to employ scientific procedures, and we need to create a climate that is conducive to scientific investigation if we intend to find accurate answers to this particular question. If we discover a need after an investigation of this kind, then I should think that it would be in order to engage in a limited amount of research to discover the best ways to teach about religion within the context of education. As I pointed out in my paper, a good deal of the discussion and ferment in this particular area of teaching-about-religion, revolves around general education courses, courses in the humanities, social studies, and the natural sciences, and so on. Some persons suggest the possibility of teaching about religion wherever it is intrinsic to the subject matter; others suggest the possibility of inaugurating courses in comparative religion and courses of this kind. Each suggestion seems to have limitations and possibilities. All I am saying here is that perhaps once again we need to observe closely and scientifically some of the experiments that may be under way in this area in future years.

The second general area of research concern that I have discussed in this paper is moral-and-spiritual-values education. Here again, I feel there are many unanswered questions, there is a lot of talk, a lot of activity, but a minimum of scientific findings. It seems to me that we need to make the same effort to obtain reliable information in this area, too.

The third area to which I have alluded in this paper may not be considered by some of you to be within the context of public education. Yet, as I tried to point out, because of its implications, because it cannot be completely divorced from our concerns and our experiences in public education, I feel it is relevant to my topic. It is the area of released-time education. We have a concern, it seems to me, with what is taking place or what isn't taking place in connection with released-time education. The quotes that I have used in the paper point up some of the current questions that are being asked with increasing frequency these days. Once more, I think research might make us somewhat more intelligent as we think in terms of the possibilities and the limitations in this particular area.

I do not expect complete resolution of the problems in these three areas to which I have referred, but I do hope for a series of small gains that will enable us to make wise decisions. Those of you who are familiar with the prolific amount of research being done in education these days must be impressed by the very limited amount of real research that is being done in the field of religion and public education. Likewise, you must be conscious of the great possibilities of this kind of research.

Finally, I want to mention in this cursory overview of my paper that this conference reflects an important trend, a new sensitivity and interest in this whole general area. It is good for educators and religionists to communicate with one another as they are doing here. Better communication, however, must await the discovery of better information.

MR. DePOISTER: Dean Dawson, I would be interested to know how one might measure the desirability of released-time programs in school. In other words, how would one measure the results to ascertain whether they are desirable or undesirable? What is the procedure by which one might learn that this is a good program to continue to intensify? We have a released-time program in the community where I live. I have some personal doubts about its desirability and some misgivings about the amount of money we are spending on it. Would you have anything to say about how we might measure the results?

DR. DAWSON: I haven't any complete design as to procedures. I am concerned with the questions, as you are, concerning the value of a program of this kind. What is happening to the youngsters? Are they becoming increasingly literate religiously? Are their attitudes changing? What is happening to youngsters who may be considered neutral or even antagonistic to the program? What is happening to the parents? What methods are being used by teachers in released-time religious education that might be improved and strengthened? What suggestions should be made to persons who are working in this particular area? There are many instruments and procedures that might be used to throw some light on these questions. I am confident that we can devise specific procedures that would yield genuinely useful results.

MR. WORNOM: Dr. Dawson, in your paper you suggest the study of textbooks to determine how religion is actually treated therein. Do you think it would be desirable to go beyond that study later and have a committee of textbook writers and others decide what might be done? Would it be valuable, for example, to have some kind of resource book that would document and illustrate the relevance of religion in teaching, let us say, American history at the elementary and secondary levels? Such a book might also serve as a guide for textbook writers and those who adopt textbooks. If it proved useful in the field of history, perhaps a similar book could be written for other disciplines?

DR. DAWSON: At one point in my paper I mentioned the possibility of developing a handbook or a manual such as you suggest. Teachers who are conscious of these problems but do not hold theological degrees feel that a manual or a book of this kind would be helpful. I think this might be a natural outgrowth of a textbook study. I was interested that some of the tables, including my own, spent some time on that possibility yesterday.

MR. SASSCER: There are some changes taking place in our American society that are being documented by David Riesman and William White, among others. If we don't take these into account when we conduct an experiment and do research in religious education, we may pat ourselves on the back for something which is merely the result of other factors in the changing social scene. I think we need to take these larger factors into account, and I don't see this point emphasized too much in your paper.

DR. DAWSON: I think that Mr. Sasscer has certainly emphasized an important point; however, I think that we have been mindful of this. In spite of an apparent religious resurgence, we still find a great deal of religious illiteracy, and I don't believe there is too much danger of attributing possible results in overcoming this illiteracy to the wrong cause.

MR. PFEFFER: What confuses me about the three areas of research is that they have completely different goals.

It startles me that released-time is even mentioned in this conference and under these circumstances. In what capacity are we here? Are we here as religionists or are we here as educationists?

Teaching about religion involves a completely different aim and objective. As part of the educative process of learning the forces in society and in history, it is undoubtedly within the competence of the public school system. However, if one is honest and committed to intellectual integrity, he doesn't approach this area with a preconceived notion, even of reverence; he doesn't approach it with a preconceived notion that it will come out well. It is conceivable that an honest and objective study of the force of religion in history may bring us to a Marxist conclusion or the conclusion of the Communists that it is not good, that it is an opiate for the people, and that it is an unfortunate and an evil power in history. In testing the effectiveness of teaching about religion, the objective is not to find out whether the pupils have been religiously committed but to discover to what extent they know, appreciate, and are cognizant of the forces of religion, good or bad, in history.

Finally, moral and spiritual values are a completely different area. Here the objective is to influence conduct and character. Religion may be relevant or irrelevant, but it is not the objective. It might very well be that one would find the best way to improve ethics and character is to divorce a person from religion completely. That is a possibility. At least, one should not have the preconceived notion that religion is necessary and desirable for that purpose.

So these are three disparate approaches, the first of which I do not think belongs in this conference. The second and third may or may not involve the commitment which seems to be assumed here.

DR. DAWSON: Mr. Chairman, I would like to say just this in reply to the speaker. I tried to make clear that these were three separate categories, each of which has really no relation to the other as far as I am concerned.

It may be that the released-time program is beyond the scope of this conference. We have religionists and educators here; so I thought it was not entirely irrelevant to this subject. If it is a waste of time to discuss it, then I submit that most of the first evening and most of your discussion, sir, which related to Terry McCollum, was irrelevant.

MR. PFEFFER: I think so.

DR. DAWSON: In the second place, regarding the teaching-about-religion approach, your contention is that we must be objective and have no predispositions. Well, when one engages in scientific investigations he should have no presuppositions, no serious biases. At least he must strive to be reasonably objective. I have tried to say this in my paper. I am not for or against this approach. I just don't know. I am interested, as I think some of you are, in finding out.

It may be that you are right, as I have also said in my paper, that religion has no significant role to play in moral-and-spiritual-values education. That is one of the big debates. All I am saying is: Let's try to find out.

CHAIRMAN JONES: It is unfortunate that I cannot recognize a number of you who want to speak now, but I think you will have that opportunity in the table discussions that follow.

Table Reports and Discussion

O<small>N</small> THE FINAL day of the conference, the table groups were asked to consider the following questions which, in a very real sense, reflect the main purpose of the conference: (1) To what extent does the group agree with the policies and recommendations of the Council's Committee on Religion and Education? (2) In what ways, if any, should the committee's published reports be amended? (3) What type of research and experimentation should be undertaken by the Council's Committee on Religion and Education?

TABLE I REPORT

Chairman: JAMES L. HANLEY
Recorder: HARRISON SASSCER

Table I addressed itself exclusively to one aspect of the Council committee's present position on the teaching of religion in the public schools, namely, whether or not public schools should commit themselves to a theistic position. Most of the group felt that public schools should not be formally committed to such a position. On the other hand, it was argued that there are far too many public school systems which, in the absence of policy statements from responsible educational bodies, take a position of indifference toward religion. A substantial minority expressed concern lest the public schools be subjected to adverse criticism in the absence of a more explicit statement from the Council's committee on the attitude of public education toward religion.

It was agreed that, as an agency concerned with the whole development of the child, the public school should not be indifferent to the religious growth of the child. Positively speaking, this seemed to mean that the child should be free to study religious events and facts as they are found in our history and in our present culture. Negatively, this seemed to mean that the school should never permit itself to become the means whereby any child is discouraged from adhering to the beliefs of his parents.

The majority of the table members believed that the public schools should not commit themselves further in this direction lest there be an infringement on the religious freedom of teachers and children. Some of the group expressed concern that commitment of the public schools to a theistic position might hasten an already detectable trend to substitute an amalgam of vaguely defined religious notions for positive religious convictions.

With regard to the research and experimentation to be encouraged by the Council's committee, the table felt that it had suggested in its previous report at least two projects that would assist both in the evaluation of progress to date as well as in the development of new approaches in the classroom. The suggested projects were a survey of teaching materials to determine their effectiveness in presenting religious questions as they arise in the subject matter and a historical survey of religion in American life and culture.

The table expressed hope that more publicity would be given to the results now being obtained in such experiments as the AACTE project on religion in teacher education. It was felt that particular attention should be given to the effectiveness with which teachers participating in such projects are able to apply their special experience in the communities they serve.

Finally, the group expressed approval of the proposal by Dr. Dawson for establishing experimental centers where teaching about religion can be introduced in public education. Two qualifications were urged by some members of the group: (1) that religious authorities be consulted in developing such programs, and (2) that such programs below the senior high school level be planned with much special caution.

TABLE II REPORT

Chairman: ROSCOE L. WEST
Recorder: DUMONT F. KENNY

Table II is on record as agreeing with the policies and recommendations of the Committee on Religion and Education. The existence of
influential religious institutions in our American society is a fact de-
serving just as unbiased study as the investigation of any other factual
area. There may be a presupposition in the minds of religiously
motivated educators that religion is an enriching value, but the factual study of religious factors does not necessarily imply that we
must prejudge whether religious influences are good or bad until the
evidence is examined. We are concerned about any situation that
tolerates a general illiteracy, including religious illiteracy; hence, we
support the committee's proposals. Fundamental research to find out
what is happening in our American communities in the area of
religion and public education is a legitimate and necessary endeavor.

In general, we believe that the establishment of a center to assess
what is being done in American communities and to study what could
be done in one or more selected communities in line with the committee's recommendations is feasible and desirable. We suggest that
the Committee on Religion and Education re-examine its reports in
the light of recent developments to ascertain whether its concepts
are broad enough, whether high school courses in comparative religion
are possible, and whether it might not be wise to set up priorities for
needed research projects. We recommend that the Council publish a
bibliography of research in this area including relevant doctoral dissertations. We recommend the distribution of bibliographies and sum-
maries published by the National Council of Churches of Christ and
other religious bodies. We underscore the importance of a good research design and the committee's responsibility in this regard. We
wish to point out that one of the reasons we have such a paucity of
empirically formulated research in this area is the difficulty inherent
in the quest. The peculiarities of research in this field should not be
overlooked or minimized. Hence, Table II feels that research projects
should be designed for particular objectives, should make full use of
all community resources, and should not overlook the suggestions and
findings in available published materials. In this connection, we call

special attention to the current issue of the *Journal of Social Issues* devoted to "Religious Conflict," Professor Loewenberg's proposal advocating research in the field of religious history, the findings of the Lilly Foundation survey of the Indianapolis school and community developments on the value of released-time activities, a forthcoming publication of the National Conference of Christians and Jews, and the result of a symposium of interesting and outstanding American scholars, "Research in Interreligious Relations." In selecting communities for experimental action research, we believe care should be taken to choose situations which represent a variety of social, ethnic, industrial, and religious conditions.

In line with the approach taken in the 1947 report of the Committee on Religion and Education, Table II makes a distinction between the factual study of religion and the teaching of moral and spiritual values in the public schools. While recognizing the importance of the latter area, the group prefers to give the former area first priority.

The group agrees with the following statement from the 1947 committee report concerning responsibility for research in the area of released-time religious education:

Finally, the appraisal of weekday religious education in terms of actual results is primarily the responsibility of those conducting it, not of the public schools. The community, however, has an obligation to determine whether its merits are such as to justify its maintenance as a joint enterprise within the community involving cooperation of the public schools and the churches and synagogues. This will involve scrutiny of standards as to teaching personnel, curriculum and equipment, as well as an appraisal of relationships between public and religious schools.

This whole matter of religious education on released time has attained such proportions that it calls for thorough study and evaluation. However, we repeat that the released-time program is not directly related to the problem with which this report is concerned. We are addressing ourselves to the responsibility of the schools in their own right, and in relation to their own program.[1]

Finally, the group emphasizes the importance of good communication and community preparation for the many intergroup problems which the launching of any research projects will entail. Even with the finest motives, fears and misunderstandings are bound to arise in our culturally pluralistic society. The necessity of involving all community resources in the planning process and in the execution of a project should not be overlooked. Public and parochial school officials, clergy of all denominations, and leaders of community organizations should be included in the planning.

TABLE III REPORT

Chairman: PAUL H. VIETH

Recorder: ISAAC FRANCK

Table III first turned its attention to Dr. Dawson's paper and the problems involved in research in the field of religion and public education. The group distinguished between measurable, quantitative aspects of religious knowledge and qualitative aspects which cannot be measured. It noted that religion itself has more than just a quantitative dimension. It also noted that it is not possible to measure a person's participation in the supernatural life of God since this is a qualitative matter, which is not susceptible to measurement. The group was unanimous in agreeing that any research in this field should take this distinction into account. Some members expressed serious doubt even about the possibility of measuring attitudes accurately in the field of religion. They pointed out that attitude-testing in this field certainly cannot consist simply of paper-and-pencil tests and that it would require depth interviewing and other complex techniques. In general, the group agreed on the need to use the most effective research techniques available in any investigation undertaken in this field.

The group then turned its attention to a consideration of the present position of the Council's Committee on Religion and Education. It was noted that there have been pressures on the Council to go beyond its present position and to recommend a theistic commitment as a goal for public education. It was noted also that the Council has been criticized from the other direction for having gone too far in recommending the inclusion of religious facts intrinsic to ordinary subject matter since this, allegedly, opens the door to religious indoctrination in the public schools. Some members of the group favored the goal of theistic commitment for the public schools; others voiced strong opposition to such a goal, both on constitutional and educational grounds. It was noted that some public school systems have a theistic commitment at the present time. Fear was expressed that a trend in this direction might eventually lead to the establishment of a first-class citizenship for those believing in God and a second-class citizenship for those who do not believe in God.

After considerable discussion, it was proposed that the group express its approval of the committee's present position favoring the inclusion in the public school curriculum information about religion when it is intrinsic to the regular subject matter and favoring by such inclusion the encouragement of students to move to deep and significant personal commitments (as stated on page 54 of the 1947 report[2]) and to a respect for the commitments of others. This was *unanimously accepted,* with the suggestion that more effective work and materials along these lines be encouraged.

Finally, in view of the present concern of many school systems about the question of a theistic base for teaching moral values and religious information, it was proposed that the American Council on Education make a study of the extent of this phenomenon and of the rationale given for it. This proposal was unanimously accepted.

TABLE IV REPORT

Chairman: HERBERT L. SEAMANS
Recorder: MAX BIRNBAUM

Table IV decided to discuss first proposals for research and study. The members agreed on the need for the following projects:

1. To develop resource materials on various religions for the use of secondary school teachers;
2. To discover the extent to which graduates of public schools and graduates of religious schools differ in religious literacy;
3. To determine the points at which references to religion and religious institutions are intrinsic to the public school curriculum and, therefore, necessary for the general education of the child;
4. To conduct historical research that will enable secondary and elementary teachers to understand better and to communicate more clearly the impact of religion on American history;

5. To examine current textbooks and practices to determine, subject by subject, what references to religion and religious institutions are actually made in the public schools today;

6. To learn how teachers actually deal with controversial questions having to do with the Reformation, the church as a community force, etc.;

7. To ascertain if there are significant differences in the ways in which teachers of different faiths and different denominations handle controversial issues;

8. To discover at what age and grade levels and in what units of work children usually ask questions of religious significance and, further, to discover the effect of classroom discussion on such children (that is, whether the discussion promotes an appreciation of religious diversity, cultivates a climate of freedom, or tends to encourage divisiveness).

In addition to these proposals for research and study, Table IV offered the following suggestions:

1. It was suggested that the word "experimentation" not be used with reference to the public school system lest it create misunderstandings and poor public relations.

2. It was suggested that the need for research not be used as a justification for doing nothing or for slowing down present work.

3. It was suggested that the Council use its good offices to stimulate research recommended by this conference through university resources.

TABLE V REPORT

Chairman: WILLIAM E. McMANUS
Recorder: A. L. SEBALY

Table V made the following recommendations in three areas of research:

1. It recommended a survey of elementary and secondary textbooks which are now in use in public schools to determine how references to religion are made. The group recommended that the books at the secondary level (grades seven through twelve) be done first and further recommended that priority be given to subjects in the following order: (1) world history, (2) American history, (3) the human-

ities area (literature, English, foreign language, etc.), and (4) science.

The group decided that a survey of world history textbooks should be given first priority at the secondary level because the major world faiths are included in a study of world history, because we are pressed as a people as we have never been before to know about other peoples in the world, because more Americans are going abroad than ever before, and because the field of American history apparently has been surveyed more adequately than world history. These conclusions do not preclude a later survey of American history textbooks; they merely express a desire to establish a priority.

2. The group recommended that the Council's Committee on Religion and Education commission a scholar to publish a historical study of the religious influences in American life.

3. The group recommended immediate consideration of ways and means to activate the experiment described in the Council's 1953 publication, *The Function of the Public Schools in Dealing with Religion,* in the chapter on "Recommendations," item A.[3] The group felt that the Committee on Religion and Education should seek a community situation in which this recommendation could be implemented now.

The group also discussed at some length the advisability of preparing a teachers manual to point out religious influences in American history; however, the consensus was that the manual probably would not be used partly because teachers have too many special manuals already.

Finally, the group discussed the feasibility of preparing a manual with suggested religious references for the guidance of textbook writers and book companies. The members were divided in their opinions about this proposal. The consensus was: "If in the judgment of the Council's Committee on Religion and Education such a proposal is practical, the project should be carried out."

DISCUSSION BASED ON TABLE REPORTS

Presiding: F. ERNEST JOHNSON

CHAIRMAN JOHNSON: We come now to our final session. We have the five reports before us, and they are open for discussion. It is not easy and perhaps not desirable to structure a discussion of this sort. I will ask you only to consider priority among the things you would like to say and to bear in mind the fact that you are now speaking to the American Council's Committee on Religion and Education. The committee will be in session shortly and will take very serious and respectful account of what is said.

MR. FRANCK: Mr. Chairman, there seems to be a disagreement between the recommendation of Table III on the one hand and of Table V on the other with respect to the need and usefulness of a handbook. I wonder whether that might not be discussed a little more. I don't recall how many classroom teachers were in our group, but there were educators who are on the educational firing line, and many of them thought that it would be useful to develop a handbook of religious information that is intrinsic to the public school curriculum. I would be interested to learn the reasons why Table V thought otherwise.

CHAIRMAN JOHNSON: Do you want to speak to that, Father McManus?

FATHER McMANUS: I doubt that I can say much more than the report, Isaac. The majority of the group was convinced that the teachers would not make use of a detailed manual of this kind. Hence, they felt that the committee would be engaging in a futile endeavor if it developed a handbook.

They also felt that the survey of textbooks, which was part of their recommendation, would necessarily require the development of certain criteria and guides that could be used not only by the people writing textbooks, but also by others—for example, classroom teachers—who were particularly interested in this problem.

MR. PURSINGER: I don't believe any workbook has ever come under attack. As teachers in the public school, we are trusted to teach about labor unions, the National Association of Manufacturers, and other things. We are trusted to have special materials on our shelves, and most of us use them. Personally, I would find use for this type of manual. Developing a handbook is quite different from putting something into the textbook where everyone is a self-appointed authority to examine it.

If we are going to achieve anything, it will have to be done through the teacher anyway. For this reason, I personally endorse the idea of developing a teachers manual.

DR. READ: From the standpoint of teacher education, there is another consideration. It may be that the teachers on the job would be too busy to use this handbook, but those who train teachers might be able to use it very effectively.

DR. KRUG: I would like to pursue this discussion a little bit further. I have worked on several state curriculum programs in which a lot of these special materials were distributed. We know a great many of them were not used.

If the purpose of this particular manual were to try to get more teachers to teach about religion, I think that it would be ineffective. On the other hand, it would be of great help to those teachers who now do and want to teach about religion. I don't know how many such teachers there are, but those who want to do this, I believe, would use it and welcome it.

A manual that contained important information in resource unit form with activity and other suggestions would be helpful. For example, it could be used through such organizations as the National Council for the Social Studies. The various state councils would, I think, make good use of it and get it to a number of teachers who would also make good use of it.

We should not expect to get 100 percent of the teachers to use this material; nevertheless, we are inclined, I think, to underestimate the number who would make use of it.

SISTER MARY JANET: In listening to this discussion, I believe that the two table groups were not talking about the same kind of manual. In Table V, we were talking about a handbook that would correspond almost to a syllabus for teaching history and that would give full place to important religious connections. We agreed that city school systems in most states already have such syllabi, which is what the teachers follow. The manual recommended by the other group sounds quite different to me and seems to me, as a practical classroom teacher, to have more merit than the one about which we disagreed in Table V.

FATHER McMANUS: I bear that out, Mr. Chairman. It was the consensus of Table V that it was considering the type of manual described by the Sister.

MR. WALTER R. CLEMINSON (Principal, Grosse Pointe High School, Michigan): A manual means different things to different people. It was also our feeling that a manual would not be used by a great many people, just as libraries are not used by a great many people. However, there would be many superintendents, who have studied this problem and attended such conferences as this, who would like to inform their boards of education and others as to what is taking place. Superintendents could make tremendous use of such a pamphlet. Of course, the teachers could use parts of it or not as they wished.

DR. KONVITZ: I think recommending a manual that singles out religious facts would be contrary to a great deal of the discussion that has taken place up to now. It would put the matter in a different orientation altogether. I thought we were interested in seeing to it that religious facts, where germane, would be incorporated into history texts. That is a totally different thing from preparing a manual which would give the appearance that a pressure group is trying to have a point of view represented. I favor the line of thought that I felt had been developed up to this point, that is, thinking of religious facts as being organic within American history and being natural and germane within a larger context. The singling out of religious facts, I think, would do violence to a great deal of the thought that has been developed.

DR. VIETH: That is not intended.

DR. KONVITZ: We are talking about a manual of religious facts, are we not?

DR. VIETH: I think Father O'Leary would clear it up.

FATHER O'LEARY: As I understood the mind of the group, we favored a teacher's resource unit that would include religious materials germane to the teaching of American history.

DR. READ: Right.

RABBI SCHAFLER: In the last paragraph of the Table I report, I want to call your attention to a clause which calls for consultation with religious authorities which I believe is desirable and necessary. Based on a specific experience that I have had, I think it is important to have religious authorities as normally constituted authorized by the public board of education. I speak from experience in this matter. A director of a particular tax-supported institution consulted with the religious leader of her own faith and then informed the religious leaders of other faiths. This was assumed to be consultation. So I feel that, as a safeguard, such a group should be duly constituted by the leading authorities supervising the public school system in that particular area.

DR. KONVITZ: Could I ask a question? Why should the religious authorities be consulted at all? If it is a question of history and if it is a question of setting up an experiment in education which is related to history, why consult them?

RABBI SCHAFLER: I think it is desirable to consult specialists with various competencies in working up a curriculum or a course of study that has to do with molding our children.

CHAIRMAN JOHNSON: There is a point here it is well to underline. We do agree, do we not, that our public schools belong to the community? They do not belong to the state in the first instance. They are subject to state control, but they belong to the people. The American idea is to have just as much local control of education as is possible. If that is the democratic requirement, then consideration has to be taken at every point of the public reaction. We found years ago in Tennessee that the people insisted on being consulted even about biology. While it may be unfortunate, there doesn't seem to be any quick way to overcome even the most obscurantist opposition.

DR. KONVITZ: But should Tennessee be the pattern for the rest of the United States?

CHAIRMAN JOHNSON: A few years ago, a university president wrote a very informing little book entitled *Render unto the People.*[4] He was very much distressed over the Scopes trial, but he said that we have to recognize that, if we intend to be democratic, we have to let the people govern themselves. He said that the final consideration is what the people want. If we are not satisfied with that, we have to help the people to want something else, but we cannot actually abrogate their rights. Well, this is controversial, to be sure.

FATHER MCCLUSKEY: I think it is a question really of the acceptance by the public. I think that no group, either our own or any similar body, can come up with ideas which will always be acceptable to everybody and impose these ideas upon the people's schools. The ultimate criterion for the success of any program, whether it involves religious literacy or religious commitment, directly or indirectly is its acceptance by the parents of the children.

I think it is unsafe to begin with a doctrinaire policy statement by a group. I think we have to begin, as this whole movement seems to me to have begun, with the dissatisfaction of large segments of American society with some of the postwar trends in our education, and I think that the supreme criterion of success must be the acceptance by parents of the children involved. For this reason, I think it is absolutely necessary that religious groups which are recognized and delegated by the parents to watch over their children should have a place in the development of such a program. I think if we do anything else, we are making the tail wag the puppy. This is a responsibility which ultimately and primarily rests with the parent.

DR. LOEWENBERG: Mr. Chairman, I should like respectfully to dissent from Father McCluskey's view as I did in the table discussion. I think it is a very dangerous principle to state the proposition the way he did. Public education involves a reciprocal relationship, and his principle implies that in certain areas one part of the contract has greater emphasis than the other. It seems to me that we in America got into a great deal of trouble after the war on questions of academic freedom because communities exerted too much influence and thus suborned the right of faculties and school systems to make their own judgments in the areas where they had supreme competence, namely, the area of determining who is qualified to teach.

MR. DePOISTER: It is very important that we ascertain on every occasion the feeling of the constituents of the public because, after all, it is the children of the people of the community who go to the schools and are affected by what they learn.

However, we are not talking about general public relations; we are talking about writing textbooks in history and social studies, perhaps literature, but particularly history. In this matter what would the public have to offer? A historian would not inquire from a Republican or a Democrat, "What would you like for me to write about your party?" If he writes in an objective, honest fashion, neither party should have objection. The same applies to the area of religion. If the historian deals with his subject objectively and honestly, he may want to consult somebody as an individual, but not as a representative of a particular religious group.

DR. KONVITZ: I want to say something relating to what Father McCluskey said. I must say that I am very greatly startled by the idea of consulting parents and people in the community generally about matters which are in my competence or Father McCluskey's competence. I had no idea that the church schools with which he is identified consult parents as to what the teachers are required to teach and how they shall teach. The parents need to be told by people who have more competence in the field of education what needs to be put into a curriculum and how it needs to be done.

I belong to a similar denomination, and I feel that there are people competent to tell me how my child should be educated. It seems to me that public school authorities need to educate the public on the rightful role and authority of the public school teacher. Only in this way can they build up the dignity and the position of the public school teacher. I can see why we would want to consult parents when there is a public-relations problem. I wouldn't, however, set them up as a board of censors or give them any idea that I must submit to their approval.

If they come to me in a difficult situation, it is my duty to explain, but do I have to go to them when what I am doing falls within my competence and not within their competence?

CHAIRMAN JOHNSON: Let's be clear about this. It does seem to me that this is an important problem, although a rather difficult one. It arises in two connections, does it not? First, there is the question whether a particular subject shall be included in the curriculum; then, if and when it is included, there is the question of how it is to be treated. Is it useful to make a distinction between these two questions? Broadly speaking, we recognize the right of the community to have something to say about the introduction of the subject matter. After the decision is made, we expect the scholars, the experts, to be permitted to devise the curriculum and to teach it.

For instance, has the public, has the community anything properly to say about whether or not there shall be sex education in the school? What would you say to that?

MISS THOMPSON: We have a law in Pennsylvania which requires sex education.

CHAIRMAN JOHNSON: Do you care to say whether you approve making that subject a matter of legislation?

MISS THOMPSON: Frankly, I haven't thought much about it. It simply is.

MR. SASSCER: I think we should not get into a discussion of law and the local control of schools. I hope we do not. I think, Mr.

Konvitz, you are concerned lest some parent storm into the superintendent's office and say, "By golly, you will teach this and that." He may insist, "I am a parent and a member of the community, and we have local control of our schools, and therefore you will teach it." This would be no more likely to happen than it would be for an irate parent of a Cornell student to tell you he didn't want you to teach Marxism. You are responsible to your board. Ultimately your board can tell you not to teach certain things.

DR. KONVITZ: I am not a peddler of ideas. I do not ask anybody's permission as to what I should teach and how I should teach. I make that decision.

MR. SASSCER: Because the board of Cornell University has made the decision that you should do it.

DR. KONVITZ: No.

MR. SASSCER: I am sorry, but I do not think there is a single schoolteacher or administrator in this room or anywhere else who is going to go far beyond what he has explicit sanction for from his community or from the community as it is represented on his board, which represents the community. At least, he will not go far beyond that without due consultation.

You may say this is undue control of academic freedom. Be that as it may, he will not go, as a practical matter, very far beyond where he thinks he can take the community with him. He may consult the board or he may consult responsible leaders within the community who are on the board. This is what local control of schools means, that you have legally constituted agencies in the locality which direct the school, and there isn't any superintendent or principal who will go beyond that.

FATHER MCMANUS: I think it might be very useful if in the remaining minutes we could invite from the group here some comments on the type of research that the committee this afternoon will want to recommend for the future, particularly the suggestions that were made on research in the textbooks and this rather ambitious experimental project to which our committee is committed.

CHAIRMAN JOHNSON: If there is no objection, we will move to that. What is your evaluation of the various suggestions made with respect to research? Who wants to speak to that?

SISTER MARY JANET: Dr. Johnson, I should like to say an additional word in favor of the project described on pages 86–88 of the Council's last report.[3] I am one of the people who had a copy of the book. I bought it when it first came out, not as a result of this conference, and I read it with great interest, especially the outline of that experiment. The point I think is of particular sigfinicance is that it is related to teacher education. I believe the key to success in the projects in which we are all interested is the teacher.

DR. HUNT: The American Association of Colleges for Teacher Education has a project in which fifteen teacher-training institutions are making pilot studies, each one initiating its own program. It is just possible that in the years that have elapsed one of those fifteen pilot schools may have undertaken a project which would be regarded as duplicating the proposal. I would like to ask Dr. Sebaly if he feels that any one of the fifteen institutions have done a project which is equivalent to this.

MR. SEBALY: None of the fifteen institutions has attempted a full-scale project like that outlined on pages 86–88 in the 1953 report, but some have approached it in general principle. I would say that in my experience in working with the colleges, that there may have been some fear or difficulty in 1953 or 1954 in trying to get an institution or community to undertake this, but I think at the present time the American Council probably would find many colleges and communities willing to attempt it. We have not done it. We haven't had the money or the resources to go ahead, but we are approaching that particular stage. I think that the project is quite feasible. Although it will require a lot of money, I think one can find communities receptive to this point of view. Until we get to the classroom, to the community, and to the teacher, much of our discussion is rather valueless because it has not been tested on a practical plane.

CHAIRMAN JOHNSON: The committee will go into session very shortly, and this will be one of the matters with which it will deal.

I am not going to make any summary. I will say only that I am greatly pleased with this conference, and I feel that it will make an important contribution to the planning of the work of the committee. Now I know you want to hear a word from our host, the President of the American Council on Education.

DR. ADAMS: Thank you, Dr. Johnson.

Ladies and gentleman of the conference, I think the thing that has impressed me most about this conference has been the sense of dedication, of earnestness, of conviction, if you please, that has characterized all of the members of the conference as they approached the various issues which have been discussed here.

The spirit of comradeship has been notable. It reflects your realization that the central issue with which we have been dealing these past three days has really been one which is a continuing issue in all educational enterprises. It involves the determination of the responsibility of educators to the community they serve, on the one hand, and to the world of learning, on the other.

Someone said a few moments ago that the teacher mustn't get too far ahead of the community. By the same token, if progress is to be made, the teacher must be a little bit ahead of the community. Just where the balance is poses a vexing problem for the future, as it has in the past. The complexity of the issue does not relieve us of the necessity of tackling the problem. It is most important that we keep our sights clearly aimed at this particular issue, because, if we teach only that which is "safe" and acceptable to the community, we have no possibility of progress. On the other hand, if we overreach ourselves and get ahead of the community too far, we can easily destroy the effectiveness of that which we do.

This, then, I think, has been the grand issue with which we have been dealing. I think you have made a signal contribution to the resolution of that issue. This is an area in which this particular issue becomes more cogent than any other that I can think of.

We are grateful to you for your willingness to come here and to address yourselves with such earnestness and with such perceptiveness to these matters.

I hope that you have enjoyed the experience, and, if my observation is correct, you have. At any rate, I think we have formed a fellowship here which we can all look back upon with great satisfaction. Thank you all very much.

Notes

Johnson, "Summary of Policies and Recommendations of the Committee on Religion and Education"

1. A summary was published under the title *Religion and Public Education: Proceedings of a Conference* (Washington: American Council on Education, 1945).
2. Washington: American Council on Education, 1947.
3. *The Relation of Religion to Public Education: The Basic Principles,* p. 54.
4. See pp. 38–39 for a discussion of the Zorach case.
5. Washington: American Council on Education.
6. See pp. 37–38 for a discussion of the Everson and McCollum cases.
7. Washington: National Education Association.
8. Discussed in William Clayton Bower, *Moral and Spiritual Values in Education* (Lexington, Ky.: University of Kentucky Press, 1952).
9. James E. Russell, ed., *National Policies for Education, Health and Social Services,* Columbia University Bicentennial Series (New York: Doubleday & Co., 1955).
10. "What Catholics Expect of the Home, Church, and School in the Religious Education of Children," an address delivered Aug. 2, 1954, at the Workshop on Home, Church, and School Relationships in the Religious Education of Children and Youth, sponsored jointly by the Department of Education of the University of Chicago and the Department of Religion and Public Education of the National Council of the Churches of Christ in the U.S.A.
11. American Jewish Committee, *Religion in Public Education, A Statement of Views* (New York: The Committee, 1955), p. 8.

Sutherland, "Public Authority and Religious Education," and Discussion

1. *McCollum* v. *Board of Education,* 333 U.S. 203 (1948).
2. *Tudor* v. *Board of Education,* 14 N.J. 31 (1953); certiorari denied 348 U.S. 816 (1954).
3. This paper discusses only public institutions. Parochial or other private institutions may, of course, teach religious matters without governmental intervention.
4. *Modern History* (Rev. ed.; Morristown, N.J.: Silver Burdett Co., 1939).
5. Mr. Justice Holmes, dissenting in *Gitlow* v. *New York,* 268 U.S. 652 (1925).
6. See Note 1 of this paper.
7. 330 U.S. 1 (1947).
8. 330 U.S. 1 at page 15 (1947).
9. 343 U.S. 306 (1952).

10. *Quick Bear* v. *Leupp*, 210 U.S. 50 (1908): Indian treaty funds may be used for a Catholic school on a reservation. *Pierce* v. *Society of Sisters*, 268 U.S. 510 (1925): a state statute requiring public school for all violates the Fourteenth Amendment. *Cochran* v. *Louisiana*, 281 U.S. 370 (1930): free public textbooks for parochial pupils do not violate the Fourteenth Amendment. *Hamilton* v. *Regents*, 293 U.S. 245 (1934): a state university may require military training, even of conscientious objectors. *West Virginia State Board of Education* v. *Barnette*, 319 U.S. 624 (1943) overruling *Minersville* v. *Gobitis*, 310 U.S. 586 (1940): public school requirement of a flag salute from conscientious objectors violates the Fourteenth Amendment. *Everson* v. *Board*, see note 6 of this paper. *McCollum* v. *Board*, see note 1 of this paper. *Doremus* v. *Board*, see notes 13 and 14 of this paper, below. *Zorach* v. *Clauson*, see note 8 of this paper. See also *Gideons* v. *Tudor*, note 16 of this paper, below.
11. N.Y. Constitution, Art. XI, Sec. 4.
12. N.J. Constitution, Art. I, Sec. 4.
13. Kentucky Constitution, Bill of Rights, Sec. 5.
14. *Doremus* v. *Board*, 5 N.J. 435 (1950).
15. 342 U.S. 429 (1952).
16. *Tudor* v. *Board*, 14 N.J. 31 (1953).
17. 348 U.S. 816 (1954).
18. *Williams* v. *Board*, 173 Ky. 708 (1917).
19. *Rawlings* v. *Butler*, 290 S.W. 2d 801 (1956).
20. *Berghorn* v. *Reorganized School District*, 364 Mo. 121 (1953).
21. *Wooley* v. *Spalding*, Sup't of Schools, 293 S.W. 2d 563 (1956).
22. *New York Times*, Dec. 1, 1951, p. 1, col. 1; March 29, 1955, p. 31, col. 4.
23. *Ibid.*, Jan. 31, 1957, p. 29, col. 2.
24. *Sholes* v. *Minnesota*, 236 Minn. 452 (1952).
25. See *Commonwealth* v. *Cooke*, 7 Am. L. Reg. 417, discussed in Pfeffer, *Church, State, and Freedom* (Boston, Mass.: Beacon Press, 1953), pp. 376–78.
26. *Brown* v. *Board of Education, Briggs* v. *Elliott, Davis* v. *County School Board, Gebhart* v. *Belton, Bolling* v. *Sharpe*, 347 U.S. 483 (1954).
27. *West Virginia State Board of Education* v. *Barnette*, 319 U.S. 624 (1943).

Bibliographical Note.—See Leo Pfeffer, *Church, State, and Freedom* (Boston, Mass.: Beacon Press, 1953). A. E. Sutherland, "Constitutions, Churches, and Schools" in *National Policies for Education, Health and Social Services*, ed. James E. Russell, Columbia University Bicentennial Series (New York: Doubleday & Co., 1955). "Religion and the State," a collection of articles in the Winter 1949 issue of *Law and Contemporary Problems.* Mr. Pfeffer's book and the papers here cited contain numerous references to decided cases and literature.

Loewenberg, *"Religion in the History of American Ideas,"* and Discussion

1. William W. Sweet, *Religion in Colonial America* (New York: Chas. Scribner's Sons, 1942); *Religion in the Development of American Culture, 1765–1840* (New York: Chas. Scribner's Sons, 1952); *The Story of Religions in America* (New York and London: Harper & Bros., 1930).
2. Perry Miller, *Orthodoxy in Massachusetts, 1630–1650* (Cambridge, Mass.: Harvard University Press, 1933); *The New England Mind: The Seventeenth Century* (New York: Macmillan Co., 1939); *The New England Mind: From Colony to Province* (Cambridge, Mass.: Harvard University Press, 1953).

3. Henry Steele Commager and Richard B. Morris, *eds.*, The New American Nation Series (New York: Harper & Bros., in progress).
4. Arthur M. Schlesinger and Dixon R. Fox, *eds.*, *A History of American Life,* 13 vols. (New York: Macmillan Co., 1927–1948).
5. Francis M. Cornford, *From Religion to Philosophy: A Study in the Origins of Western Speculations* (London: Arnold, 1912) ; Jane Ellen Harrison, *Prolegomena to the Study of Greek Religion* (3rd ed., Cambridge, England: University Press, 1922).
6. Sterling P. Lamprecht, *Our Religious Traditions* (Cambridge, Mass: Harvard University Press, 1950).
7. New York: Ronald Press, 1956.

Farrell, "Religious Matter in the Teaching of American History," and Discussion

1. Published by the Edward W. Hazen Foundation (New Haven, n.d.). "In spite of the widespread current interest in history among theologians, the deepest currents in Protestant theology, particularly in Europe, can only be described as *anti-historical*. These currents find their source in Kierkegaard, Barth, in Berdyaev, and in secular philosophers of the existentialist school." (P. 16.)
2. "No opposition will be found between Christianity and history, in the sense that would make history only an emanation of evil. The Catholic Church has never taught such a doctrine." Translation in the London *Tablet*, CCVI (Sept. 24, 1955), 292.
3. See *Theory and Practice in Historical Study: A Report of the Committee on Historiography,* Social Science Research Council Bulletin No. 54 (New York: The Council, 1946). There have been disagreements with the findings of the committee, as for example by Chester M. Destler, "Some Observations on Contemporary Historical Theory," *American Historical Review,* LV (April 1950), 503–29.
4. New York: Harcourt, Brace & Co.
5. In his work *An Historian's Approach to Religion* (New York: Oxford University Press, 1956).
6. I, 13.
7. Princeton, N.J.: Princeton University Press, 1926. A comment in the October 1954 issue of the *American Historical Review* (LX, 10), by Frederick B. Tolles is in point: "What Jameson did—and it was no trifling achievement—was to bring American church history within the purview of American historians—to take, as it were, the first steps toward giving this neglected orphan child a home and a standing within the family of historical disciplines."
8. Boston, Mass.: Little, Brown & Co., 1941.
9. The best account of early Virginia is now Wesley Frank Craven, *The Southern Colonies in the Seventeenth Century* (Baton Rouge: Louisiana State University Press, 1949).
10. Boston, Mass.: Houghton Mifflin Co., 1930, pp. 54 f.
11. One of my Episcopalian students, William Hogue, has made an evaluation of the Great Awakening as it affected the Anglican Church in his doctoral dissertation, "The Church of England in the Northern Colonies and the Great Awakening" (MS; Mullen Library, Catholic University of America, 1954).
12. A recent study is *The Development of Academic Freedom in the United States* by Hofstadter and Metzger (New York: Columbia University Press, 1955).

13. See Ralph Gabriel, *The Course of American Democratic Thought* (New York: Ronald Press, 1956).
14. Gilbert H. Barnes, *The Anti-Slavery Impulse* (New York: Appleton-Century, 1933).
15. Ray A. Billington, *Protestant Crusade, 1800-1860* (New York: Rinehart & Co., 1938).
16. Henry J. Browne, *The Catholic Church and the Knights of Labor* (Washington: Catholic University of America Press, 1949).
17. Julius W. Pratt, *Expansionists of 1898* (Baltimore: Johns Hopkins Press, 1936), pp. 279 f.
18. Anson Phelps Stokes, *Church and State in the United States* (New York: Harper & Bros., 1950).

Sister Mary Nona, O.P., "Some Religious Aspects of Elementary American History"

1. Cited in Henry Johnson, *The Teaching of History* (New York: Macmillan Co., 1940), p. 42. A 1795 text by McCullough went into four editions; the fourth edition, consulted by the writer, is entitled *A Concise History of the United States from the Discovery of America Till 1813.*
2. Johnson, *op. cit.,* p. 60.
3. These changes are described briefly in Johnson, *op. cit.,* chap. 3.
4. Committee on American History in Schools and Colleges, American Historical Association, *American History in Schools and Colleges* (New York: Macmillan Co., 1944).
5. Quoted in Johnson, *op. cit.,* p. 40.
6. The Association, *op. cit.,* p. 74.
7. Cardinal Gerlier of Toulouse, in a 1956 address. Quoted in the Davenport *Messenger,* Jan. 17, 1957. Archbishop John Ireland in 1913 stated the same position: "Personal conscience is the ultimate asylum of the soul, in presence of civil or ecclesiastical society. Both Americanism and Catholicism bow to the sway of personal conscience."
8. Committee on Religion and Education of the American Council on Education, *The Function of the Public Schools in Dealing with Religion* (Washington: The Council, 1953), p. 7.
9. McCullough, *op. cit.,* p. 14.
10. Samuel Eliot Morison, *Admiral of the Ocean Sea* (Boston: Little, Brown & Co., 1941), p. 167.
11. Merle Curti, *The Growth of American Thought* (2nd ed.; New York: Harper & Bros., 1951), p. 35.
12. Works like those of Thomas Jefferson Wertenbaker, *The Puritan Oligarchy* (New York: Chas. Scribner's Sons, 1947), and George Waller, ed., *Puritanism in Early America* (Boston, Mass.: D. C. Heath & Co., 1950), counteract the exaggerations of Puritanism which are often given as factual.
13. Given varying names by historians, the New England system of government is described by Wertenbaker (*op. cit.,* p. vii) as a Puritan oligarchy, or Bible state.
14. See Herbert Bolton, *Wider Horizons of American History* (New York: Appleton-Century-Crofts, 1939), chap. 3, "The Mission as a Frontier Institution in the Spanish-American Colonies." Detailed description of the work of the missions is given in Pius Barth, *Franciscan Education and the Social Order in Spanish North America* (Chicago: University of Chicago Press, 1950).

15. Barth, *op. cit.,* p. 298, states that the friars introduced the Spanish language at the request of the government, and with some reluctance.
16. A clear explanation is given in Mabel Casner and Ralph Gabriel, *The Story of American Democracy* (New York: Harcourt, Brace & Co., 1955), p. 169.
17. *New York Times,* Sept. 22, 1953.
18. An early judgment of Lincoln's religion was given by Lord Charnwood in his *Abraham Lincoln* (New York: Henry Holt & Co., 1917), pp. 439 ff. A recent summary of such judgments is found in J. G. Randall, *Lincoln the President,* Vol. 4, *The Last Full Measure* (New York: Dodd, Mead & Co., 1955), chap. 16, "God's Man."
19. Roy Basler, *Abraham Lincoln: His Speeches and Writings* (Cleveland, Ohio: World Publishing Co., 1946), pp. 568, 616, 728, 761.
20. Paul Angle and Earl Schenck Miers, eds., *The Living Lincoln* (New Brunswick, N.J.: Rutgers University Press, 1955), p. 640.
21. O. D. Foster, quoted in Shirley Graham and George D. Lipscomb, *Dr. George Washington Carver, Scientist* (New York: Julian Messner, Inc., 1944), p. vi.
22. A popular adult biography is Rackham Holt, *George Washington Carver* (New York: Doubleday & Co., 1944).
23. Foster, *loc. cit.*
24. Graham and Lipscomb, *op. cit.,* p. v.

In addition to the works listed above, those which are listed below are of special pertinence to the subject of Sister Nona's paper and to the subject of the conference.

BOLTON, HERBERT E. *The Spanish Borderlands.* New Haven, Conn.: Yale University Press, 1921.
DAVIS, MOSHE. *Israel.* New York: Harper & Bros., 1956.
DAWSON, CHRISTOPHER. Religion and the Rise of Western Culture. London: Sheed & Ward, 1950.
HERBERG, WILL. *Protestant-Catholic-Jew.* New York: Doubleday & Co., 1955.
IDELSOHN, A. Z. *Jewish Music.* New York: Tudor Publishing Co., 1944.
LATHAM, EARL. ed. *The Declaration of Independence and the Constitution.* Boston, Mass.: D. C. Heath & Co., 1949.
SLOYAN, GERALD S. *Christian Concepts in Social Studies in Catholic Education.* Washington: Catholic University of America Press, 1950.
THAYER, V. T. *Religion in Public Education.* New York: Viking Press, 1947.
TYLER, ALICE FELT. *Freedom's Ferment.* Minneapolis: University of Minnesota Press, 1944.
WARE, CAROLINE F., ed. *The Cultural Approach to History.* New York: Columbia University Press, 1940.
WESLEY, EDGAR BRUCE. *Teaching Social Studies in Elementary Schools.* Boston, Mass.: D. C. Heath & Co., 1946.

Dawson, *"The Next Decade of Research and Experimentation Relating to Religion and Public Education"*

1. *Moral and Spiritual Values in the Public Schools* (Washington: National Education Association, 1951).
2. John S. Brubacher, "The History and Philosophy of Education," in *College Reading and Religion* (New Haven, Conn.: Yale University Press, 1948).
3. *The Function of the Public Schools in Dealing with Religion* (Washington: American Council on Education, 1953), pp. 85–90. See also Note 3 below.
4. *Ibid.,* p. 86.
5. *Ibid.,* p. 83.

Table Reports and Discussion on "The General Problem"

1. *The Relation of Religion to Public Education* (Washington: American Council on Education, 1947), p. 27.
2. "The intensive cultivation of religion is, and always has been, the function of religious institutions. To create an awareness of its importance is a responsibility of public education. In creating such an awareness the school is but rounding out its educational task, which culminates in the building of durable convictions about the meaning of life and personal commitments based upon them. The school cannot dictate these convictions and commitments, but it can, and should, foster a sense of the obligation to achieve them as a supreme moral imperative and to that end bring its students into contact with the spiritual resources of the community."
3. The recommendation appears on pages 86–88 and in its entirety reads as follows:
   "A. The American Council on Education should develop a plan for an experimental project to include such studies and experiments as may be needed to inquire into the desirability and feasibility of factual study of religion in the public elementary and secondary schools and in teacher education institutions. To make this recommendation more explicit, we propose that the experimental project include the following provisions:
   "The principal functions of the Council with respect to this project should be: (1) to develop a basic, but flexible, plan for studies and experiments in cooperation with selected communities, school systems, and teacher education institutions; (2) to secure the funds required for implementation of this project; and (3) to provide general administration and supervision as needed.
   "The project should be operative for a limited period, perhaps for three calendar years, exclusive of the time required to make necessary arrangements for its inauguration.
   "The Council, in consultation with responsible administrators concerned, should select a few teacher education institutions, each of which should select one or more public school systems in its immediate area, for participation in the project. In cooperation with the Council these institutions and school systems should determine the number, character, and scope of particular studies and experiments to be undertaken in the respective situations. Each cooperating institution and school system should, of course, provide adequate administration and supervision for activities related to the project for which it is directly responsible. It may be desirable in some instances for public school systems to work directly with the Council, but we believe the normative policy should be participation through a teacher education institution.
   "The Council should secure and allocate funds to each teacher education institution and school system participating in the project, as agreed upon, for consultative and secretarial service, conferences, travel expenses, equipment, and materials. It is assumed that teacher education institutions and public school systems will make substantial financial contributions to the project by the participation of administrators, supervisors, and teachers in the actual conduct of studies and experiments.
   "The cooperating teacher education institutions and school systems should make the findings of studies and experiments available to the Council for distribution to the educational profession in suitable reports.
   "The principal objectives of studies and experiments undertaken should be to answer certain questions about the desirability and feasibility of factual study of religion in the public schools and in teacher education institutions, such as the following:

"1. In what curriculum areas and at what maturity levels of students is factual study of religion desirable and feasible?

"2. What aspects of religion and religious institutions intrinsic to particular curriculum areas are appropriate for factual study at different maturity levels of students?

"3. What special preparation do teachers need for guiding students in such study?

"4. How can such study be conducted in public schools without offense to minority groups—without infringing the religious liberty of any teacher or student?

"5. In what particular curriculum areas and in what aspects of these areas, if any, do teachers and students need additional, or more adequate, materials?

"6. What are the criteria for evaluating such study?

    a) For evaluating the judgments of teachers?

    b) For evaluating the judgments of students?

    c) For evaluating the judgments of parents?

    d) For evaluating the judgments of administrators, supervisors, boards of education, and religious leaders?

"7. What further studies and experiments are needed, if any, before adoption of policy?"

4. Umphrey Lee. *Render unto the People* (Nashville, Tenn.: Abingdon-Cokesbury Press, 1947).

AMERICAN COUNCIL ON EDUCATION

Arthur S. Adams, *President*

The American Council on Education is a *council* of national educational associations; organizations having related interests; approved universities, colleges, teachers colleges, junior colleges, technological schools, and selected private secondary schools; state departments of education; city school systems and private school systems; selected educational departments of business and industrial companies; voluntary associations of higher education in the states; and large public libraries. It is a center of cooperation and coordination whose influence has been apparent in the shaping of American educational policies and formation of educational practices duri